Collins

Teacher's Guide

CAMBRIDGE IGCSE® ENVIRONMENTAL MANAGEMENT

David Weatherly and Nicholas Sheehan

William Collins' dream of knowledge for all began with the publication of his first book in 1819.
A self-educated mill worker, he not only enriched millions of lives, but also founded a flourishing publishing house. Today, staying true to his spirit, Collins books are packed with inspiration, innovation and practical expertise. They place you at the centre of a world of possibility and give you exactly what you need to explore it.

Collins. Freedom to teach.

Published by Collins
An imprint of HarperCollins*Publishers*
1 London Bridge Street
London
SE1 9GF

Browse the complete Collins catalogue at
www.collins.co.uk

10 9 8 7 6 5 4 3

ISBN 978-0-00-819044-6

British Library Cataloguing in Publication Data
A catalogue record for this publication is available from the British Library.

Commissioned by **Anne Mahon**
Project managed by **Rachel Allegro**
Proofread by **Louise Robb**
Typesetting by **QBS**
Cover design by **Gordon MacGilp**
Printed and bound by CPI Group (UK) Ltd, Croydon, CR0 4YY

HarperCollins PUBLISHERS Since 1817

CONTENTS

Introduction

Welcome to the Teacher's Guide for *Collins Cambridge IGCSE® Environmental Management* which has been written to support the teaching and learning of the Cambridge IGCSE Environmental Management (0680) and O Level (5014) syllabuses for first examination from 2019.

Contents of the Teacher's Guide

The Teacher's Guide enables you to consolidate the students' core knowledge and understanding of environmental management gained from the Student's Book. In addition, the Teacher's Guide has also been designed to support you to expand upon and extend the thinking of the students so that they are able to grasp more complex concepts and subject matter, master additional skills, and, in particular, comprehend the holistic and interconnected nature of environmental management. Each chapter in the Student's Book is therefore matched by a corresponding chapter in the Teacher's Guide. Each of the sections in the Teacher's Guide has the same format, consisting of:

Links to other chapters

This enables you to see at a glance how the learning objectives of each topic in the Student's Book is linked to the subject content covered in other topics and chapters. Opportunities can then be taken to demonstrate how environmental management requires an interrelated and cross-cutting approach, by encouraging students to make connections and build up a multi-dimensional understanding of the subject.

Extension content and related activities

This section provides supplementary material designed to widen and stretch student knowledge and understanding of some of the topics in each of the Student's Book chapters. Here, students are challenged particularly to handle information from a variety of sources and to reach conclusions and make judgements about a wide range of environmental issues through tasks which enable them to consolidate and extend their thinking.

Supplementary case studies

Each section in the Teacher's Guide also contains additional topical and relevant case studies from all over the world to both complement and extend those in the Student's Book. These case studies are more exacting than those in the Student's Book and consequently serve to advance student understanding of key principles and concepts, as well as enabling evaluative and reflective thinking.

Data response and decision making exercises

In each section of the Teacher's Guide, you will find a comprehensive data response and decision making exercise to use with students. These have been carefully written to support students to interrogate, interpret and critique data from a range of sources related to the topics in the Student's Book. In addition, through problem solving and decision making exercises, students are assisted to appreciate some of the complexities of environmental management and to consolidate their understanding of what sustainable development entails.

Answers to the data response and decision making exercises can be found at **www.collins.co.uk/EnvMgmtIGCSE**

1 Rocks and minerals and their exploitation

Introduction

This section reinforces and extends student learning by:

- Consolidating and developing the factual material in the Student's Book that students will be required to recall and explain (AO1)
- Advancing student thinking through providing more challenging content and activities than those in the Student's Book, which extend some areas of the specification and require the synthesis of information and the application of knowledge and understanding to unfamiliar contexts (AO2)
- Enabling students to grasp that the effective management of environmental issues requires a coherent and holistic approach to problem solving through the principles of sustainable development (AO3)

This is achieved through the provision of:

- Extension content and related activities that secure and progress student knowledge and understanding through tasks that require handling information from a variety of sources to reach conclusions and make judgments
- Supplementary case studies that reinforce and advance key principles and concepts and support evaluative thinking
- A decision making or problem solving exercise that encourages students to appreciate the complexities of environmental management and the pivotal role of the principles of sustainable development in achieving successful outcomes

Links to other chapters

The exploitation of rocks and minerals generates very significant environmental management issues. The most obvious challenge is of course that all rocks and minerals are finite and non-renewable natural resources and their exploitation is currently occurring at a time of both an increasing global population and the desire to improve life quality for everyone. Population growth in LEDCs accounts for almost all of the world's annual increase of 80 million people. It is also in these countries that the most significant leaps in living standards will occur during the remainder of this century. Historically, securing rising living standards has always been achieved through increasing natural resource consumption. The management issue of how existing reserves of rocks and minerals can be conserved through sustainable development, alongside discovering new reserves and further processing waste from generations past, is therefore crucial. All minerals are extracted from ore, and rising global energy demand is placing huge pressures on these reserves. The burning of fossil fuels is a major contributory factor to both anthropogenic global warming and acid rain. In addition, the worldwide transportation of rocks and minerals, both as a raw material and in semi-processed form, presents serious potential environmental risks. Rock is the parent material of soil and is therefore central to thinking about the sustainability of attempting to increase agricultural yields and productivity, and the risks of environmental damage through erosion, land degradation and desertification. A third of all the freshwater consumed by the world's population is extracted from rock aquifers, which in many parts of the world are being exploited at a much faster rate than they are being replenished. Increasing pollution of these rock-based water reserves from surface percolation of toxic materials, such as pesticides and chemicals like mercury used in mineral processing, presents an additional environmental management challenge. The link between rocks and minerals and atmospheric pollution has already been highlighted in terms of carbon dioxide and sulfur dioxide emissions. It is crucial therefore for students to see rocks and minerals in the broader context of holistic sustainable management of the environment. For example, conserving existing rock and mineral reserves through their more efficient use, recycling and reusing does more than ensuring they last longer. This improved management can be cleaner and safer and therefore have direct positive impacts on atmospheric and water pollution and biodiversity long term. Finally it is worth reflecting that perhaps rocks and minerals are most profoundly linked to natural ecosystems since they form the abiotic element of communities of living things with which all organisms interact and are interdependent.

Rocks and minerals and their exploitation topic	Links to other subject content	Section
Formation of rocks	Earthquakes and volcanoes	6
Extraction of rocks and minerals from the earth	Fossil fuel formation Energy resources and the generation of electricity Soil composition Oceans as a resource	2 2 3 5
Impact of rock and mineral extraction	Atmospheric pollution – causes and impacts Impact of oil pollution	7 2
Managing the impact of rock and mineral extraction	Managing atmospheric pollution	7
Sustainable use of rocks and minerals	Opportunities presented by natural hazards	6

Extension content and related activities

Extraction of rocks and minerals from the Earth

When the feldspar component of the igneous rock granite decomposes, it forms fine white clay-based mineral called kaolinite, more commonly referred to as kaolin or china clay. The three largest kaolin producing countries are the United States, Brazil and the United Kingdom. In Devon and Cornwall in southwest England, 1350 people are employed in the china clay industry, which generates over US$200 million a year for the region. The traditional way to extract kaolin from granite is through surface or opencast mining. This involves blasting high-pressured water at the granite to separate the kaolin out into water based slurry. Through a process of suspension and filtration, the fine kaolin particles then settle and separate from coarser materials such as sand and gravels. As with all surface mining, the impact on the environment is usually very significant. Huge open pit mines are created, which often subsequently flood when mining ends, and they are surrounded by piles of white mining waste. Generally, to obtain one tonne of refined kaolin, it is necessary to remove at least nine tonnes of waste material from the mine, including sand, rock and overburden.

Fig. 1.1 China clay workings, Cornwall, UK.

Fig. 1.2 China clay extraction hose, Cornwall, UK.

Fig. 1.3 Kaolinite.

Read the briefing paper about kaolin from the British Geological Society at **https://www.bgs.ac.uk/downloads/start.cfm?id=1362**. From this information, produce a simple mind map or concept map to show the huge variety of modern-day uses of kaolin.

Most of the kaolin produced in Brazil comes from surface mines within the Amazon Basin. Read through the *Natural ecosystems and human activities* section in the Student's Book and draw a simple table showing the possible advantages and disadvantages of such mining for local communities and the environment.

Impact of rock and mineral extraction

The Student's Book case study on pages 21–23 details the development, restoration and reuse of the BHP Island Copper Mine at Port Hardy, British Columbia in Canada. Currently there are nine major metal mines and ten major coal mines operating in British Columbia. There are also 35 major industrial mineral mines, two smelters and many smaller mining operations throughout the province.

Fig. 1.4 Provinces of Canada.

Fig. 1.5 Copper Mountain in an open pit porphyry mine in British Columbia, Canada. It is the third-largest copper mine in Canada.

The Mining Association of British Columbia has recently undertaken an assessment of the economic impact of the mining industry on British Columbia. Key findings included:

- The mining industry currently spends over US$5 billion a year directly related to mining, which includes salary costs, capital costs (obtaining land and mining rights, construction, machinery), exploration and development, environmental controls (reclamation and waste permits) and community projects (grants and donations).
- A further US$3.9 billion is spent indirectly, relating to mining through the purchasing of goods and services by mining companies from other industries and services, for example, environmental consultants and accounting services.
- The mining industry employs 21 112 people directly in mining operations.
- At least another 16 590 people are employed indirectly by the mining industry. These people include all of those working for engineering, catering, security and transport companies to whom mining industries subcontract work.
- A further 8000 jobs across the province have been created or 'induced' as a result of the 37 702 direct and indirect employees that spend their salaries on goods and services from other providers such as supermarkets, restaurants, clothes shops, houses and cinemas. This is known as the 'multiplier effect'.
- The total 45 702 direct, indirect and induced mining jobs represent 2 per cent of all employment in British Columbia. As a result of the opening of new mines, a further 15 000 job opportunities are likely to arise over the next five years.
- The mining industry pays US$495 million a year in taxes that the provincial government is able to spend on improving public services such as hospitals, schools, transport and the police force to benefit all of the 4.6 million residents of the province.

In 2014, the government of British Columbia granted permission for a new US$5.3 billion mine to be operated by the Seabridge Gold mining company (known as KSM) in the far north of the province. It will tap into one of the largest gold and copper deposits in the world. Seabridge estimates it will be able to mine 1.1 million kilograms of gold and almost 5 billion kilograms of copper over the 52 years that the mine will operate. The company says the project will create 1800 jobs during the construction phase and more than 1000 permanent jobs once it is operating to full capacity. The mine will become the largest single employer in the area. In your own words, describe and explain why the opening of the mine is likely to have a positive economic impact on the area. Use the information in the diagram below and that provided by the Mining Association of British Columbia (http://www.mining.bc.ca) to help your thinking.

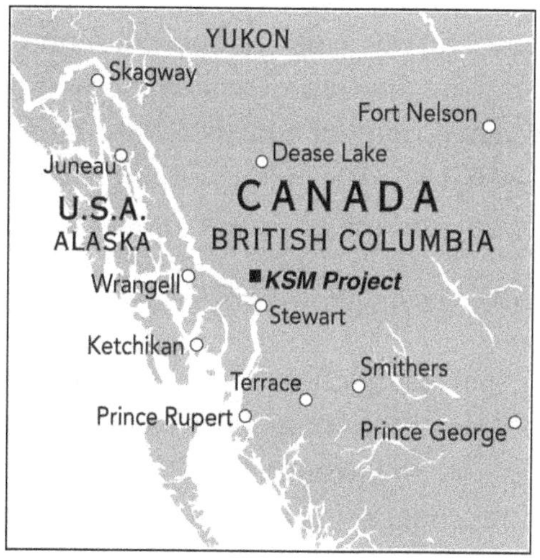

Fig. 1.6 Location of KSM.

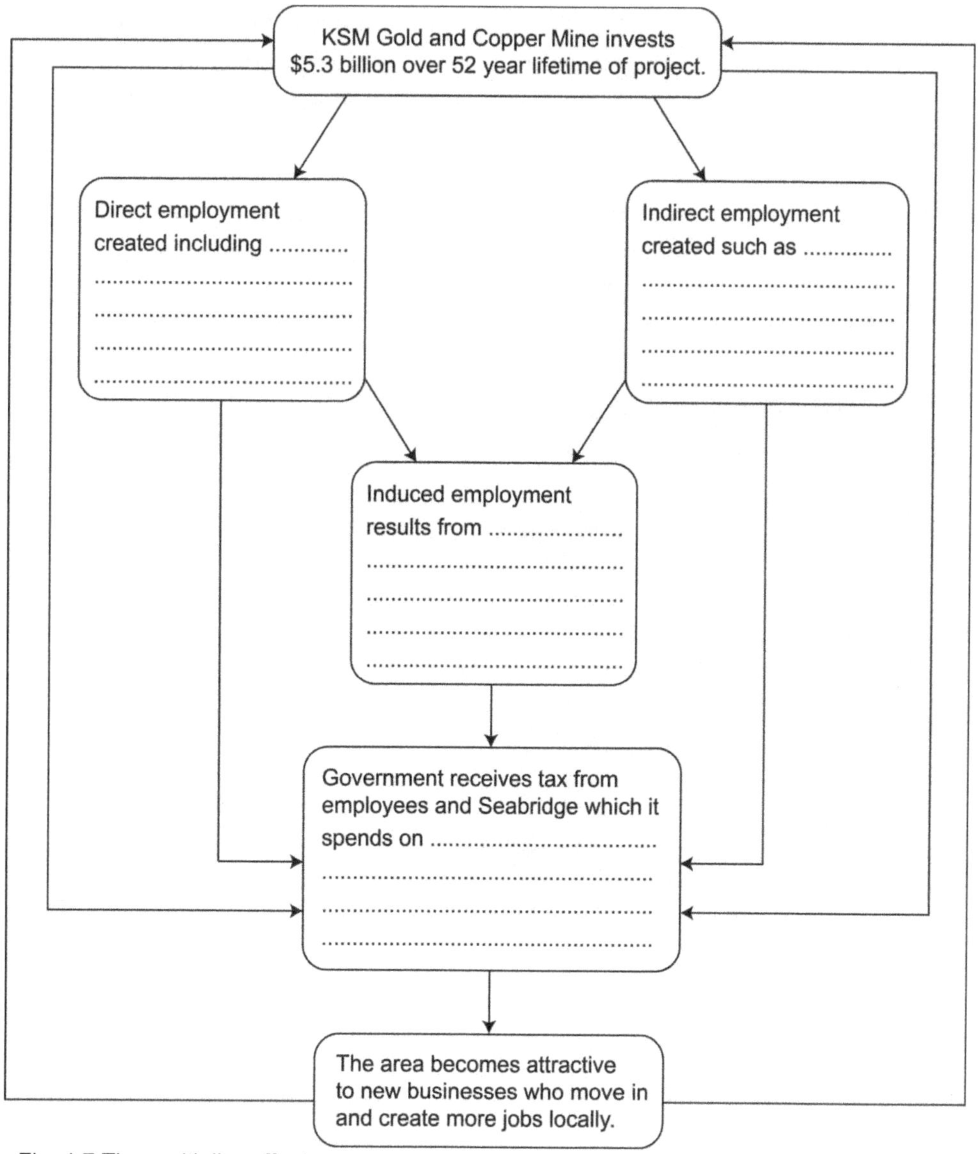

Fig. 1.7 The multiplier effect.

Sustainable use of rocks and minerals

Recycling involves the collection and separation of metals that have reached the end of their useful life and reprocessing them to become useable products once again. Increasing recycling rates of construction materials such as concrete and brick, industrial materials such as glass used in manufacturing processes and metals like tin and aluminium is very important if rocks and minerals are to be used more sustainably in the future.

There are environmental benefits to be achieved through increasing recycling rates such as:

- The energy needed to re-melt and recycle scrap metal is a fraction of that required to extract the metal from its ore and refine it. Not only does this have environmental benefits such as lowering fossil fuel consumption, but it also reduces manufacturing costs for the reprocessing company.
- For construction minerals such as sand and gravel, the use of recycled demolition waste reduces the need to open new quarries.
- The more efficient recycling of scrap and waste means that much less material has to be disposed of in landfill waste sites.

The recycling of minerals used in manufacturing processes presents the greatest sustainability challenge for the future. This is because the valuable physical properties of minerals are either destroyed or dispersed so widely during manufacturing that recovering them in their original form is very complex and expensive. Glass is an exception. It is 100 per cent recyclable and can be recycled endlessly without loss of purity.

Using the information at **http://www.recycling-guide.org.uk/science-glass.html** and **http://www.gpi.org/recycling/glass-recycling-facts**, together with the film at **https://www.youtube.com/watch?v=6R8YObQbE88**, create a flow or loop diagram to illustrate the stages of recycling glass.

Fig. 1.8 Woman recycling glass bottle.

Connecting the rocks and minerals topics

The Pilbara covers a remote area of 507 896 sq km in Western Australia. Only 63 million people live in the area, which stretches all of the way from the Indian Ocean to the border with Northern Territory. There are currently 45 000 people working in the Pilbara and 18 500 of these jobs are in the iron ore mining industries alone. Iron ore is Australia's largest single export commodity and of the 400 million tonnes it sells each year to countries such as China, 95 per cent comes from the Pilbara.

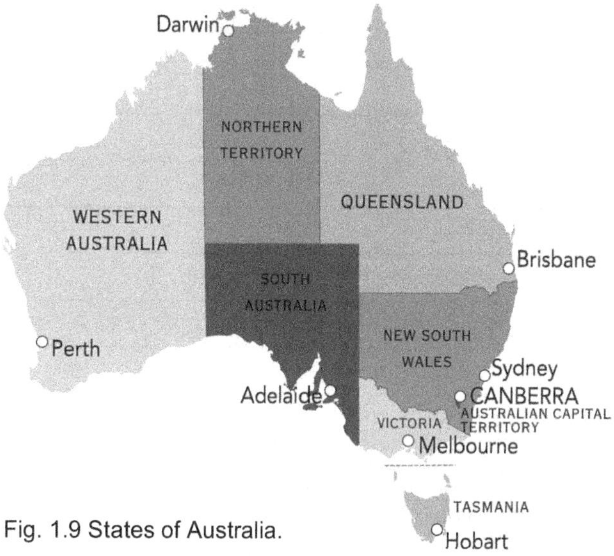

Fig. 1.9 States of Australia.

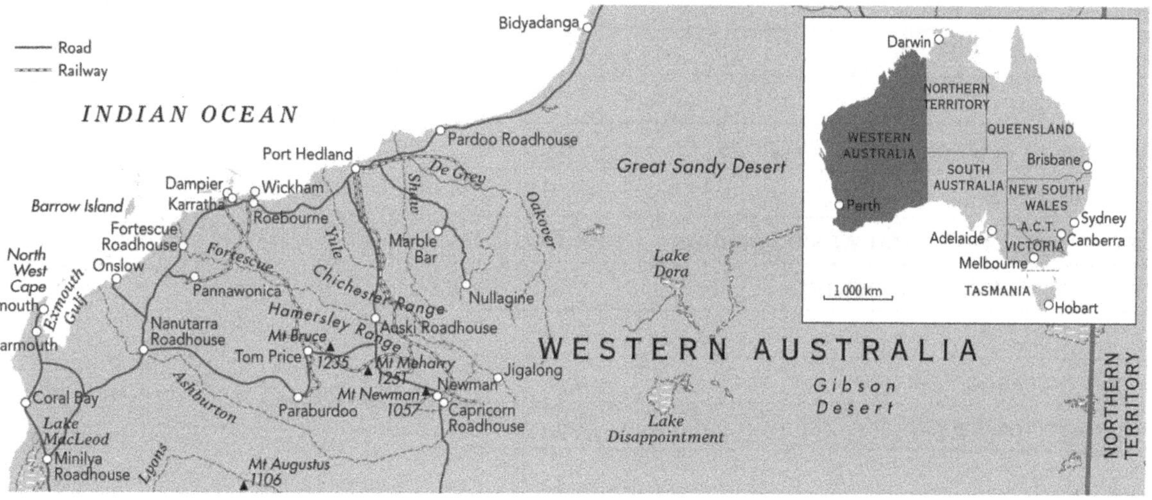

Fig. 1.10 Pilbara region of Australia.

Fig. 1.11 A truck being loaded with dirt and ore.

Fig. 1.12 Rain coming to the Pilbara region.

Exports of iron ore from the Pilbara earn the Australian government US$46 billion a year. In addition to this the Pilbara produces 85 per cent of Australia's crude oil and 70 per cent of its natural gas from the offshore Carnarvon Basin. Look at the table of data below about employment in the Pilbara. What do you think would happen to the people of the Pilbara if the demand for iron ore, and other minerals it produces, from other countries around the world suddenly dropped and prices crashed?

How will people working in indirect mining jobs such as real estate, the retail trade and construction be affected if the prosperity of the mines dropped and they made less profit?

Industry	Jobs
Mining	18 500
Construction	8404
Accommodation and food services	2467
Transport, postal and warehousing	2354
Education and training	1527
Manufacturing	1445
Health care and social assistance	1424
Administrative and support services	1380
Public administration and safety	1369
Professional, scientific and technical services	1366
Retail trade	1349
Other services	1101
Rental, hiring and real estate services	689
Wholesale trade	626
Electricity, gas, water and waste services	456
Agriculture, forestry and fishing	163
Financial and insurance services	144
Arts and recreation services	99
Information, media and telecommunications	93

The Australian government is worried about the lack of what it calls *economic diversity* in the Pilbara. This means that it thinks that people in the region are too reliant on just one activity – mining. In 1992, the Pilbara Development Commission was set up with the task of developing the region sustainably in the future. Its two most important tasks are to bring new companies with different kinds of jobs to the region and to persuade at least another 100 000 people to move in from other parts of the country.

Consider what the government might do to try to persuade people to move to a town such as Newman in the Pilbara. In particular, think about what someone with a business would require as well as what someone looking for work might need to consider when moving from a city such as Brisbane.

Fig. 1.13 Location of Newman.

Fig. 1.14 Panoramic photo of Newman.

Supplementary case study 1

The Eden Project

The Eden Project is one of the most famous visitor attractions in the UK. Since its opening in 2001, over ten million people have travelled from across the world to experience it. It is a very good example of the reuse of a decommissioned mine to ensure that it continues to contribute economically to the community of the local area and region. The project is located in a former kaolinite pit close to the town of St Austell in Cornwall, UK. The attraction consists of a number of features, including a Mediterranean and tropical biome, outside temperate gardens and exhibitions and activities that focus on achieving more sustainable lifestyles.

Fig. 1.15 Eden Project geodesic domes.

Fig. 1.16 Inside the Eden Project.

Visit **http://www.edenproject.com/** and complete the following:

- What is the purpose of the project?
- Provide an overview of the attractions awaiting visitors. What can they see and do?
- Make a list of some of the ways in which the project considers itself to be a good example of sustainability and sustainable development.
- Since 2001, the Eden Project has brought economic benefits (wealth and prosperity) to the local area, but there have been some social impacts (wellbeing of people) as well. On a copy of the table below, make some notes about what you think some of these benefits and costs might be. When you have finished, go to **https://getrevising.co.uk/grids/the_eden_project** and add to your table any points made here that you may not have considered.

Possible economic benefits	Possible social impacts or costs

a) Explain what 'infant mortality' measures.

....

....

....

....

b) Explain what 'access to improved sanitation' measures.

....

....

....

....

c) Suggest what type of work many of the children are likely to be doing instead of attending school.

....

....

....

....

2. Guinea is one of the most mineral ore rich countries in the world. At current world prices it possesses US$222 billion worth of bauxite reserves (used to manufacture aluminium) that will last another 444 years at the current rate at which it is being mined. The following is an extract from the Central Intelligence Agency (CIA) fact book for 2016:

"Guinea is a poor country that possesses the world's largest reserves of bauxite and largest untapped high-grade iron ore reserves as well as gold and diamonds. In addition, Guinea has fertile soil, ample rainfall, and is the source of several West African rivers. Guinea's hydro potential is enormous and the country could be a major exporter of electricity. The country also has tremendous agriculture potential."

a) What is iron ore used to manufacture?

....

b) Explain what a 'fertile' soil is.

....

....

....

c) Explain using a labelled diagram how water can be used to generate electricity.

d) Although Guinea has a small population, and a wealth of natural resources and potential for farming, it remains the eighth poorest country in the world. Suggest why this is.

....

....

....

....

....

....

....

....

....

3. Guinea has the largest untapped reserves of bauxite in the world. The government of the country has recently announced a ten year plan to increase production of the mineral through opening at least eight new mines. All current bauxite mines are surface opencast mines and new mines will use the same extraction methods.

Fig. 1.23 Bauxite mine in Sangaredi, Guinea, West Africa.

a) Describe how minerals such as bauxite are extracted using surface mining methods.

....

....

....

....

b) In the box below, suggest one positive and one negative environmental, economic and social impact that opening eight new opencast mines could have in Guinea.

	Positive impact	**Negative impact**
Environmental		
Economic		
Social		

4. Read the following passage about bauxite in Guinea:

Supervisor David Smith states that one of his excavators, complete with rotating shovel, can extract up to 750 tons of rock an hour. This would be enough to fill seven trucks.

Bauxite earth is transported by truck to the station, where it is then moved onto a freight train and taken to the provincial capital Kindia. It is then taken to Conakry port where it will travel to Ukraine by boat. In Ukraine, aluminium is made from the bauxite and exported to locations all over the world. Even though Guinea has been independent for over 50 years, there is still no industry to convert bauxite into aluminium.

a) On the grid provided below draw a bar graph to display the following data.

Date	**Price per tonne US$***	**Date**	**Price per tonne US$***
June 2011	162	June 2014	93
June 2012	135	June 2015	63
June 2013	115	June 2016	52

*Price of a dry metric tonne of bauxite ore on world market June 2011 to June 2016.

b) By what percentage did the price of a tonne of bauxite ore fall on the world market between June 2011 and June 2016?

....

c) Aluminium is a lightweight, corrosion-resistant metal, used mainly in the aerospace industry, as a construction material in buildings, in food packaging, motor vehicles and trains. Draw a simple line graph below to show how the price of a refined tonne of aluminium (US$) changed on the world market between November 2015 and July 2016.

Date	**Price per tonne (US$)**
November 2015	1435
December 2015	1510
January 2016	1535
February 2016	1535
March 2016	1600
April 2016	1540
May 2016	1670
June 2016	1665
July 2016	1680

d) By what percentage did the price of a tonne of refined aluminium rise on the world market between November 2015 and July 2016?

....

e) Suggest why it would make more economic sense for the government of Guinea to invest in building processing factories that will convert the bauxite ore they already mine to aluminium metal, rather than opening new mines to extract more ore.

....

....

....

....

....

....

....

f) Because Guinea is the eighth poorest country in the world, it is going to have to apply for loans from richer MEDCs to cover the cost of opening new mines or constructing new ore refining plants. Suggest why MEDC governments, banks and multinational businesses are likely to look more favourably on loaning money to pay for opening new mines rather than building ore processing factories.

....

....

....

....

....

....

....

....

5. In September 2015, the government of Guinea began talks with the China International Water and Electric Corporation (CRE) to build a US$2 billion hydropower dam. Lansana Fofana, a government energy ministry official, announced that the idea of the 550 megawatt Souapiti dam "is to feed the mining industry". He said, "We want to build refineries for our bauxite and become an exporter of electricity". Souapiti will be built on the Konkoure River, about two kilometres upstream from the 240 megawatt Kaleta dam completed by CRE in July 2015. The Kaleta dam project tripled Guinea's electricity production. The reservoir behind the Souapiti dam will be huge, allowing both hydroplants to function even when the river loses most of its flow during the six-month dry season. It will require at least 15 000 people to be resettled from massive areas of flooded land. The Export-Import Bank of China is likely to loan the government of Guinea the money to build the dam and plant. The loan will then be paid back with interest once income is being earned from the sale of its electricity. The bank loaned three-quarters of the US$526 million needed to build the Kaleta complex.

a) Guinea earns US$6 billion a year from goods and services it sells to other countries. This sum is referred to as its Gross Domestic Product (or GDP). Suggest why borrowing US$2 billion from an overseas bank, that will have to be repaid with interest, could be risky.

....

....

....

....

....

....

b) Huge multipurpose dam projects can have environmental, economic and social impacts. Using examples of projects that you have studied, what would you advise Lansana Fofana to consider carefully to ensure that the Souapiti project is a sustainable development for the environment and for the people of the country.

....

....

....

....

....

....

....

Answers to these questions can be found at **www.collins.co.uk/EnvMgmtIGCSE**

2 Energy and the environment

Introduction

This section reinforces and extends student learning by:

- Consolidating and developing the factual material in the Student's Book that students will be required to recall and explain (AO1)
- Advancing student thinking through providing more challenging content and activities than those in the Student's Book, which extend some areas of the specification and require the synthesis of information and the application of knowledge and understanding to unfamiliar contexts (AO2)
- Enabling students to grasp that the effective management of environmental issues requires a coherent and holistic approach to problem solving through the principles of sustainable development (AO3)

This is achieved through the provision of:

- Extension content and related activities that secure and progress student knowledge and understanding through tasks that require handling information from a variety of sources to reach conclusions and make judgments
- Supplementary case studies that reinforce and advance key principles and concepts and support evaluative thinking
- A decision making or problem solving exercise that encourages students to appreciate the complexities of environmental management and the pivotal role of the principles of sustainable development in achieving successful outcomes

Links to other chapters

Understanding the complex links between population growth, increasing levels of economic development and rising demand for energy are vital for students studying this qualification. The environmental management challenges associated with the increasing demand are significant. Rising demand for energy is not simply caused by population increase. Instead, a combination of rising numbers and increasing affluence is leading to greater domestic consumption of electricity in lower-income countries. However, this consumption is far outweighed by domestic demand in high-income countries. The proliferation of energy consuming devices in the average household has been exponential and it is important to explore this temporal change with students. Rising demand for energy and the associated mineral extraction, processing, transportation and consumption in thermal power stations all have significant environmental impacts. It is important to note how dependent humans are on fossil fuels and how the use of fossil fuels and the associated carbon dioxide emissions link across all the chapters in the Student's Book.

The supply and demand for energy, the associated greenhouse gas emissions and attempts to reduce these are key themes that are seen throughout. It is vital that students are encouraged to think synoptically and to identify the links between each area. For example, a rising and economically developing population will demand more food – particularly meat. This causes an increase in grain production for animal feed – which uses energy in the production and transport (as well as water, soil erosion and potential deforestation). This in turn leads to a rising demand for energy, which causes an increase in demand for fossil fuels. The production and transport of oil can impact oceans when spilt. The burning of fossil fuels impacts atmospheric process – both locally and globally, which in turn impacts ecosystems and increases vulnerability to hazards such as flooding and tropical cyclones.

It is important to allow students time when working through each unit to develop and explore links such as these. Further useful links are shown in the table below.

Energy and the environment topic	**Links to other subject content**	**Section**
Fossil fuel formation	Extraction of rocks and minerals from the Earth	1
Energy resources and the generation of electricity	Extraction of rocks and minerals from the Earth Multipurpose dam projects Oceans as a resource	1 4 5
Energy demand	Increasing agricultural yields Human population distribution and density	3 8
Conservation and management of energy resources	Managing human population size Deforestation	8 9
Impact of oil pollution	Impact of rock and mineral extraction Impact of water pollution Atmospheric pollution – causes and impacts	1 4 7
Management of oil pollution	Managing pollution of fresh water Managing atmospheric pollution	4 7

Extension content and related activities

Energy resources and the generation of electricity

Each country in the world will use a range of different energy sources to produce electricity – some renewables like wind power, but mostly non-renewables like oil, coal and gas. There are some exceptions, however, such as Germany, which already generates 74 per cent of its power needs from renewable sources. The range of sources used is described as the energy mix of a country.

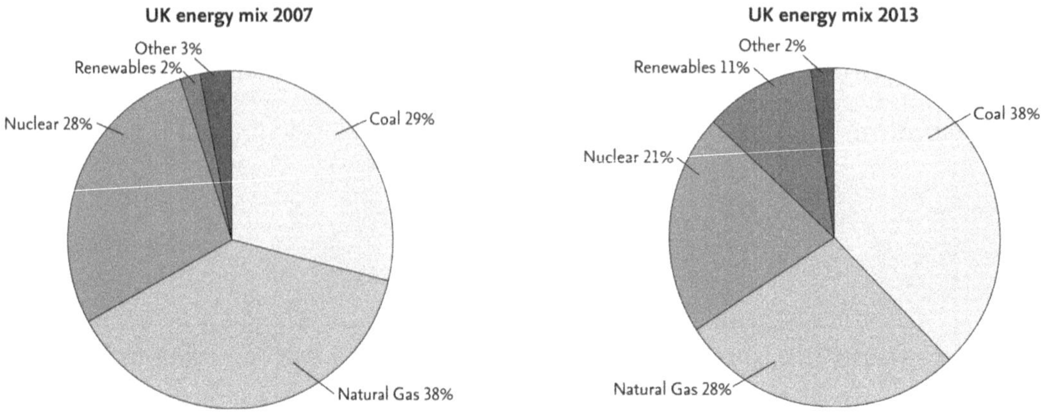

Fig. 2.1a and 2.1b UK energy mix in 2007 and 2013.

UK coal imports – largest source (per cent) 2012
Russia 40%
Colombia 26%
USA 24%

UK crude oil – largest source (per cent) 2012
Norway 50%
Nigeria 12%
Russia 11%
Algeria 6%

UK gas imports – largest source (per cent) 2012
Norway 55%
Netherlands 15%
Qatar 27%

In the UK, and in many other countries, the energy mix has changed significantly over time. As sources of energy are discovered, exploited and exhausted, the way a country generates its electricity will also need to change. For example, the UK had plentiful supplies of accessible coal, so this was used in the earliest power stations. The invention of nuclear power led to the development of nuclear power stations in some parts of the country. This began a decline in the use of coal, which accelerated with the discovery of oil and natural gas reserves in the North Sea, and the closure of most coal mines in the 1980s.

Figures 2.1a and 2.1b show how the UK energy mix has shifted since 2007, when natural gas and nuclear power accounted for over 50 per cent of electricity produced. By 2013, this had shifted again as renewables began to increase in importance and the UK took advantage of importing low-priced coal from abroad. The UK is, however, still predominantly reliant on non-renewable fossil fuels for electricity generation, and in 2013 the country became a net importer of these for the first time, as reserves in the North Sea are in decline. The UK is also needing to phase out older nuclear power stations, as well as those older coal- and gas-fired power stations that emit the most carbon dioxide into the atmosphere.

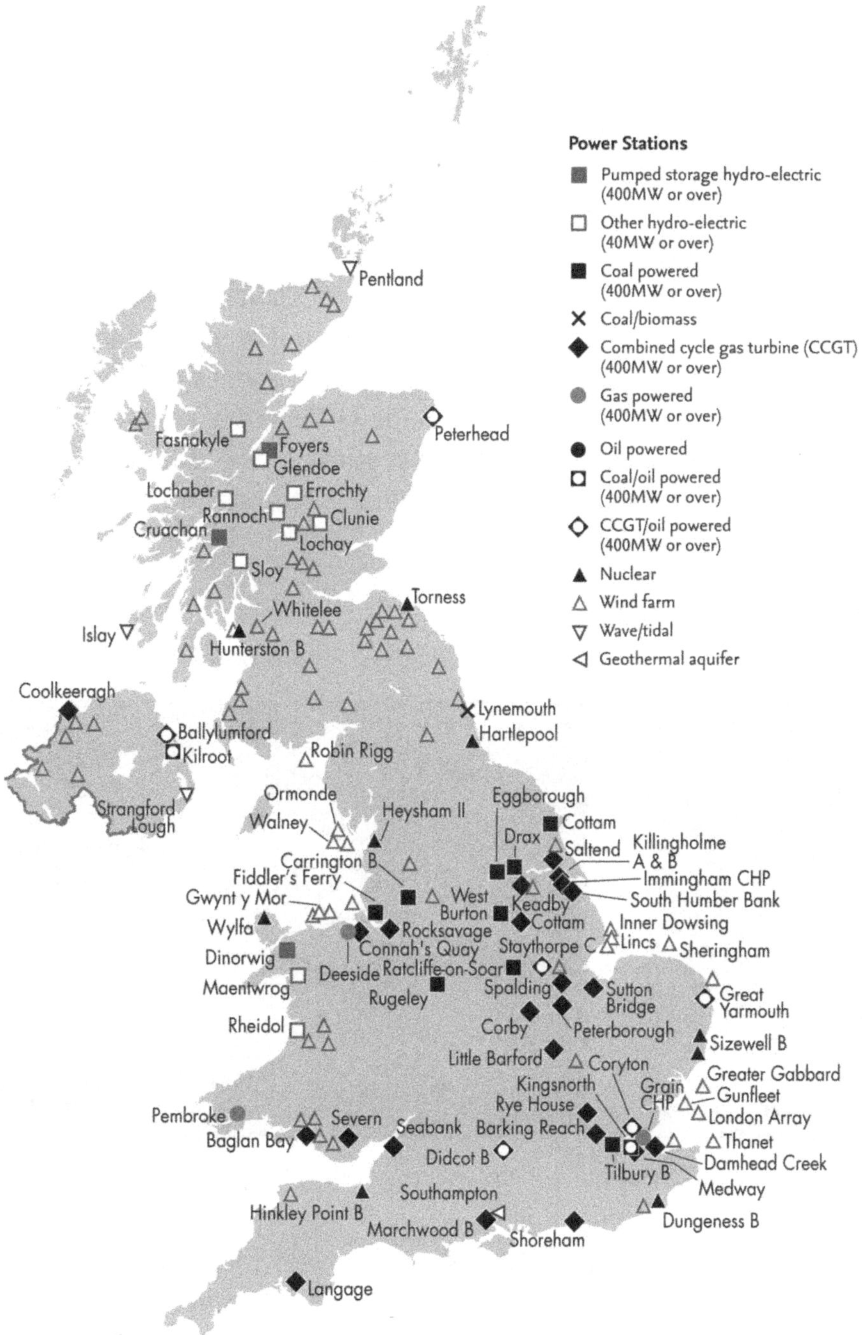

Fig. 2.2 Power station locations in the UK.

A country that is heavily reliant on the import of energy sources, or one that is reliant on non-renewable sources, could be described as energy insecure because they do not control access to the resources and they are vulnerable to sudden interruptions in supply or price increases. Around the world, many countries face challenges with their current energy mix – and what this means for security and keeping the lights on.

Consolidating your thinking

Examine the map of the UK electricity generating power stations, the pie charts showing the UK energy mix over time and the data tables that show the key countries the UK uses as sources of imported energy. Such data is available for most countries around the world.

Use the information provided here for the UK as an example, and research your own country. Use your research to compare and contrast the energy mix of the UK with that of your own country. You might wish to present your comparison as an infographic with the title 'Comparing the energy mix'. Try to include maps, graphs and images. You could cover past and current patterns, the distribution of power stations, the pathways that the energy imports take and how sustainable you consider the current position to be. How reliable do you think the UK's energy imports are? How does this compare to the situation in your country? Is your country more or less energy secure than the UK? You might want to consider using a website like **http://piktochart.com/**, **http://www.easel.ly/** or **http://infogr.am/** to help you.

Supplementary case study

Fracking in North Dakota

The USA is currently experiencing a domestic energy boom with the discovery and exploitation of unconventional oil and gas sources like those found in North Dakota. This has drastically reduced its reliance on foreign energy imports and increased the short-term energy security of the world's largest consumer of energy. However, the USA is still reliant on non-renewable fossil fuels for 67 per cent of its energy needs, which significantly adds to global carbon emissions. One possible solution to the UK's energy needs is to explore and exploit the huge potential reserves of natural gas locked up in shale rocks found beneath some areas of the country. Supporters of this move point to the USA and suggest the UK could also experience a vital domestic energy boom through exploiting its gas reserves in shale rocks. However, this is not without huge controversy and there is significant local opposition to the drilling, with many groups arguing that this is not a sustainable solution.

Population boom in Williston, North Dakota

There are four years between the two aerial images below. What changes can you describe?

Fig. 2.3a Farmland outside of Williston, North Dakota, 2009.

Fig. 2.3b Farmland outside of Williston, North Dakota, 2013.

The images show a farm outside of Williston in North Dakota in the USA, which was a sleepy agricultural town with a population of 12 512 in the year 2000. By 2013, its population had reached an estimated 20 085. The mayor believes it is even higher, with an estimated 30 000 people calling Williston home. This area of North Dakota has a semi-arid climate with freezing temperatures possible from late September to mid-May each year. Prior to 2006, the majority of jobs in the area were on farms or in local shops. Today, this area has the lowest unemployment rate in the USA and the Walmart store pays wages that are double its national average. However, soaring rent costs mean some people have to sleep in their cars and the area has experienced an increase in social problems like drug dealing, prostitution, domestic violence and other crimes. The infrastructure and services here have struggled to grow at a quick enough pace to support the rise in population.

Fig. 2.4 The Bakken Shale Formation – an extensive source rock for oil and one of the largest locations of fracking in the USA.

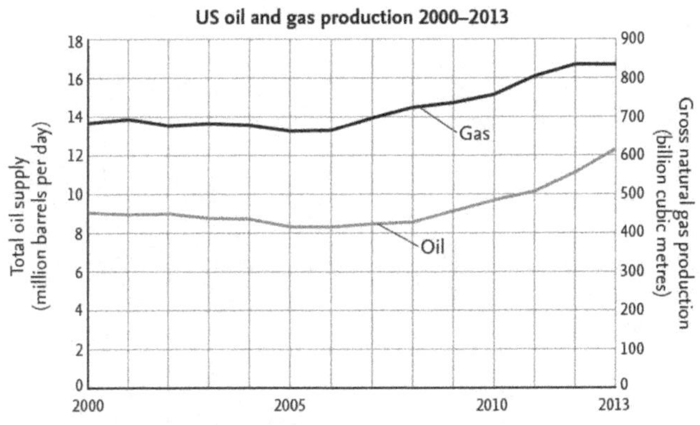

Fig. 2.5 Production of gas and oil in the USA.

Fig. 2.6 Jobs in the oil and gas industry in the USA.

Fig. 2.7 Camps built for oil workers, North Dakota, USA.

Fig. 2.8 Business has increased at refineries across North Dakota.

Fig. 2.9 Fast-food restaurant advertising for new workers, North Dakota.

Fig. 2.10 New housing units to accommodate large influxes of workers, North Dakota.

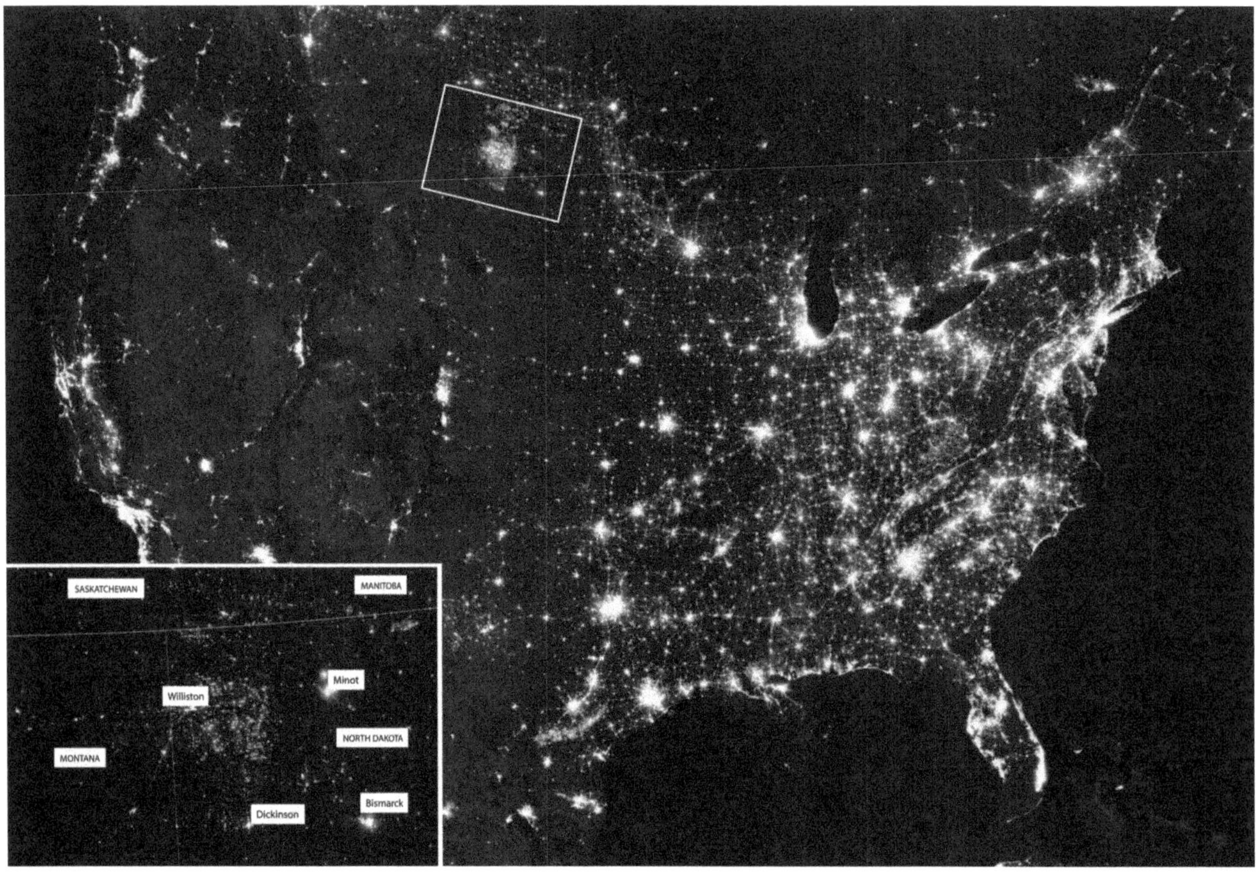

Fig. 2.11 Gas flares from North Dakota are visible from space.

Consolidating your thinking

Examine the range of photographs and graphs in Figures 2.3–2.11. Use these images to answer this question: why is the population of Williston, North Dakota increasing so fast?

Data response and decision making exercises

1. The data below shows total energy consumption for three countries between 1990 and 2015, as well as global energy consumption.

	Total energy consumption in MTOE (million tonnes oil equivalent – a unit of energy defined as the amount of energy released by burning one million tonnes of crude oil)			
Year	**USA**	**China**	**India**	**World**
1990	1967	681	195	8136
1995	2121	885	252	8589
2000	2312	1003	316	9388
2005	2350	1794	394	10 940
2010	2285	2487	541	12 181
2015	2281	3014	700	13 147

a) Plot this data as a line graph on the grid below.

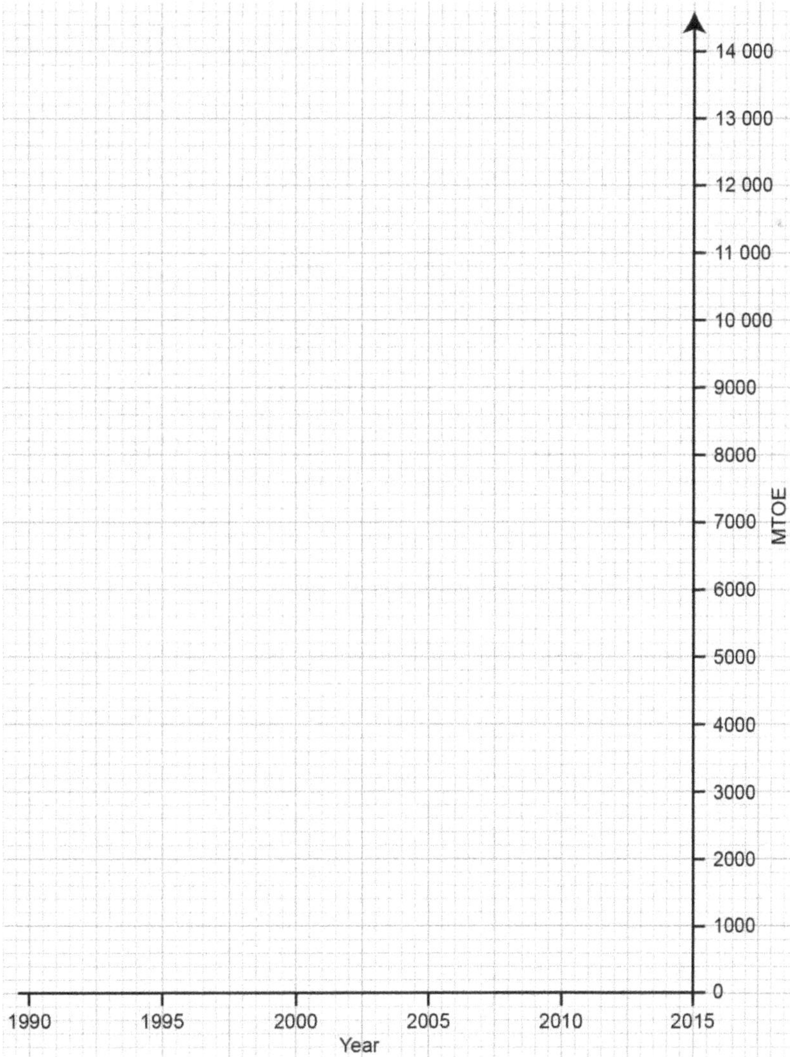

b) Describe the trend in world energy consumption from 1990 to 2015. Ensure you use statistics in your response.

....

....

....

....

c) By how many MTOE did China's total energy consumption change between 1990 and 2015?

....

d) Compare energy consumption in the USA with that in China over time.

....

....

....

....

....

e) The energy consumption of China and India has increased rapidly over time. Suggest reasons for this increase.

....

....

....

....

....

....

....

....

....

....

f) Identify two possible environmental management challenges caused by this increase in consumption. For each, suggest a possible solution.

....

....

....

....

....

....

....

....

....

....

....

2. This graph shows global energy use by source over time. It is a compound line graph, so the total amount of energy used is shown by the top line, but each proportion underneath is representative of the energy source.

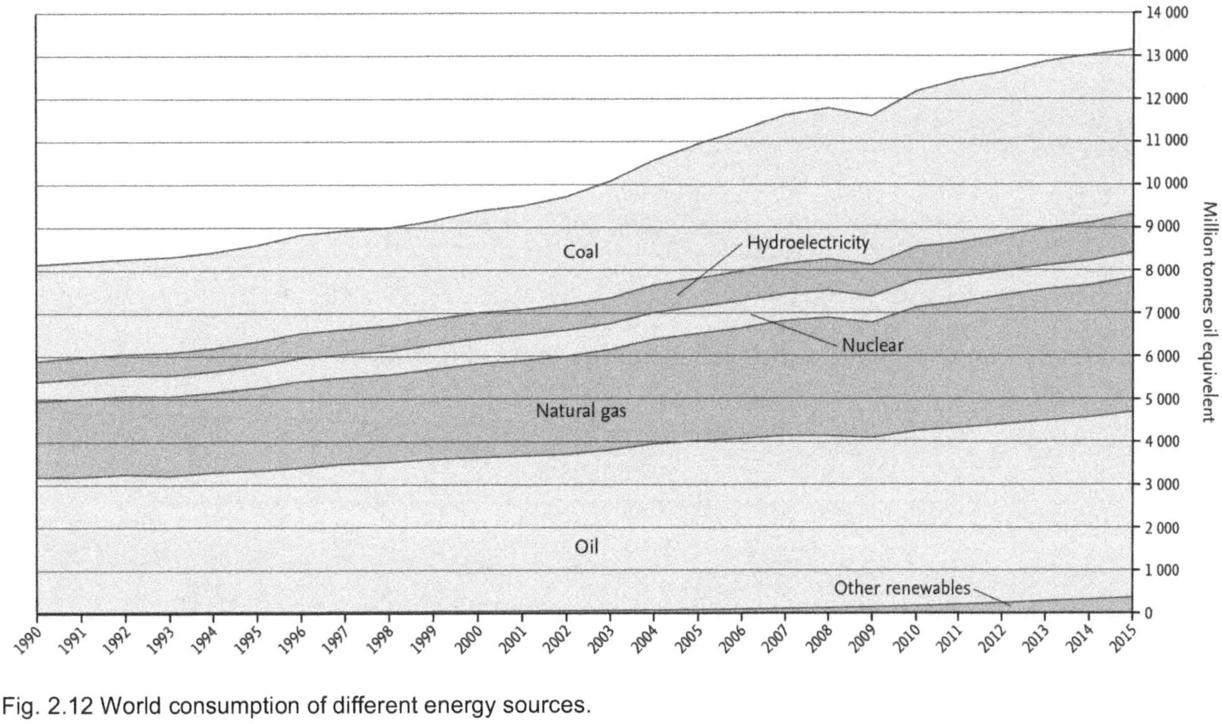

Fig. 2.12 World consumption of different energy sources.

a) Describe how the proportion of oil used has changed since 1990.

....

....

....

....

....

....

....

....

....

....

....

b) Which energy source has seen the greatest growth since 1990? Use statistics in your answer.

....

....

....

....

....

....

c) Which types of fuel dominate the global energy mix in 2015?

....

....

....

....

....

....

d) In your view, is the world likely to move away from the use of fossil fuels in the next 10 years? Use the graph, plus your own knowledge and understanding to justify your conclusion.

....

....

....

....

....

....

....

....

....

....

....

....

....

....

....

....

....

....

....

....

....

....

....

....

....

3. The pie charts below show the energy mix of Brazil.

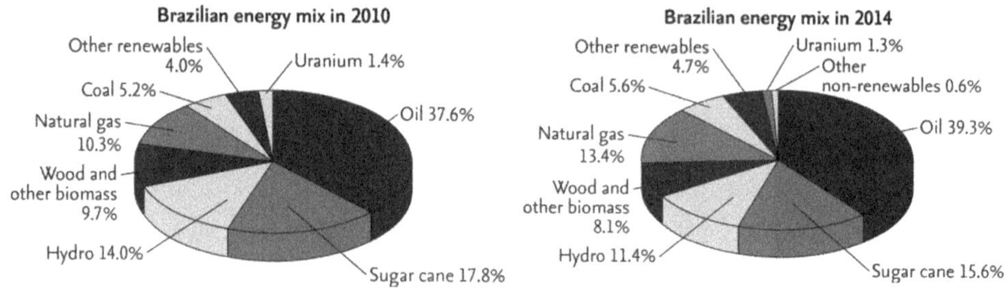

Fig. 2.13 Location of Brazil.

Fig. 2.14a and 2.14b Brazilian energy mix 2010 and 2014.

a) Define the key terms 'energy mix' and 'energy security'.

b) Describe the changes in Brazil's energy mix between 2010 and 2015.

c) What proportion of Brazil's energy comes from non-renewable sources? Has this changed over time?

....

....

....

....

....

....

d) Major HEP projects require construction of large scale dams across rivers. Describe and explain two advantages and two disadvantages of these projects.

....

....

....

....

....

....

....

....

....

4. Read the following extract from a news report from June 2016:

The Brazilian government has suspended a major HEP project in the Amazon rainforest whilst it investigates the impact on indigenous people in the region. The project would include 40 dams (5 major and 35 smaller projects) in the Tapajós river basin. This is part of a wider plan to develop 24 gigawatts of hydropower by 2024 to ease the electricity shortages that affect some places frequently. The largest dam – the 8000 MW São Luiz do Tapajós (SLT) dam – would be 7.6 km wide and flood hundreds of square kilometres of rainforest. The project would also be used to create an industrial waterway to allow soybeans produced inland to be shipped easily to North America and Europe. If built, the dams on the Tapajós would flood an area the size of greater London, Paris and Amsterdam combined. There is significant environmental opposition to the project from around the world, but Brazil argues such a project is needed to meet demand shortages from renewables.

Fig. 2.15 A traditional fishing village on the Rio Tapajos that would be flooded under the new plans.

Fig. 2.16 Aerial view of a hydroelectric power plant in northeastern Brazil.

a) Using your own research and the information here, outline the arguments for and against building the São Luiz do Tapajós dam in the Amazon rainforest.

For	**Against**

In recent years, Brazil has found an estimated 50 billion barrels of oil in deep water (2000 m) 300 km off the coast. These finds are the most significant of the 21st century and have the potential to lift millions of Brazilians out of poverty and increase energy security. The oil fields are in water deeper than the Gulf of Mexico (where the Deepwater Horizon disaster occurred) and occur in complex geology with the reservoirs reported to contain toxic gases. Accessing this oil presents major engineering challenges, as well as causing environmental concerns over possible spills and the carbon dioxide emissions caused by accessing and consuming the oil. Each well is estimated to cost US$300 million – four times the cost of drilling a shallow water well. Currently, a low oil price means that exploiting these wells is not a cost-effective solution to an energy shortage at this time. One answer would be to develop more renewable projects, but these have also been plagued with difficulties. Prolonged drought has reduced river levels and stopped HEP projects from functioning. The projects are often located a long way from urban centres. Furthermore, HEP projects that flood tropical forests often face acidic water conditions that reduce the efficiency of large-scale dams as turbine blades have to be replaced more frequently.

Meeting energy demand for a growing urban population is a challenge for the Brazilian government – especially at a time of low oil prices, a shrinking economy and rising public debt. An estimated 11 million people live in shanty towns known as favelas, and perhaps here people have a solution: small-scale household-based renewable solar projects. There has been a recent growth in these projects in favelas, and local councils and mayors are taking an interest in smaller-scale projects as a short-term solution to keep the lights on.

b) Why is it necessary to change the current energy mix in Brazil? Think about local, national and global issues.

....

....

....

....

....

....

....

....

....

....

....

....

The Brazilian government has a range of approaches to consider when dealing with decisions about future energy supply.

i. **Business as usual** – continue to use fossil fuels (some of which are imported) and current renewables whilst exploiting offshore gas and oil finds as soon as possible.

ii. **A multi-energy solution** – diversify the energy sources to make best use of what is available in the country. This could include:

- developing small scale energy projects
- developing new renewable energy sources such as solar and wave energy – both of which have high potential in the country
- increasing biofuel production to reduce dependence on oil imports
- building nuclear power stations – Brazil has large deposits of uranium
- building new HEP projects
- developing refining capacity to reduce imports of oil products and natural gas, whilst building oil and gas thermal power stations
- developing the use of carbon capture and storage in power stations

iii. **Energy conservation** – reducing the amount of energy consumed.

c) Using your own research, the information here and the Student's Book, consider the options available to Brazil. If you were advisor to the Minister of Energy in Brazil, what suggestions would you make on how to meet demand for energy in Brazilian cities – both now and in the future?

....

....

....

....

....

....

....

....

....

....

....

....

....

Answers to these questions can be found at **www.collins.co.uk/EnvMgmtIGCSE**

3 Agriculture and the environment

Introduction

This section reinforces and extends student learning by:

- Consolidating and developing the factual material in the Student's Book that students will be required to recall and explain (AO1)
- Advancing student thinking through providing more challenging content and activities than those in the Student's Book, which extend some areas of the specification and require the synthesis of information and the application of knowledge and understanding to unfamiliar contexts (AO2)
- Enabling students to grasp that the effective management of environmental issues requires a coherent and holistic approach to problem solving through the principles of sustainable development (AO3)

This is achieved through the provision of:

- Extension content and related activities that secure and progress student knowledge and understanding through tasks that require handling information from a variety of sources to reach conclusions and make judgments
- Supplementary case studies that reinforce and advance key principles and concepts and support evaluative thinking
- A decision making or problem solving exercise that encourages students to appreciate the complexities of environmental management and the pivotal role of the principles of sustainable development in achieving successful outcomes

Links to other chapters

One of the key determinants of agricultural productivity anywhere in the world is the nature of the soil with which farmers are presented. Soil is derived from the rocks that make up the thin outer crust of the Earth and is constantly recycled through the stages of the rock cycle. The fertility of soil, combined with its drainage characteristics, structure and texture, has a huge influence on its workability and potential for farming. The other fundamental natural determinant of patterns of agriculture and their yield potential is the availability of water. Global water distribution is very uneven, and consequently, the obtainability and quality of water has a huge influence on the agricultural prospects of any location. As a result, one very important reason for commissioning huge multipurpose dam projects is to bring irrigation water to currently dry areas, where the soil offers potential for commercial farming. Similarly, agricultural activity both contributes to, and suffers the consequences of, water pollution from domestic and industrial sources. Managing farms in a way that conserves water resources and reduces to a minimum their negative impacts on the natural ecosystems upon which all life depends is a core element of sustainable development. With the prospect of an additional three billion people on Earth by the end of the century, demand for food, particularly in LEDCs, will continue to rise. Maintaining the integrity of ecosystems while supplying such a demand presents the world with one of its greatest environmental management challenges.

Agriculture and the environment topic	Links to other subject content	Section
Soil composition	Extraction of rocks and minerals from the Earth	1
Soils for plant growth	Water supply Opportunities presented by natural hazards Ecosystems	4 6 9
Agriculture types	Water usage Population structure Human population distribution and density	4 8 8
Increasing agricultural yields	Energy demand Water supply The water cycle	2 4 4
Impact of agriculture	Atmospheric pollution – causes and impacts Deforestation	7 9
Causes and impacts of soil erosion	Flooding Deforestation	6 9
Managing soil erosion	Drought Managing forests	6 9
Sustainable agriculture	Managing atmospheric pollution Measuring and managing biodiversity	7 9

Extension content and related activities

Increasing agricultural yields

The Green Revolution is the term used to describe a programme of agricultural development in the 1960s and 1970s, designed to increase food production in some of the poorest countries of the world such as India, the Philippines, Brazil and Mexico, where populations were growing rapidly. The programme focused on introducing the modern commercial and intensive farming technologies common in MEDCs, to countries where farming was still largely traditional, small scale and subsistence based. The overriding objective was to boost food production through:

- The adoption of high yielding varieties of cereal crops, especially dwarf hybrid wheats and rice, which matured more quickly than traditional varieties and allowed for two or even three crops a year to be grown.
- The widespread use of chemical-based pesticides and fertilisers.
- Controlling and regulating water supply through the construction of irrigation schemes using diesel and electric pumps.
- The introduction of farm machinery such as tractors and threshers.
- Reforming land ownership by amalgamating smaller, less profitable farms to form much larger single units where new technologies such as machinery could be used most efficiently.
- Improving the general infrastructure of rural areas, especially the road network, to enable farm produce to reach national and international markets more quickly.
- Establishing facilities such as credit banks from which farmers could borrow money to invest in improving their farms.
- The use of multiple cropping where a field is used to grow two or more crops throughout the year, so that a field constantly has something growing in it.

Successes

The Green Revolution brought about huge increases in food production throughout what was then referred to as the Developing World. Some argue that it saved a billion people from the prospect of famine and starvation during the period 1960–1980 when the world's population grew by two billion and experienced a peak annual growth rate of 2.1 per cent in 1970. In the Philippines, the introduction of the IR8 rice semi-dwarf high-yielding rice plant known as 'miracle rice' increased rice production from 3.7 to 7.7 million tonnes a year between 1960 and 1980. In India, the same plant when used with fertilisers increased rice yields from 0.01 tonnes per square kilometre using traditional methods to 0.1 tonnes per square kilometre by 1995. Brazil's vast inland cerrado region was regarded as unfit for farming before the 1960s because the soil was too acidic and poor in nutrients. However, from the 1960s, vast quantities of lime (pulverised chalk or limestone) were poured on the soil to reduce its acidity, and by the 1990s, between 14 million and 16 million tonnes of lime were being spread on Brazilian fields each year. The quantity rose to 25 million tonnes in 2003 and 2004, equalling around 0.05 tonnes of lime per square kilometre. As a result, Brazil has become the world's second biggest soybean exporter and, as a result of the massive increases in animal feed crops such as oats made possible by the Green Revolution, Brazil is now the biggest exporter of beef and poultry in the world. The Green Revolution also contributed to developing manufacturing industries such as engineering firms producing farm machinery and irrigation equipment in the countries in which it operated. In addition, many of the thousands of dams that were constructed to provide irrigation water also generated hydroelectricity, which further encouraged businesses and industrial growth. Hydroelectricity transformed the lives of millions in rural areas where wood was the only source of heat and light.

Problems and issues

Whilst the food increases that occurred during the Green Revolution were considerable and welcomed in the countries in which they occurred, the programme has been criticised for the following reasons:

- Traditional, mostly subsistence and self-sufficient, family farms were converted very quickly to intensive commercial practices using expensive fertilisers, pesticides, irrigation systems and seeds. For example, the traditional system of farmers saving seeds for sowing the following year quickly disappeared and was replaced with farmers having to buy expensive hybrid plant seeds every season. Farmers were encouraged to borrow the money required for inputs such as machinery from credit banks. Millions were made destitute and lost their farms in years when crops failed or yields were less than expected because they were unable to pay back loans on time.
- When small farms were consolidated to create larger single units, hundreds of thousands of family farmers were displaced from their land and livelihoods. This was because the new larger commercial farms used a lot of machinery and technology rather than manual labour, which made their work superfluous to requirements.
- Those farmers, driven off the land either by debt and land consolidation or because their work was replaced by machines, migrated to towns and cities. Rural–urban migration increased greatly during the Green Revolution and this created many problems in urban areas. Most migrants could not find regular work in urban areas and therefore could not afford regular housing either. Such displaced migrants ended up living in very high-density shanty towns like favelas without running water, electricity, adequate sanitation or work.
- Intensive farming methods associated with the Green Revolution, such as pesticides and fertilisers, have been responsible for a number of environmental problems. For example, in the Philippines, pesticides used to control diseases of hybrid rice plants also killed fish and vegetables that farmers grew in the paddy fields to supplement their diets.
- The Green Revolution has led to the loss of agricultural crop biodiversity as it relied on just a small number of hybrid varieties of plants. Traditional varieties of rice and wheat that have been bred in traditional ways over thousands of years, and that have many positive genetic traits, have been lost.
- The continuous monoculture of crops on the same land led to serious soil erosion and land degradation in many areas. In order to keep yields high, farmers resorted to felling forested areas to expand their farmland. This had a serious effect on local ecosystems, particularly in tropical and semi-tropical regions.
- Although the Green Revolution improved food security in many poor countries, it did contribute to widening the gap between the rich and the poor as wealthier and better-educated people had better access to credit and land than their poorer counterparts.
- In a number of places, the Green Revolution was held responsible for serious health problems experienced by local people. For example, in the Punjab region of India, a number of studies made a link between heavy use of chemical pesticides and increased incidence of cancer. Another study in the same region in 2009 revealed that 20 per cent of wells sampled had nitrate levels (from nitrogen-based fertilisers) above the human safety limit laid down by the World Health Organization.

Summarise the benefits and costs of the Green Revolution programme on an enlarged copy of the table below.

	Advantages	**Disadvantages**
Economic		
Social		
Environmental		

Impact of agriculture

In LEDCs, farmers with smallholdings that decide to convert to producing cash crops for export can encounter very serious problems. Read the following passage written by a small cash crop farmer on the island of St Lucia in the Caribbean and summarise, in your own words, the main reasons why the farmer feels powerless to improve his life.

Fig. 3.1 St Lucia.

Fig. 3.2 Worker harvesting bunches of bananas, River Doree Plantation, St Lucia.

I have a small farm of just 0.04 sq km in the hills above the capital city of Castries. I grow bananas that are sold in supermarkets in the United Kingdom. The tropical climate of St Lucia is ideal for growing bananas as it is hot and wet all through the year – the average daily temperature is 25 °C and in most years there is over 2000 mm of rainfall. As a result the growing season here is always twelve months long. Being on a hillside is an advantage too as the water drains away well and the roots of the banana trees are never waterlogged, which they would hate. Growing bananas is very hard work for me because I can't afford things such as chemical pesticides to spray on the trees to kill off insects and other pests. I have to use the traditional method of covering my banana bunches with polyethylene bags to protect them from the wind, attacks by insects and birds and to keep them at the right temperature. The time between planting a banana plant and the harvest of the banana bunch is between 9 and 12 months and all of the work to ensure that the crop is as healthy and large as possible has to be done by hand. Having to constantly be doing things such as weeding; propping up the trees to ensure they don't break under the weight of the banana bunches; irrigating when we have dry periods; and washing and packing the fruit in boxes by hand means that I work long hours, seven days a week. Often when serious storms and hurricanes (my greatest fear) are forecast, I spend all night on the farm as well just to be on hand if anything should happen.

When I was young and working with my father on the farm, we used to take our bananas to the market in Castries where lots of buyers (people representing companies in the United Kingdom) used to come and offer to buy our bananas. Because our bananas have always been of high quality, the buyers would compete with each other to get them and as a result we could negotiate a good price. Sadly those days are gone. Today just a few supermarkets control all of the buying of bananas and they all want the same thing – to offer their shoppers food at the lowest possible prices and to keep their profits as high as possible. The result for a small producer such as me is that I am left with no choice – the supermarkets control all of the trade – and I have to sell at very low prices. If this wasn't hard enough to bear, the supermarkets insist on the very highest standards of banana production – if there is the slightest bruise or blemish on it, or if it is the wrong shape and length for example, they will reject it. Sometimes I am left with perfectly lovely fruit that I have no option but to sell to local families at a price lower than it cost me to grow them in the first place. Perhaps the worst thing for me is that being such a small farmer I can't compete with the massive plantations of multiple square kilometres in countries such as Ecuador, Costa Rica, the Philippines and Colombia, which use a lot of modern technology including chemical pesticides and fertilisers. They can produce bananas at a much lower cost than me and still make a decent profit. It's really hard some months to feed my family and to find the fees to send my two children to school. I think they deserve better for all the hours of work I put in, seven days a week, 365 days a year. Put it this way – if a supermarket shopper buys a kilo of my bananas in the United Kingdom for, say 68 pence (US$0.9), I will receive less than 7 pence (US$0.09) from the sale. This doesn't seem very fair to me but I am powerless to do anything about it.

An increasing number of small banana farmers in St Lucia are now 'Fairtrade certified'. Watch the film at **https://www.youtube.com/watch?v=wpGMeQXyr5w** in which Nick Hewer travels to St Lucia to meet Retina and Stephen, two Fairtrade banana farmers. What benefits does being a Fairtrade farmer bring? Consider particularly the advantages of minimum pricing, the Fairtrade premium and being able to set up cooperatives.

Connecting the agriculture and environment topics

Biofuels are substances extracted from crops that have just been harvested and then burned to release energy. There are three main types of biofuel – ethanol, biodiesel and biojet fuel. Ethanol is used in engines that burn petrol, biodiesel in engines that burn diesel, and biojet fuel is used in aeroplanes. Ethanol is commonly made from crops such as maize, wheat and sugar cane, and biodiesel from soya beans and palm oil. At present, an estimated 6 billion litres of ethanol and 250 million litres of biodiesel are produced worldwide each year. Ethanol is commonly mixed with petrol for use in car engines. Most petrol sold in European and North American countries now routinely includes ethanol. Biodiesel can be used directly in diesel vehicle engines without any modifications being required.

Growing food crops for biofuel extraction is increasing. In 2004, only 1 per cent of the world's crop land was used to grow biofuel crops but by 2030 this will increase to over 4 per cent. This overall average figure hides important regional differences. In MEDC regions such as Europe, it is likely that over 15 per cent of cropland will be planted for biofuels by 2030 and 10 per cent in the United States and Canada.

The growing of biofuels is a contentious environmental management issue with strong views on either side of the argument.

Arguments in favour of biofuel production from food crops

- Biofuels are sustainable renewable resources that reduce the worlds' dependence on non-renewable fossil fuels such as oil and natural gas.
- Biofuels are much cleaner than fossil fuels and contribute to reducing greenhouse gas emissions because they are 'carbon neutral'. This means that the amount of carbon dioxide they release into the atmosphere on combustion is the same as the amount of carbon absorbed by the plants as they grew.
- For countries without their own reserves of fossil fuels, growing their own biofuels can be a means of reducing economic dependence on other countries around the world through no longer having to import so much energy. Such countries can become more self-sufficient in terms of their energy supplies and therefore save money on expensive imports.
- Growing and processing biofuels can boost the economy of countries through the jobs that are created and the taxes that workers and successful companies pay to the government.

Arguments opposing biofuel production from food crops

- Using food crops to make biofuels means that those crops are no longer available for human consumption. There are worries that this could lead in time to food shortages for people in some parts of the world, particularly in MEDCs.

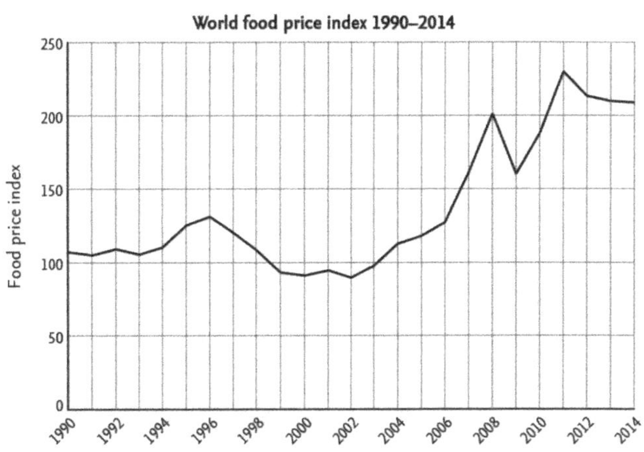

Fig. 3.3 World food price index 1990–2014.

- Increasing biofuel farming has been identified as an important factor explaining the massive increase in food prices that has occurred around the world in the last ten years. Since 2000, the average world prices for rice rose by 217 per cent, wheat by 136 per cent, maize by 125 per cent and soybeans by 107 per cent.
- As more farmland is taken to grow biofuel crops, other farms have to increase their yields of food crops to compensate. This encourages them to use very intensive methods such as increasing the use of chemical fertilisers, pesticides and irrigation. This can lead to serious environmental side effects such as eutrophication, bioaccumulation and the salinisation of soils.
- Creating new land on which to grow biofuels such as palm oil is a major factor contributing to deforestation, particularly in tropical regions such as Borneo. Relatively little land is needed for oil rigs and pipelines compared to the size of the vast underground oil fields that they tap into (not least because many oil fields are offshore). The same is not true of biofuels: enormous amounts of land are needed to grow the crops.
- The process of growing biofuel crops (such as making fertilisers and pesticides and providing irrigation) and then processing the plants consumes a lot of energy – most of which comes from burning fossil fuels. When this is taken into account, producing biofuels can eventually produce more carbon dioxide than the fuels themselves, except when they are burned.
- Biofuel crops are frequently grown year after year on the same land. This practice of monoculture leads to nutrient depletion and land degradation and makes the soil more vulnerable to erosion and desertification.

How does the biofuel life cycle diagram in Figure 3.4 suggest that ethanol is a carbon neutral source of energy for cars?

Why do some people believe that producing biofuels such as ethanol may in fact create more carbon dioxide than they save?

How could you modify Figure 3.4 to show this? Draw a labelled sketch to illustrate your thoughts.

Explain in your own words how growing biofuel crops on farmland can have negative effects on both the environment and people.

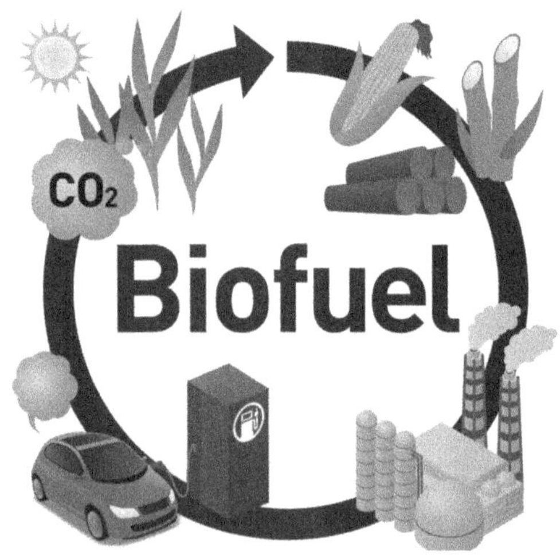

Fig. 3.4 Biofuel life cycle.

Supplementary case study 1

Soil salinisation in Australia

Salinisation occurs when the water contained in soils evaporates in high temperatures. This has the effect of drawing soluble salts of sodium, magnesium and calcium by capillary action from the subsoil to the surface, where they accumulate in high concentrations. Over time, the build-up of soluble salts in this way leads to the land becoming degraded and unusable as most plants find the salts toxic. An increase in salt can reduce the ability of plants to absorb water through their roots by osmosis, cause leaf burn resulting in poor growth and death. Irrigation of farmland in dry regions throughout the world is a major cause of soil salinisation. For example, in Mexico 15 per cent of all farmland (amounting to 30 000 sq km) is salinised.

Nearly 20 per cent of the irrigated land of Australia is affected by salinisation. Approximately 25 000 sq km of farmland are now unusable for farming as a result of salinisation, and this figure could rise to 170 000 sq km by 2050. Much of this land is the most productive farming land in Australia. Lost agricultural production from this salinised farmland costs the Australian government US$130 million a year in lost income.

Fig. 3.5 Farmland damaged by salinisation in Western Australia.

Salinisation has occurred in dry land regions of Australia such as the southwest of the state of Western Australia for three main reasons:

- All water (even natural rainwater) contains some dissolved salts. When the plants use the rainwater, the salts are left behind in the soil and build up there. This natural salt level can range from 0.005–0.02 tonnes per square kilometre every year.
- Irrigation often has the effect of raising the water table (the level of the groundwater held in underground aquifers) in dry land regions to within two or three metres of the surface. The naturally occurring salts in the groundwater are then raised by capillary action to the surface of the soil.
- The introduction of European-style farming over one hundred years ago has resulted in the felling of 15 billion indigenous trees in Western Australia alone. Current figures put the continued loss of woodland to farmland at 3000 sq km a year. Native trees are deep rooted and have a high demand for water, which ensured that the water table level remained well below the surface. These trees were replaced by farm crops and livestock pasture plants that have much shorter roots and use less water. Slowly but surely, the water table has risen, bringing the salt up with it.

Management practices

Two approaches have been taken to manage the challenge of soil salinity in Australia – prevention and reclamation. The main prevention method has been to ensure that no more native woodland is cleared from areas at greatest risk of salinisation. In addition, millions of deep-rooted native trees have been planted to lower the water table, which prevents soluble salts being drawn up to the surface by capillary action – the main cause of salinisation. Other prevention strategies have included avoiding building dams at sites where the water table is high; ensuring that soils are always covered by good pasture cover; and avoiding constructing deep water drainage systems. Reversing soil salinity is very difficult and may take tens or even hundreds of years to achieve. However, when planted in saline soil areas, a hybrid gum tree called saltgrow has shown that it is able to completely remove salinity in damaged soils, which allows new grasses and shrubs that are not salt resistant to establish themselves. Leaching is another method used to remove salts from contaminated soils. It involves allowing up to 20 per cent of irrigation water to percolate through the soil at a rapid rate. This has the effect of filtering out salts in a solution that has salt concentrations five to ten times higher than that of the irrigation water.

Supplementary case study 2

Agricultural 'land grabbing' in Africa

Between 2008 and 2013, the price of food around the world increased hugely. Over this period, the price of rice, for example, increased by 217 per cent and the cost of wheat by 136 per cent. The United Nations Food and Agricultural Organization estimates that in the last ten years alone global food prices have risen by 83 per cent. Although the world's population was increasing by 80 million a year throughout this time, this growth in numbers was not responsible for the hike in prices. The increase in global food production has kept pace with the increase in the number of people living in the world.

The steep increase in the price of food was caused by five factors:

- Between 2003 and 2013, the price of oil rose from an average of US$30 a barrel to over US$100. This had an important 'knock on' effect for farming as it made fuel for machinery used on farms, together with transport costs of taking produce to market, much more expensive. In order to maintain profit levels, farmers raised the price of their farm products.
- Oil is an important raw material used in the manufacture of chemical fertilisers. Higher oil prices therefore led to very rapid increases in the cost of fertilisers. The increases in prices that occurred in six common fertilisers over the twelve month period, 2010–2011, is shown in the graph below. Because farmers had to pay more for fertilisers, they recouped this extra cost by increasing the prices of the food they produced.

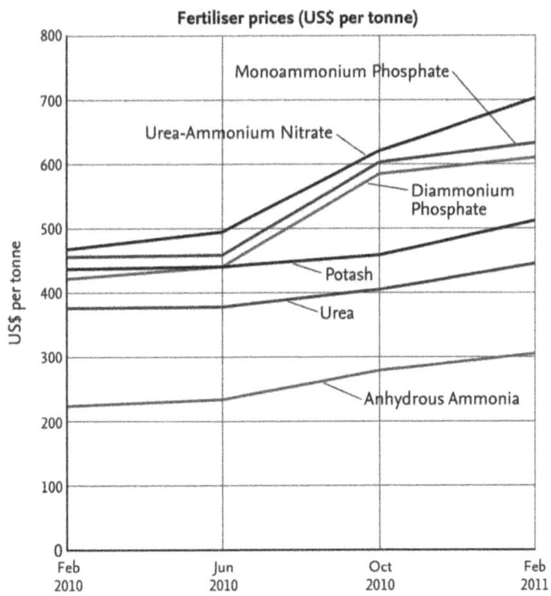

Fig. 3.6 Prices of different fertilisers in 2010–2011.

- A steady increase in the use of food grains such as wheat to manufacture biofuels like ethanol rather than to feed people has reduced the supply of cereal crops. Currently, 100 million tonnes of food grain (5 per cent of the world's yearly harvest) is used to manufacture biofuels and this proportion is increasing. A reduction in supply of some food crops has contributed to price increases in staple foods.
- Extreme weather events such as the prolonged drought between 2007 and 2012 in Australia led to less food crops being produced globally. For example the drought in Australia directly caused a 98 per cent drop in the country's rice harvest and serious reductions in the amount of wheat it was able to export. This was serious as Australia is

the second largest wheat exporting country in the world. Less food availability led directly to price increases.

- Hundreds of millions of people in countries such as China are adopting a more 'western' diet and eating habits as a result of rapid economic development and increasing prosperity. The consumption of more processed foods and particularly meat by people in these countries has increased demand for farm produce around the world. The desire for more meat has led directly to an increase in the price of grain. The production of 1 kg of beef requires 7 kg of grain feed and uses twelve times the amount of water needed to produce 1 kg of wheat and more than five times the amount of farmland.

Land grabbing in Africa is occurring as a result of rising food prices and increased demands for food in countries such as India, China, Saudi Arabia and the United Arab Emirates. It involves companies or government organisations in these countries buying or leasing land in much less economically developed African countries to use to grow more food for people back at home. Over 600 000 sq km of farmland in African countries has been 'grabbed' in this way.

Country	**Land acquired by foreign investors (sq km)**	**Country**	**Land acquired by foreign investors (sq km)**
Democratic Republic of the Congo	82 503	Republic of Congo	6640
Sudan	32 814	Liberia	64 980
Tanzania	19 177	Sierra Leone	4236
Mozambique	14 969	Gabon	4072
South Sudan	14 085	Madagascar	3691
Ethiopia	10 014	Nigeria	3623
Uganda	8589	Cameroon	2950
Morocco	7000		

Table 3.1 African nations with most land grabbed by foreign companies and government agencies.

Ethiopia has sold or leased over 10 000 sq km of land to foreign companies and governments since 2007. The majority of this land is in the most fertile areas of the west and south of the country such as the Gambella region, which is comparable in size to the area of Belgium.

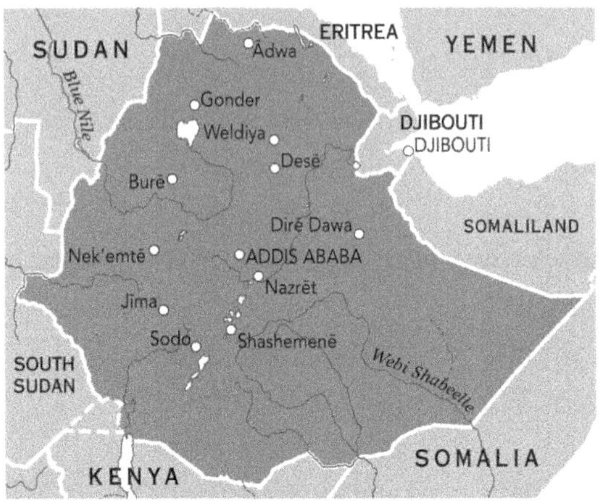

Fig. 3.7 Ethiopia.

Here, countries such as Saudi Arabia and China are already growing over a million tonnes of rice a year to supply their own populations. India is also a major purchaser of land. In India an increasing population and the trend of using more of its own farmland to produce biofuels rather than food means that the government sees buying cheap fertile land and water resources in poorer countries such as Ethiopia, as a solution to its food problems.

Data response and decision making exercises

1. The data in the table below shows changes in managed honeybee colonies in the United States between 1945 and 2005.

Year	Number of honeybee colonies (millions)	Year	Number of honeybee colonies (millions)
1945	5.5	1980	4.4
1950	5.5	1985	4.3
1955	5.4	1990	3.2
1960	5.0	1995	2.5
1965	4.7	2000	2.5
1970	4.0	2005	2.4
1975	4.4		

Table 3.2 Changes in managed honeybee colonies in the US between 1945 and 2005.

a) Plot this data as a line graph on the grid below.

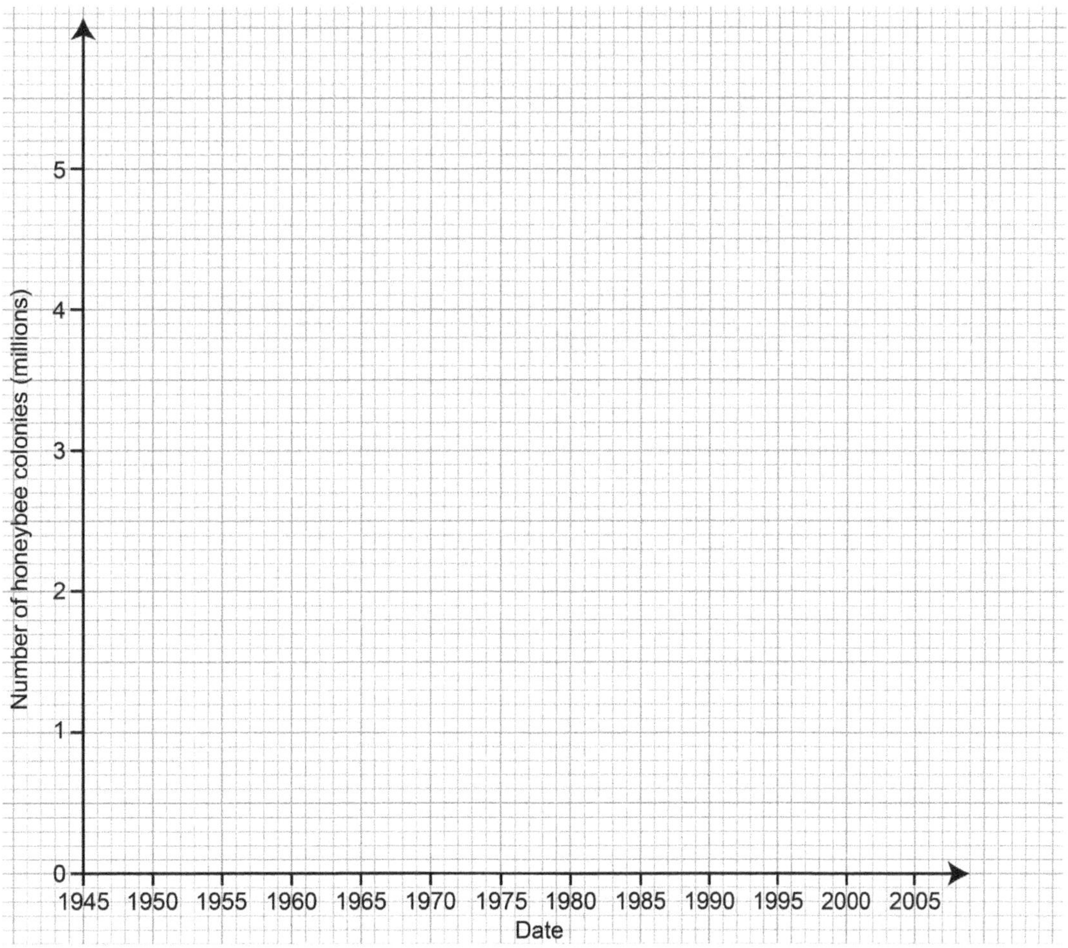

b) By how many millions did the number of colonies fall between 1945 and 2005?

....

c) Which five-year period recorded the largest single fall in colony numbers?

....

d) At the current rate of decline from 2000 to 2005, in which survey year will researchers record less than two million bee colonies for the first time?

....

2. Throughout North America, Europe and many parts of Asia and Oceania, wild bee populations (as well as managed bee colonies) are facing a very serious decline.

Fig. 3.8 European honeybee *Apis mellifera*.

Ecologists place much of the blame for this on intensive commercial farming practices. Explain how each of the following practices can threaten wild bee numbers.

a) Misuse of chemical pesticides

....

....

....

....

....

b) Loss of habitats such as wildflower meadows, scrubland and forests

....

....

....

....

....

c) Air pollution

....

....

....

....

....

d) Use of genetically modified (GM) crops

....

....

....

....

....

3. Wild bees and other invertebrate creatures such as butterflies and midges, together with vertebrate organisms like bats, are vitally important crop pollinators. Pollination involves the transport of male gametes or sperm cells to the female reproductive organs of seed plants. It is an example of one kind of interaction between species in a habitat.

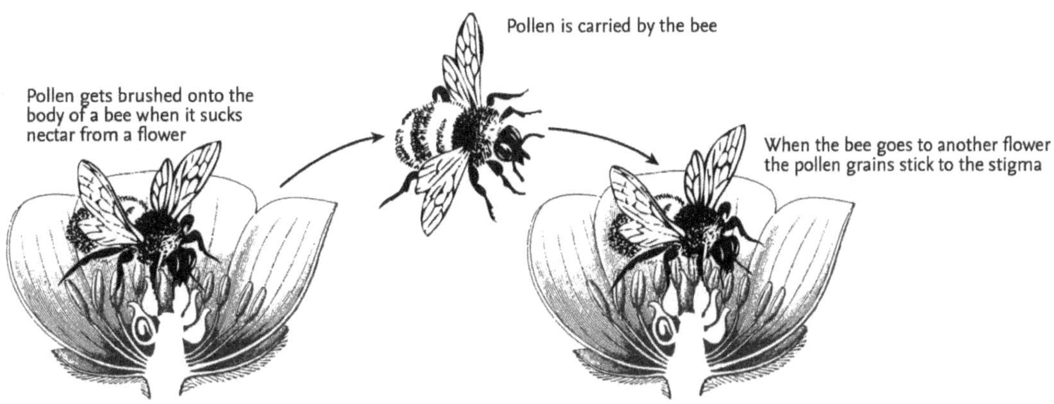

Fig. 3.9 Pollination by bees.

Explain what these three other types of interaction involve.

a) Competition

....

....

....

b) Predation

....

....

....

c) Mutualism

....

....

....

4. It is estimated that pollinators are worth at least US$5 billion a year to European commercial farmers. This is because 80 per cent of all crops grown on farms in Europe depend directly on wild insects, bats and birds for their pollination. If there were no wild pollinators then farmers would have to pay to hire captive honeybee hives that would then be transported to their farms to do the job instead.

a) If this situation were to occur in the future, describe and explain one very likely effect it would have on food shoppers around the world.

....

....

....

....

b) If the pollination of food crops in the future came to rely on a single species of captive bee, why could this be a serious risk to the security of global food supplies?

....

....

....

5. In July 2009 the global agribusiness company, Syngenta, launched a five year programme called Operation Pollinator to provide essential habitat and food sources for pollinating insects across Europe. The project aims to boost the numbers of pollinating insects on commercial farms and protect biodiversity, which in turn increases crop yields and farmers' incomes.

a) What does biodiversity mean?

....

....

b) What does it mean when a farmer improves crop yields?

....

....

c) An important element of the Operation Pollinator programme is to create new areas of habitat for pollinators such as planting field margins around crops with wild flowers.

Fig. 3.10 A rapeseed field margin sown with pollen and nectar rich wildflowers for bees and insects in Northamptonshire, England.

As well as creating new habitat for pollinating insects, explain why wildflower margins will also boost the numbers of a variety of birds and mammals living on farmland.

....

....

....

....

....

6. Operation Pollinator is considered to be a good example of sustainable agriculture because it seeks to improve yields on commercial farms in a way that conserves and improves the natural ecosystems on which all farming depends. Describe and explain how each of the following strategies are also good examples of sustainable farming practices.

a) Organic fertilisers

....

....

....

b) Livestock and crop rotation

....

....

....

c) Biocontrol of pests and diseases

....

....

....

d) Weeding by hand

....

....

....

e) Trickle drip irrigation and rainwater harvesting

....

....

....

7. Creating new land for both subsistence and commercial agriculture is the single most important cause of deforestation in the world. Define the following terms.

a) Deforestation

....

....

....

b) Subsistence agriculture

....

....

....

c) Commercial agriculture

....

....

....

8. The central African country of Cameroon has a population of 20 million and is one of the poorest countries in the world. It is similar in area to Sweden and is ranked 147th out of 183 counties by the World Bank when measuring Gross Domestic Product at purchasing power parity per person. Life expectancy at birth is 55 years (South Korea: 81 years), infant mortality is 56 per 1000 live births (South Korea: 4 per 1000) and access to improved water supplies stands at 76 per cent (South Korea: 100 per cent). Just under half of the country is covered by tropical rain forest.

Fig. 3.11 Location of Cameroon.

In 2015, Cameroon produced 300 000 tonnes of the agro-industrial crop palm oil. By 2020, the government intends to increase production by 50 per cent to 450 000 tonnes. This expansion in palm oil production will almost certainly bring both benefits and negative impacts.

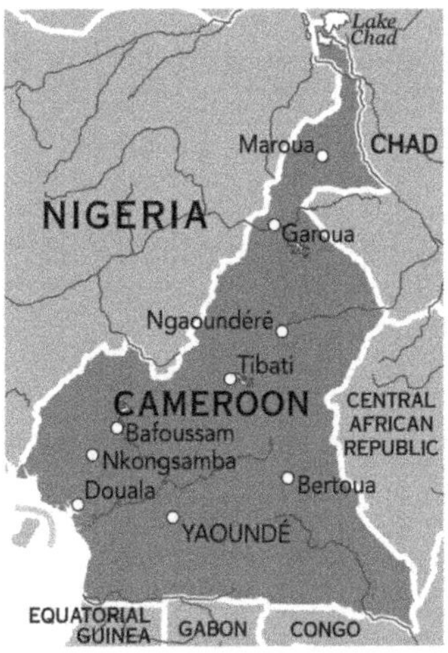

Fig. 3.12 Cameroon.

Consider some benefits that might arise under the following headings.

a) Employment and living standards

....

....

....

b) Income to the government

....

....

....

c) Development of new road and railway infrastructure

....

....

....

Now consider some negative impacts under the following headings.

d) Deforestation and biodiversity

....

....

....

e) Impact on indigenous peoples

....

....

....

f) Greenhouse gas emissions

....

....

....

Answers to these questions can be found at **www.collins.co.uk/EnvMgmtIGCSE**

4 Water and its management

Introduction

This section reinforces and extends student learning by:

- Consolidating and developing the factual material in the Student's Book that students will be required to recall and explain (AO1)
- Advancing student thinking through providing more challenging content and activities than those in the Student's Book, which extend some areas of the specification and require the synthesis of information and the application of knowledge and understanding to unfamiliar contexts (AO2)
- Enabling students to grasp that the effective management of environmental issues requires a coherent and holistic approach to problem solving through the principles of sustainable development (AO3)

This is achieved through the provision of:

- Extension content and related activities that secure and progress student knowledge and understanding through tasks that require handling information from a variety of sources to reach conclusions and make judgments
- Supplementary case studies that reinforce and advance key principles and concepts and support evaluative thinking
- A decision making or problem solving exercise that encourages students to appreciate the complexities of environmental management and the pivotal role of the principles of sustainable development in achieving successful outcomes

Links to other chapters

Water is the world's most important natural resource and the fundamental component of both biotic and abiotic elements of ecosystems upon which all life on Earth relies. Agriculture, for example, would not be possible without it. The constant movement of water through the closed system of the hydrological cycle has been a major determinant of atmospheric conditions and weather patterns anywhere in the world for billions of years. Pollution of this atmospheric water through human economic activities poses serious environmental management challenges, such as acid rain, in many regions of the world today. Ocean and other saline water accounts for almost all the water found on Earth. Maintaining the integrity of ocean ecosystems as a sustainable source of resources like fisheries and energy supplies, to meet the demands of a rapidly growing global population, presents another critical and immediate environmental issue. Pollution of oceans, particularly as a result of pumping or transporting oil, is an ever-present threat to fragile marine habitats and the biodiversity that lives within them. Human life depends on a tiny fraction of the world's water that is held in freshwater reserves. These freshwater reserves are unevenly distributed, which creates water-rich and water-poor regions in which shortages occur. Millions of people lack access to both safe drinking water and improved sanitation facilities and are affected by water-borne diseases as a result.

Water and its management topic	Links to other subject content	Section
Global distribution of water	Oceans as a resource	5
The water cycle	Increasing agricultural yields Flooding	3 6
Water supply	Increasing agricultural yields Soils for plant growth Drought	3 3 6
Water usage	Agricultural types	3
Water quality and availability	Human population distribution and density	8
Multipurpose dam projects	Energy resources and the generation of electricity	2
Water pollution and its sources	Earthquakes and volcanoes Atmospheric pollution – causes and impacts	6 7
Impact of water pollution	Impact of oil pollution	2
Managing pollution of fresh water	Management of oil pollution Tropical cyclones Managing atmospheric pollution	2 6 7
Managing water-related disease	Changes in population size	8

Extension content and related activities

Water quality and availability

Latin America and the Caribbean, with water reserves of 13 867 billion cubic metres and available water reserves per person of 22 162 cubic metres, is the most water-rich region in the world. However, the one country that is the exception to this rule is Peru. All of Peru suffers from either physical or economic water shortage. The situation is worse along the narrow strip of land between the Andes Mountains and the Pacific Ocean. Here is where the Atacama Desert is found (the driest hot desert in the world), with an annual average rainfall of only 6 mm a year and home to 70 per cent of the country's population (21 million). Eight million people live in the city of Lima alone, and this number increases by 100 000 a year. It is the second driest capital city in the world after Cairo in Egypt. Over one million residents in Lima do not have access to improved water supplies or sanitation facilities.

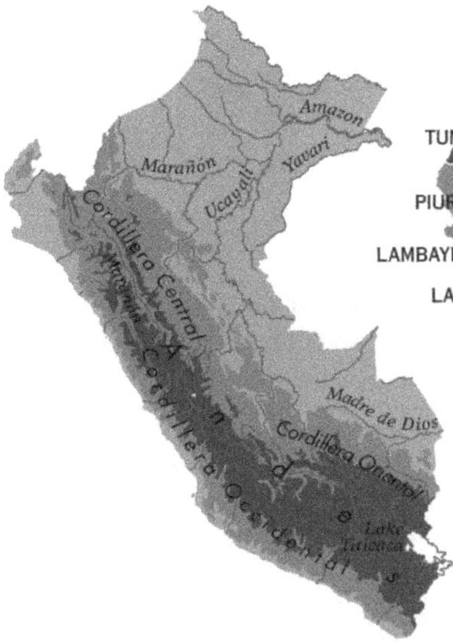

Fig. 4.1 Peru.

Fig. 4.2 Districts of Peru.

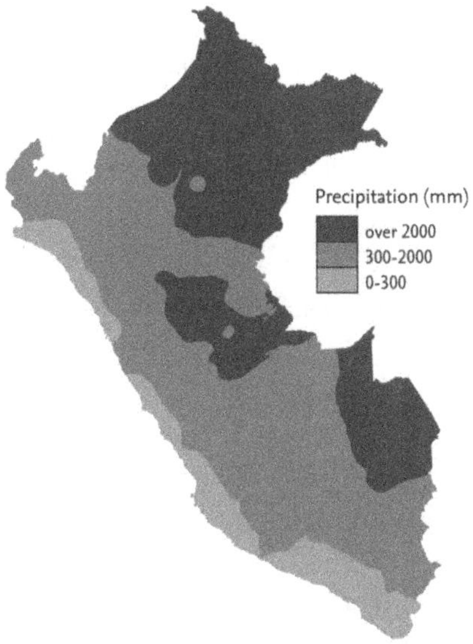

Fig. 4.3 Annual precipitation in Peru.

Fig. 4.4 In the Bellavista neighbourhood in Peru, water is often contaminated and unsafe for drinking.

Fig. 4.5 Panoramic view of Lima.

With only two per cent of Peru's available water reserves, but eight out of ten of the country's people, the city of Lima is facing major water supply problems. At the same time that the population of the city is growing rapidly, its main source of water is drying up. Currently the city gets most of its water from the Rio Rimac and two other rivers that flow out of glaciers high in the Andes Mountains. However these glaciers are melting rapidly. Estimates indicate that glaciers in the Peruvian Andes have lost a third of their surface area since 1970 as a result of global warming. Ironically, water supply will actually increase slightly in the next few years as more of the glaciers melt, but a massive decline is predicted after 2030.

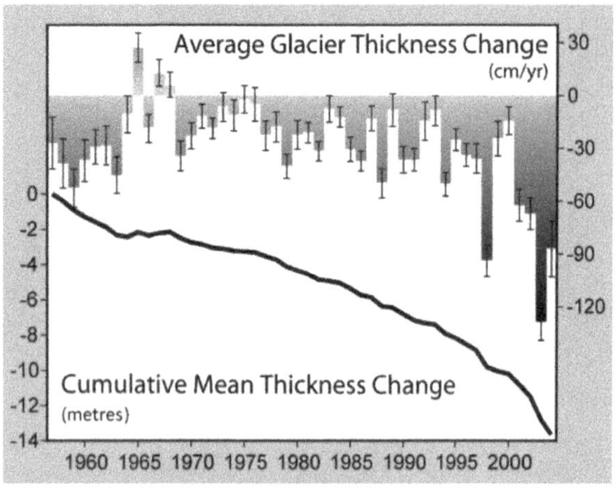

Fig. 4.6 Average glacier thickness change.

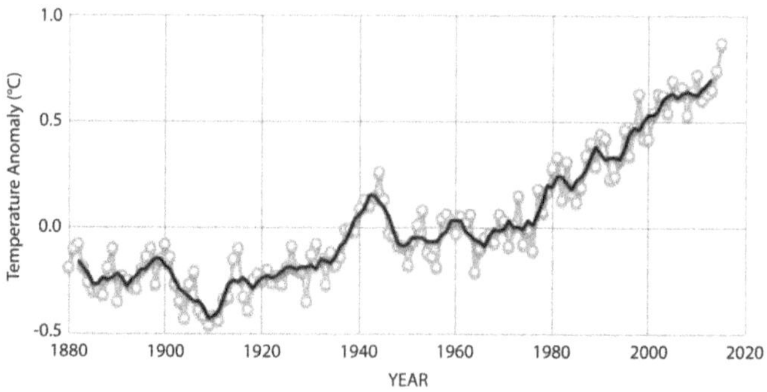

Fig. 4.7 Global land-ocean temperature index. The grey line represents the annual mean, and the black line represents the 5 year mean.

Describe what has happened to the glacier whose data is shown in Figure 4.6 since the 1960s and suggest why it has happened using the information in Figure 4.7.

Water shortages affect those in Lima without running water the most as they have to rely on expensive water deliveries by truck. One third of the city's population live in shanty dwellings known as barriadas. People living in barriadas have to pay much more for water than anyone else in the city despite being the poorest residents.

Fig. 4.8 A typical barriada in Lima, Peru.

Fig. 4.9 A fog catcher in South America.

Many of the inhabitants of the barriadas in Lima have become 'fog catchers' as they look to source drinking and irrigation water from water droplets in the atmosphere. Giant nets are used to create artificial condensation surfaces. The water droplets condense on the nets and then fall to the bottom to be collected for drinking or to be channelled away to crops.

Now read the newspaper article at: **http://www.theguardian.com/global-development/2012/sep/19/peru-fog-catchers-water-supplies**

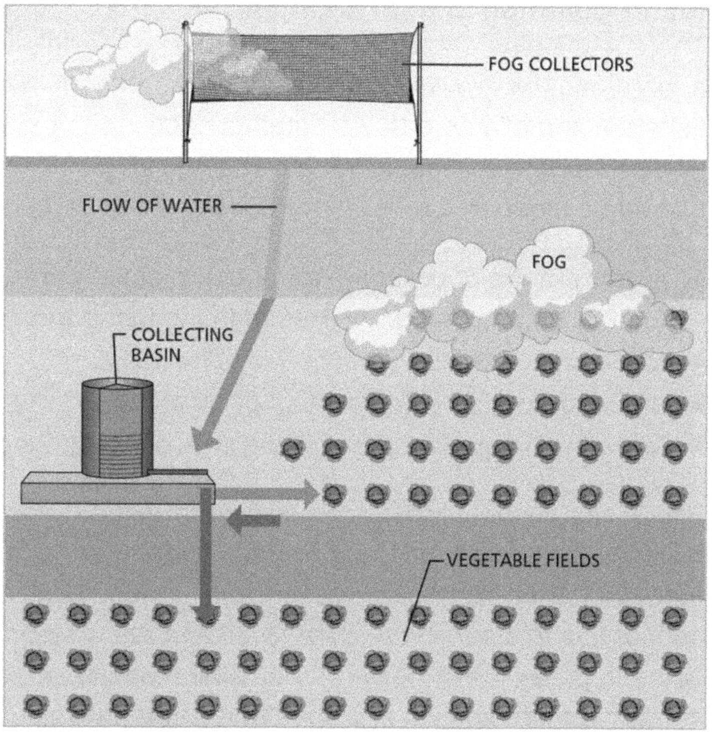

Fig. 4.10 The diagram above shows how giant nets (known as 'fog catchers' or 'fog collectors') can be used to create artificial condensation surfaces.

- Make a list of all the ways the poorest communities of Lima benefit from collecting water by 'fog catching'.
- What is the cost of a 'fog catcher' and where has the money required come from?
- In what ways do you think 'fog catching' could be a good example of sustainable development for the poorest people in Lima?

Water pollution and its sources

The oceans play a vital role in regulating the Earth's climate by distributing heat from the equator and by providing the planet's human population with resources such as marine fisheries and oil and gas. As humans continue to exploit these resources at an increasing rate, and as the world's population grows and living standards improve, greater pressure is being placed on these natural systems. Some of the impacts of this growing pressure include:

- a wide range of pollution from human activity, including nutrient pollution from farms, heavy metals such as mercury from manufacturing industries, oil pollution and human sewerage
- overfishing and the depletion of fish stocks
- the degradation or 'bleaching' of coral reefs
- climate change leading to rising sea levels and increased coastal erosion and flooding

Plastic is a resource that is processed from the refining of crude oil. In the United States two million plastic food and drink containers are used every five minutes. Greenpeace estimates that 100 million tonnes of plastic waste is generated every year in the world and at least 10 per cent of this ends up in the oceans. Plastic is non-biodegradable and will take hundreds of years to break down slowly into smaller particles. Once in the oceans, it moves around in the currents before settling in places where the wind and currents are weaker.

Oceanographers have identified two massive plastic 'garbage patches' in the Pacific Ocean. The Western or Great Pacific Garbage Patch is around 1 760 000 square kilometres in size. The plastic is often suspended on or below the surface in a plastic soup. Up to 70 per cent of plastic sinks, so it is also found on the seabed.

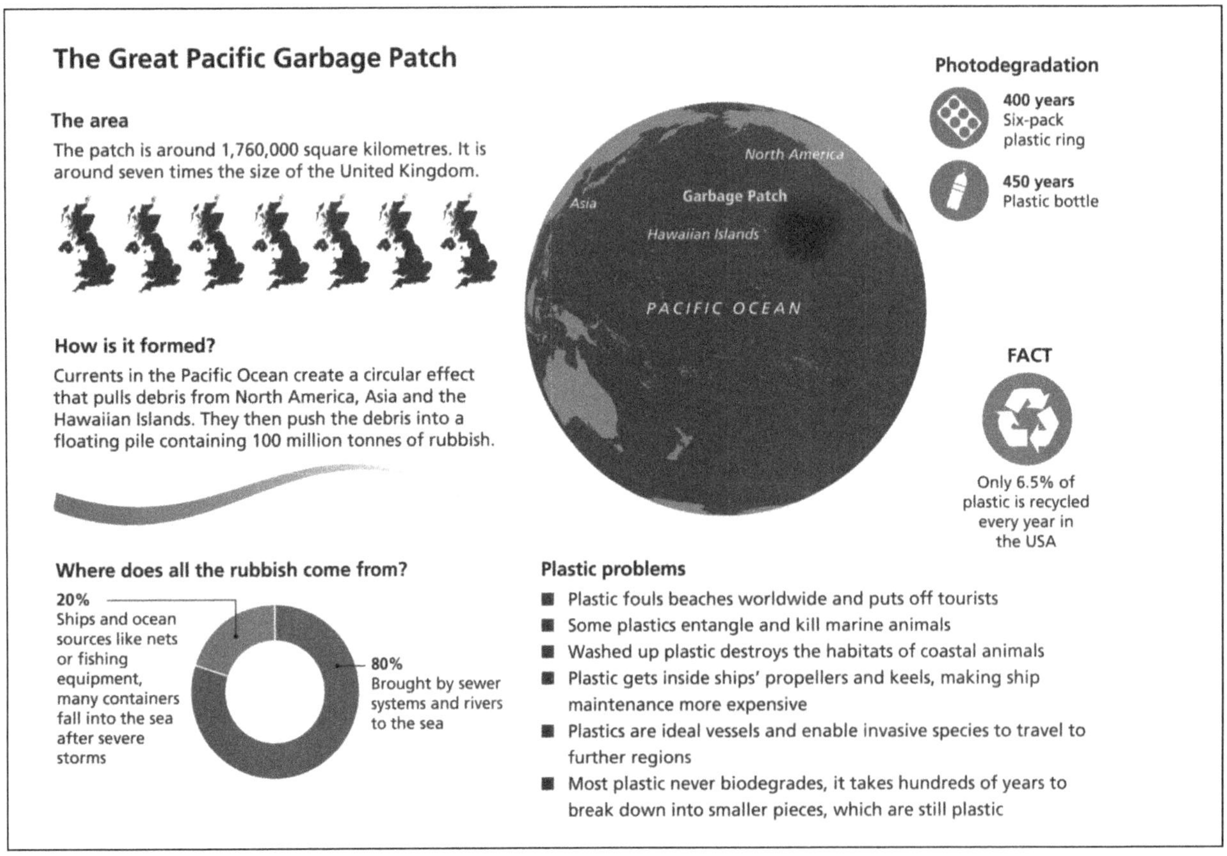

Fig. 4.11 The Great Pacific Garbage Patch.

- How does the area of the Great Pacific Garbage patch compare to that of the UK?
- Why does the plastic rubbish accumulate at this particular location?
- Give three examples of where this plastic rubbish comes from.
- Describe two problems that result from plastic pollution in the Great Pacific Garbage Patch.

The Ocean Cleanup Foundation has developed the first feasible method to clean up the world's ocean garbage patches. Their objective is to remove at least half of the Great Pacific Garbage Patch by 2022. Go to **http://www.theoceancleanup.com/technology/** which explains the process they use. Then, draw a series of labelled diagrams to describe and explain how plastic pollution is caught and removed from the ocean.

Fig. 4.12 Plastic waste washed up on a beach in Panama.

Connecting water and its management topics

The only continent drier than Australia is Antarctica. Records show that since the 1860s, a severe drought has occurred in Australia, on average, every eighteen years. The worst drought ever to affect Australia occurred between the years 2003 and 2012. The year 2006 was the driest on record for many parts of the country. Since the beginning of the 1990s there has been a marked decrease in annual rainfall totals in several regions of Australia, which many scientists attribute to the effects of global warming on weather patterns. The worst hit area is the southwest of Western Australia where there has been a decline of over 20 per cent in average winter rainfall since 1990. Meteorologists predict that this will drop by a further 20 per cent by 2100. This has created huge water management issues for the state capital city of Perth, which is home to 1.8 million people (78 per cent of everyone who lives in Western Australia). Perth is not only one of the most geographically isolated cities in the world, but it is also becoming one of the driest in Australia.

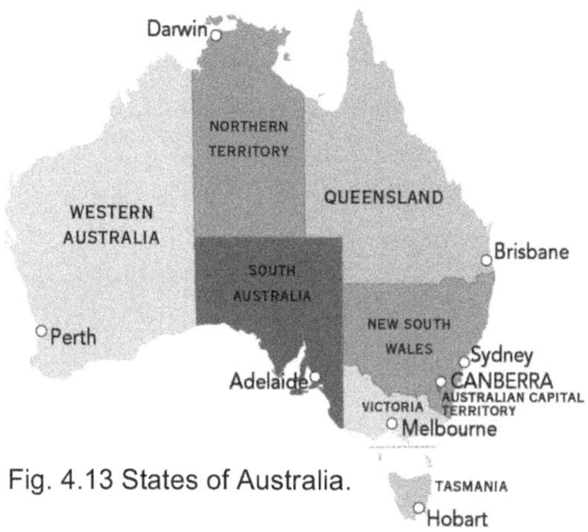

Fig. 4.13 States of Australia.

Fig. 4.14 Perth city, Australia.

Fig. 4.15 Western Australian cities, towns, settlements and road network.

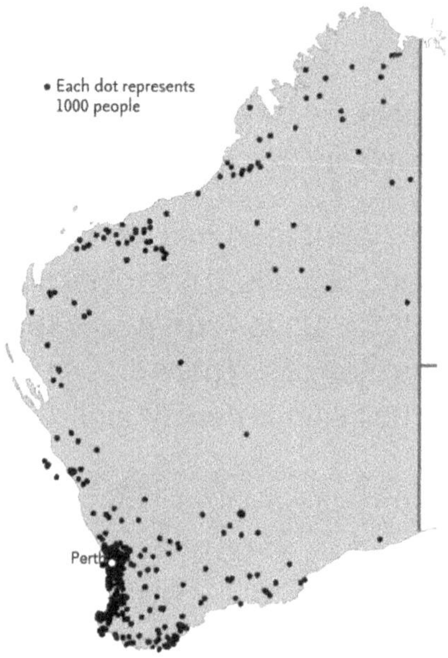

Fig. 4.16 Distribution of Western Australian population.

In 2015, rainfall in Western Australia was the lowest ever recorded. Australia's Climate Council estimates that water flow from rainfall into the reservoirs supplying most of Perth's water has dropped by 80 per cent since 1970. Over the summer of 2015, more water in Perth's reservoirs was lost through evaporation than flowed into them from run-off by way of rivers in the winter. By the end of 2015, water in the reservoirs was down to just 23 per cent of capacity. This was because the reservoirs received just 72.4 billion litres of water – far less than the 300 billion litres currently consumed each year by its residents.

Western Australia's Water Corporation, a government agency, has produced a long-term plan to solve Perth's water supply problems and to ensure the sustainability of water for generations to come. The plan sets out three objectives to be achieved by 2030:

- Reduce water use by 15 per cent by working with households, businesses and communities.
- Increase water recycling to 30 per cent for use in parks, gardens and in industry.
- Develop 70–100 billion litres of new water sources, including desalination, groundwater replenishment and securing groundwater sources.

Go to **http://www.watercorporation.com.au/water-supply-and-services/solutions-to-perths-water-supply** and make brief notes about how each of the following strategies will help to deliver the objectives of the plan:

- desalination
- water recycling
- reducing water use
- storm water
- groundwater
- groundwater replenishment
- dams

Supplementary case study 1

Eradicating poliomyelitis

Poliomyelitis, or polio for short, was once a disease feared worldwide and its incidence has a long recorded history. The stone carving in Figure 4.17 created in Ancient Egypt over three thousand years ago shows a man with a crutch who has been disabled by the disease. Polio is very contagious and is caused by a virus that enters the body through the mouth and then multiplies in the intestine. It then leaves the body in the faeces of the infected person. In places where there is poor sanitation infected faeces can contaminate drinking water. As a result, the virus can infect large numbers of people very quickly. Babies and young children under the age of five years are particularly vulnerable to the disease. An infected person may also spread the virus to others through their saliva and mucus when they sneeze. It can also be passed through food when infected people do not wash their hands adequately after defecating. There is also evidence that flies can spread the virus from infected faeces to food. Most people infected with the poliovirus have no signs of the illness and are never aware that they have been infected. These symptomless carriers can spread the disease to thousands of other people before someone develops symptoms.

Fig. 4.17 Egyptian carving of a person with polio.

The poliovirus invades the nervous system of humans and initial symptoms of polio include fever, fatigue, headache, vomiting, stiffness of the neck and pain in the limbs. On average, one in every two hundred infections leads to irreversible paralysis (usually in the legs), which often occurs within hours. Among those paralysed, up to 10 per cent die when their breathing muscles become immobilised.

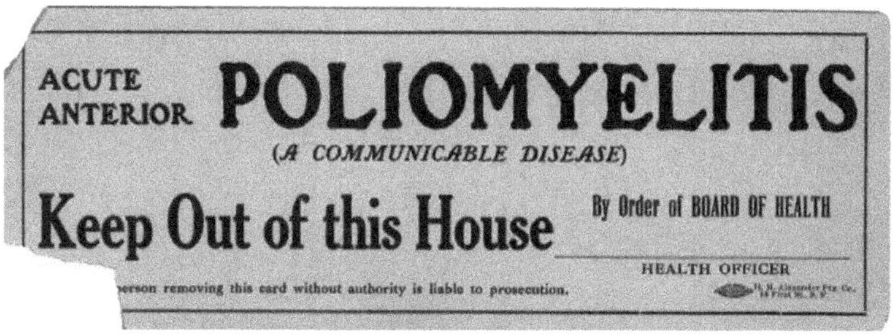

Fig. 4.18 A 1910 United States of America Board of Health quarantine card warning that the premises are contaminated by poliomyelitis.

There is no cure for polio but it can be prevented through giving a vaccine to children. The goal of the Global Polio Eradication Initiative, co-ordinated by the World Health Organization of the United Nations, is to eradicate the incidence of polio by 2018. This was established in 1988, and since 1988, 2.5 billion children have been immunised against polio worldwide. The programme has made spectacular progress towards achieving its objective. Polio cases have decreased by over 99 per cent since 1988, from an estimated 350 000 cases then to just eleven in 2016. The United Nations estimates that there are fifteen million people today who are able to walk who would have otherwise been paralysed by contracting polio. In addition, an estimated 1.5 million childhood deaths have been prevented. Today only two countries, Afghanistan and Pakistan, remain polio endemic (regularly found among people), compared with 125 in 1988.

If a sufficient number of children are fully immunised against polio the virus will be unable to find susceptible children to infect and will die out. However, as long as one single child remains infected, then all children will remain at risk of contracting the disease. Economic modelling suggests that the eradication of polio will save at least US$50 billion over the next twenty years, mostly in the world's poorest countries.

Fig. 4.19 Newspaper reports announcing a breakthrough in vaccinating for polio in 1955.

Fig. 4.20 A child being given polio vaccine drops in Chaman, Pakistan.

Supplementary case study 2

Aswan High Dam

The Aswan High Dam was constructed by the Egyptian government between 1960 and 1970 at a cost of approximately US$750 million. It is a multipurpose dam as its three main objectives are to control flooding along the lower course of the River Nile, provide water for irrigation and generate hydroelectricity for homes and for industry. The dam is 111 metres high and has a width of 4000 metres. Behind the dam is the huge Lake Nasser reservoir with a storage capacity of 169 million cubic metres of water.

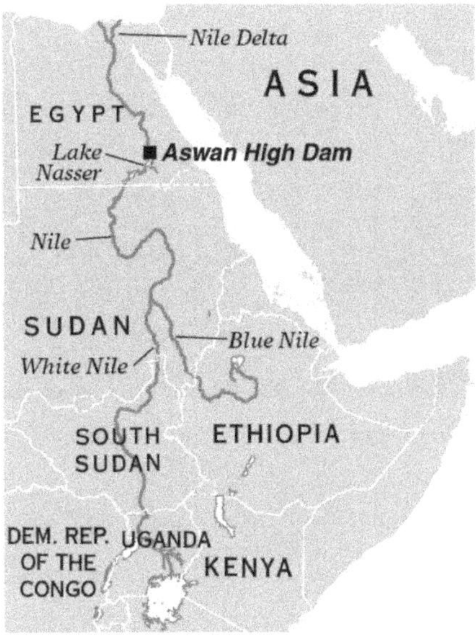

Fig. 4.21 Location of the Aswan High Dam.

Fig. 4.22 The Aswan High Dam.

Like many multipurpose dams around the world, the effects of the Aswan High Dam have been very controversial. After fifty years, the costs and benefits of what was one of the first modern multipurpose dams in the world can be accurately evaluated.

Benefits

- Before the dam was constructed, the Nile Valley was often affected by devastating floods in high water years that destroyed farmers' crops and also periods of drought during low water years when crops died and famine occurred. The dam now prevents these extreme events, which saves the Egyptian government US$15 million a year.
- Irrigated land in Egypt has increased by 30 per cent as a result of the water it can make available from its Lake Nasser reservoir. About half a million farming families have settled onto the 8400 sq km of new irrigated land. Another 4200 sq km of land already under irrigation is now able to produce two crops of rice and sugar cane a year rather than one, through the availability of additional water. This increased agricultural production is worth US$200 million a year.
- Over 40 per cent of Egypt's entire electricity production now comes from the Aswan High Dam – a source of electricity that does not produce greenhouse gas, is predictable in cost and easy to maintain. Electricity production from the dam is worth US$150 million in sales every year to domestic and industrial users.

- The dam has hugely improved navigation for ships along the River Nile. For example before the dam was constructed, water levels in winter were often too shallow to allow navigation by tourist cruise ships. Today, the depth of the river is sufficient all year long – navigation that benefits the country by US$7.5 million a year.
- New fishing fleets now operate on Lake Nasser, and fish processing and packaging industries have grown along its banks as a result.

Fig. 4.23 An irrigation channel running between crops in the Nile Valley.

Fig. 4.24 Tourist cruise ships on the Nile near Aswan.

Costs

- The construction of the dam, together with the flooding required to create Lake Nasser reservoir, resulted in the forced resettlement of over 100 000 people. New communities were built for these people and irrigated farmland provided. While most were relocated three to ten kilometres from their original homes, some were moved 45 kilometres away. This caused high levels of stress-related illnesses and sometimes food shortages when the new farmland was not as fertile as that which had been lost below the reservoir.
- Twenty-two famous archaeological sites, such as the Great Temple of Abu Simbel, were saved (at considerable cost) from flooding. However, other sites, including the Buhen Fort, were lost forever below the water of Lake Nasser.
- Before the construction of the High Dam, the water table (the height of the groundwater) in the Nile valley ranged from eight to nine metres. This was too deep to allow salts dissolved in the groundwater to be drawn to the surface in summer through capillary action when evaporation was at its highest. The building of the dam put an end to annual river flooding along the valley and the water table level gradually increased in height, which led to waterlogging. Salinisation (the build-up of soluble salts in the soil) increased because the distance between the surface and the groundwater table was small enough (1-2 metres) to allow water to be pulled up by evaporation. Small concentrations of soluble salts then slowly built up in the valley soils, which seriously affected crop yields. As a result, the government had to install sub-surface drainage systems to prevent further salt build-up and to flush out existing salts in the soil over 20 000 sq km of farmland. The cost of this work totalled US$3 billion.

- Before the construction of the High Dam, the River Nile deposited fertile sediments of sand, silt and clay on fields along its valley through its annual floods during late summer. This annual flooding provided ideal conditions for farming for over 5000 years. Now, most of this fertilising silt and sediment never reaches the farmland and remains trapped in the Lake Nasser reservoir behind the dam wall. To replace this estimated loss of at least forty million tonnes of fertile silt, farmers along the Nile valley now have to buy one million tonnes of expensive chemical fertilisers to spread on the land as a replacement. Much of this artificial fertiliser is washed off into the river, causing problems of eutrophication and deoxygenation.

- Fishing in the Mediterranean Sea has also been seriously affected by the fact that nutrients are no longer carried into the sea dissolved in the waters of the River Nile. The sardine catch in the Mediterranean Sea each year has dropped by over 50 per cent, resulting in many job losses and a decline in the number of fishing boats.

- Because the River Nile now carries less sediment and silt, its water is much clearer and sunlight penetrates deeper. Because of this and the increased presence of chemical fertilisers in the water, much more algae grows. This has increased the costs of drinking water treatment to ensure it is entirely hygienic for human consumption.

Fig. 4.25 Colossus of The Great Temple of Ramesses II, Abu Simbel, Egypt.

Data response and decision making exercises

1. Diarrhoea is the second leading killer of babies and young children in the world. The United Nations Children's Emergency Fund (UNICEF) estimates that this water-borne disease accounted for 9 per cent of all deaths among children under the age of five worldwide in 2015. This equates to over 1400 young children dying each day or about 530 000 children in a year. Most deaths from diarrhoea occur among children less than two years old.

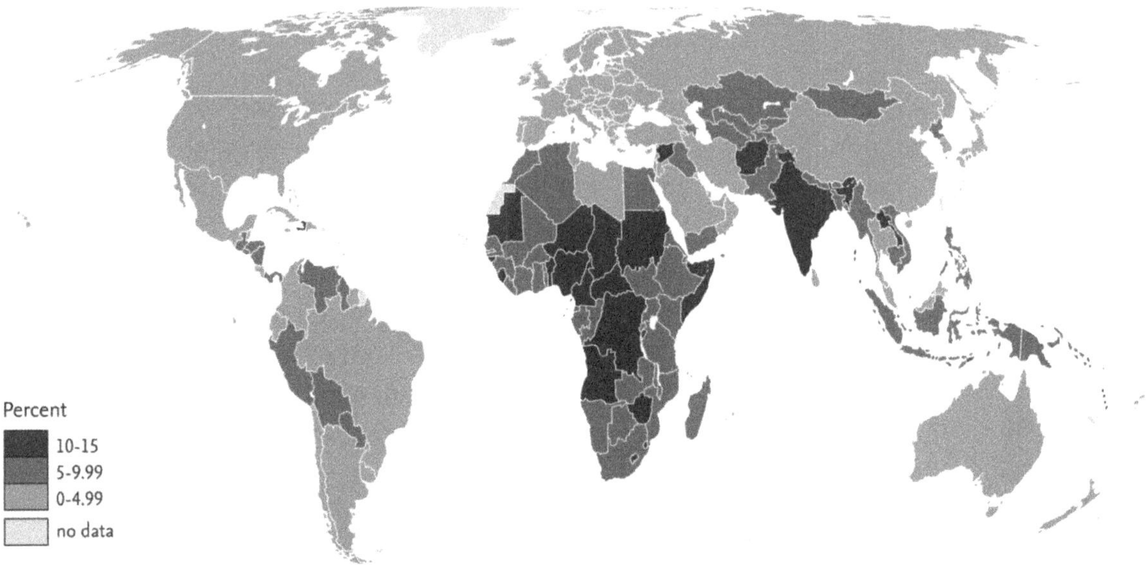

Fig. 4.26 Percentage of deaths among children under 5 years of age, attributable to diarrhoea, by country.

a) Describe the general distribution of countries in the world where diarrhoea accounts for 10 per cent or more of childhood deaths.

....

....

....

....

b) The most severe threat to life posed by diarrhoea is dehydration. Explain what dehydration is and why you think it presents such a threat to babies and young children.

....

....

....

....

....

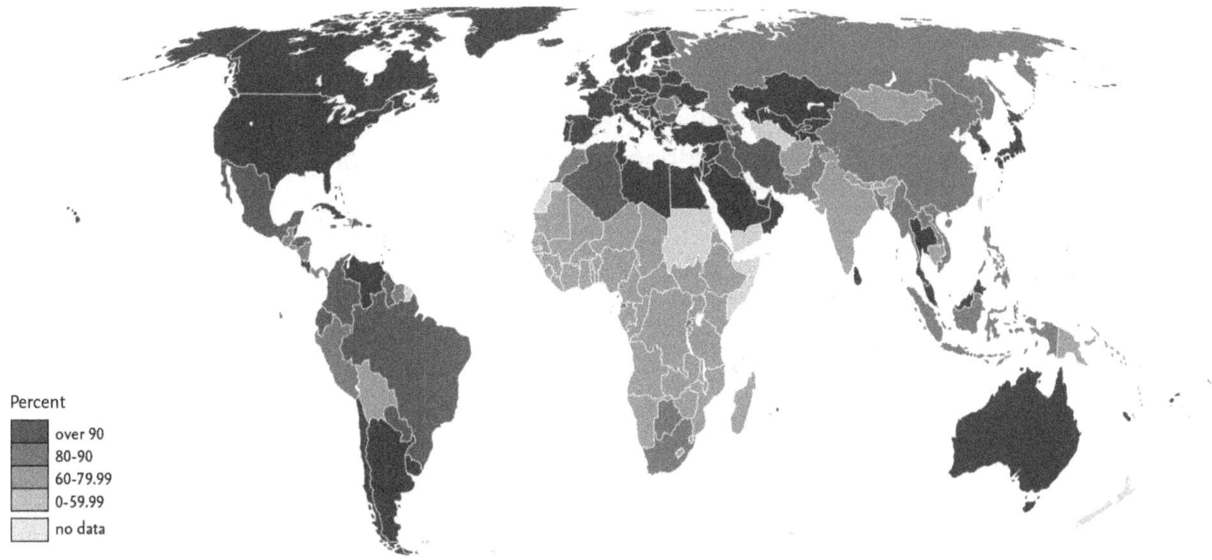

Fig. 4.27 Percentage of population with improved sanitation by country.

c) The map in Figure 4.27 shows the proportion of the population using improved sanitation facilities. Explain what you understand by the term 'improved sanitation'.

d) How does the information in Figure 4.27 help to explain the distribution of deaths as a result of diarrhoea in Figure 4.26 that you described earlier?

2. The country of Cambodia in Southeast Asia has one of the highest incidences of diarrhoea amongst children of any country in the world. Diarrhoea accounts for 20 per cent of all deaths of children aged under five, which translates to 10 000 overall deaths each year.

Fig. 4.28 Location of Cambodia.

Fig. 4.29 Cambodia.

a) UNICEF is working with the government of Cambodia and other partners in the country to reduce childhood deaths caused by diarrohea. One important part of its work is educating children about the importance of handwashing using soap. Suggest why this simple and inexpensive change could reduce childhood deaths from diarrhoea in Cambodia by up to 40 per cent.

....

....

....

....

....

....

....

Another focus of UNICEF's work in Cambodia is to provide every home with a toilet. The cost of doing this is a challenge in Cambodia, which is one of the poorest countries in Asia. Over two million people survive here on less than US$1.20 a day.

Fig. 4.30 Pumping raw sewage out of a gutter on a city street in Phnom Penh, Cambodia.

b) Using examples of improved sanitation that you have studied in other countries of the world, describe what UNICEF could do in Cambodia that would be cheap and effective.

....

....

....

....

....

....

....

....

3. UNICEF estimates that 7 million out of 15 million Cambodians are unable to access safe drinking water – most of them poor and living in rural areas. Improving the quality of rural water would make a huge contribution to reducing child deaths resulting from diarrhoea in the country. Water for Cambodia is a non-government organisation (NGO) working in Cambodia, which since 2006 has been building and installing biosand water filters in rural homes that produce clean drinking water directly from contaminated sources. Each filter is constructed of a concrete case about a metre tall and a 10 centimetre square within which there are layers of sand and gravel.

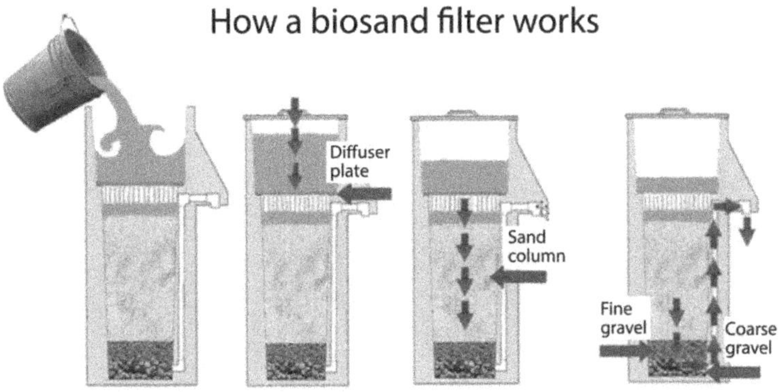

Fig. 4.31 A biosand filter.

Fig. 4.32 A boy in Cambodia taking safe drinking water from a sand filtration device.

a) Suggest how the sand filter removes up to 98.5 per cent of bacteria from contaminated water.

....

....

Read the following information about biosand filters from Water for Cambodia:

"A family receiving a biosand filter pays a nominal fee and is actively involved in the installation, giving them a vested interest in maintaining the filter. Also, instruction in filter operation and maintenance, as well as basic education in hygiene and sanitation, is provided. Biosand filters in general require very little maintenance (occasional stirring up of the top few inches of sand and scooping the suspended sediment) and are still functioning effectively at other sites more than 10 years after installation. Filters are manufactured locally using local materials. After passing through the sand and gravel, the now clean water travels through the copper pipe and out the spout using the force of gravity alone. There are no moving or mechanical parts to break. One filter can produce enough clean water for a family of 6–8 for many years."

b) Explain why installing biosand filters is a good example of sustainable development for people in rural Cambodia.

....

....

4. The figures in Table 4.1 show changes in the total number of deaths of children aged under five years in the world since 1990 calculated by UNICEF.

Year	Deaths in millions
1990	12.7
1995	11.0
2000	9.8
2005	8.3
2010	7.0
2015	5.9

Table 4.1: Deaths of children under five years, 1990–2015.

a) On the grid below, draw a simple bar graph to show these figures.

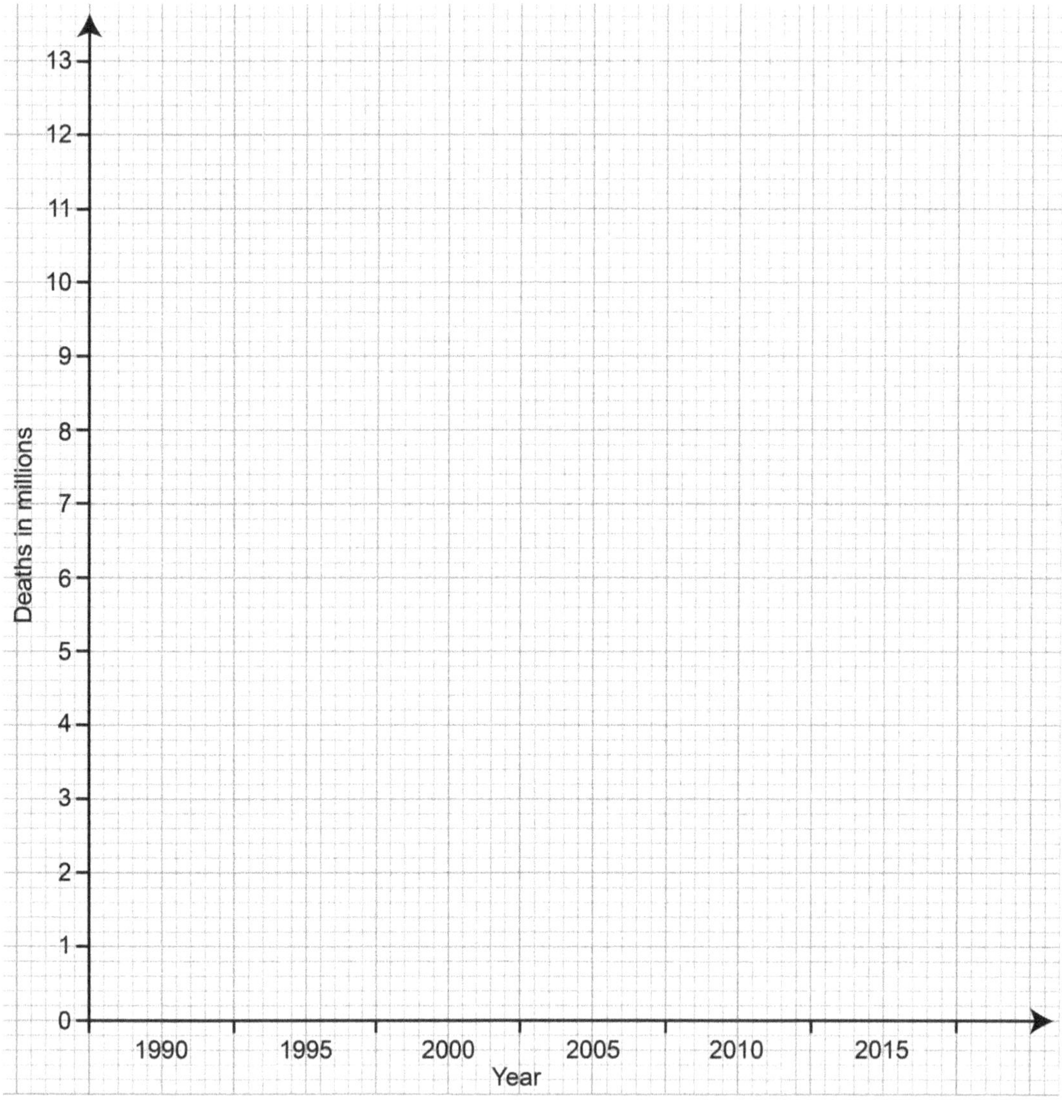

b) By how many million did deaths fall between 1990 and 2015?

....

c) Which five-year interval showed the greatest decline in deaths?

....

During this period, the total annual number of deaths in children under five years from diarrhoea decreased by more than 50 per cent from over 1.2 million to half a million. This is because of education programmes to improve hygiene such as hand washing, installing improved toilet systems and improving the quality of drinking water, particularly in rural areas. Another factor has also contributed to this dramatic decline in deaths. Children with diarrhoea can be treated easily with a simple and cheap oral rehydration solution (ORS) that involves drinking water with small amounts of salt, sugar and zinc added.

Fig. 4.33 A woman gives a boy some of the oral rehydration solution, Benin, Africa.

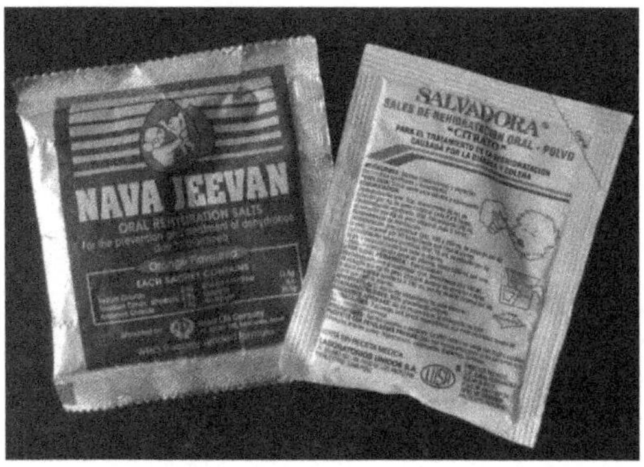

Fig. 4.34 Packets of oral rehydration solution from Nepal (left) and Peru (right).

d) Thousands of lives are now being saved across the world through the use of ORS. Suggest why even though cheap ORS has been available since the 1950s, they have not had a major lifesaving effect on children until fairly recently.

....

....

....

....

5. Rotavirus is the leading cause of diarrhoea in children and it cannot be treated with antibiotics or other drugs. Rotavirus and the deadly diarrhoea it causes can, however, be prevented through vaccinating children. For example, Ghana introduced rotavirus vaccination in 2012. By 2014, the number of children aged 0-11 months admitted to hospital with severe diarrhoea dropped from 4817 cases to 2711.

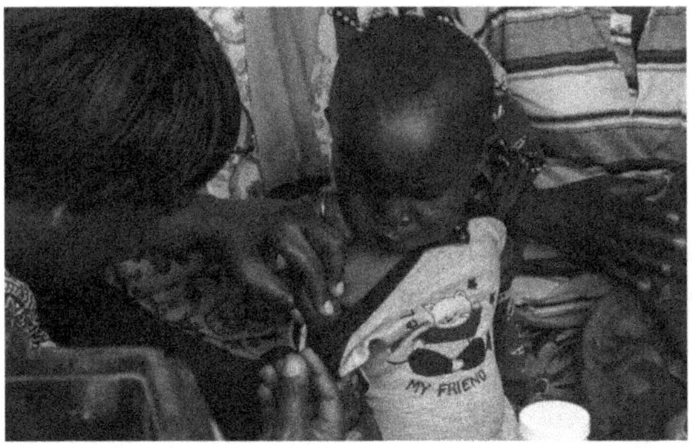

Fig. 4.35 Vaccinating a baby against rotavirus.

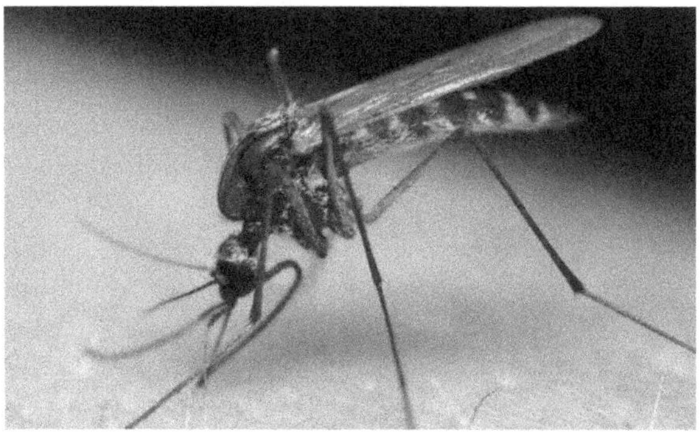

Fig. 4.36 Anopheles mosquito.

While progress is being made in Ghana in reducing child deaths from diarrhoea, the country is finding controlling malaria, another water-borne disease spread by the anopheles mosquito, a much greater challenge. In Ghana, approximately 20 000 children still die from malaria every year (25 per cent of all deaths of children under the age of five). Even if a child survives, the consequences from severe malaria such as convulsions or brain dysfunction can hamper long-term development and schooling. The economic burden of malaria is estimated to cost Ghana at least US$2 billion a year.

a) Using a diagram, show how anopheles mosquitoes spread malaria.

b) Explain why malaria is proving to be a very difficult disease to fight and conquer.

....

....

....

....

....

....

....

Answers to these questions can be found at **www.collins.co.uk/EnvMgmtIGCSE**

5 Oceans and fisheries

Introduction

This section reinforces and extends student learning by:

- Consolidating and developing the factual material in the Student's Book that students will be required to recall and explain (AO1)
- Advancing student thinking through providing more challenging content and activities than those in the Student's Book, which extend some areas of the specification and require the synthesis of information and the application of knowledge and understanding to unfamiliar contexts (AO2)
- Enabling students to grasp that the effective management of environmental issues requires a coherent and holistic approach to problem solving through the principles of sustainable development (AO3)

This is achieved through the provision of:

- Extension content and related activities that secure and progress student knowledge and understanding through tasks that require handling information from a variety of sources to reach conclusions and make judgments
- Supplementary case studies that reinforce and advance key principles and concepts and support evaluative thinking
- A decision making or problem solving exercise that encourages students to appreciate the complexities of environmental management and the pivotal role of the principles of sustainable development in achieving successful outcomes

Links to other chapters

The resource potential of the oceans is vast and the exploration, production and consumption of these resources are themes that link across all chapters of the Student's Book. In many ways, the use of the oceans tends to be less of a focus than the human impact upon the land – which is more visible and seen as a more immediate environmental management challenge. However, the oceans are under significant pressure and show signs of environmental degradation. Exploring the importance of the oceans in climate regulation and as a carbon sink will link directly with the atmosphere section. The oceans are also a vast and mostly untapped source of energy. The development of ocean-based wind, wave and tidal energy schemes is vital if attempts to move the energy mix to more renewable forms of energy are to succeed. Furthermore, it is important for students to understand the role that desalination could play in securing potential freshwater supplies in the future.

Perhaps the most visible impacts of human activities are the issues of unsustainable consumption of certain marine species and the accumulation of plastic waste in the Pacific and Atlantic Oceans. The impact of overfishing and, in particular, bycatch on marine ecosystems cannot be underestimated. Destructive fishing policies, net design and illegal fishing are having an increasingly visible toll on the abundance of marine species. How this is managed in the coming years is a vital issue. Examples of local sustainable management can be used to develop sustainable local solutions to other environmental issues. Exploring this at the local scale with students could be a useful engaging route into the topic. It is also important to consider how oceans are used as a resource to hold waste. The exponential increase in the use of a variety of plastics in everyday life has led to a huge accumulation of plastic waste in between the major ocean currents in both the Pacific and Atlantic Oceans. This has a major impact on marine ecosystems, the human food chain, the extraction of oil and the associated increase in demand caused by unsustainable use of plastic, which is explored further in this chapter.

Oceans and fisheries topic	**Links to other subject content**	**Section**
Oceans as a resource	Extraction of rock and minerals from the Earth Energy resources and the generation of electricity Global distribution of water	1 2 4
World fisheries	Ecosystems	9
Impact of exploitation of the oceans	Energy demand Impact of oil pollution	2 2
Management of the harvesting of marine species	Measuring and managing biodiversity	9

Extension content and related activities

Ocean currents and marine pollution

The oceans are under increasing pressure. They provide humans with a significant resource base that is being increasingly exploited. As we continue to exploit these resources and the human population expands, we are placing increasing pressure on the natural systems and this is having profound impacts on the oceans – now and in the future. Some of these impacts are summarised below:

- a wide range of pollution from human activity
- rising sea levels and the impact on coasts and rates of erosion
- unsustainable fishing practices
- climate change and the change in the chemistry of the ocean
- the loss of marine species and coral reefs
- conflict over access to resources and the impact on the environment

A clearly visible sign of our impact on the seas and oceans is marine litter found on the coast. Our beaches are scattered with fascinating pieces of debris that wash in on a rising tide. Storm waves also deposit huge amounts of material onto beaches. In Cornwall, UK, thousands of pieces of LEGO® have been washed up over the past 20 years. Many people scour the beaches of the world for interesting flotsam and jetsam, and searching for plastic LEGO® sea creatures, flippers and dragons whilst walking on beaches has become a hobby for many people. People in the USA have also reported finding LEGO® sea creatures on the shore. Could these discoveries be related?

In February 1997, the container ship, Tokio Express, was heading from Rotterdam to New York when it was hit by a freak wave. The ship listed 60 degrees one way, then 40 degrees the other. Over 60 steel containers and their contents were lost into the sea off the southwest coast of England.

Fig. 5.1 The Tokio Express.

Fig. 5.2 LEGO® has been washed up all over the world.

One container contained over 4.8 million pieces of LEGO®, of which it is believed over 3 million would have floated. Since 1997, the marine themed LEGO® has been washing up on beaches across the UK, Holland, Ireland, USA and even Australia. In the southwest of the UK, the LEGO® is being pushed onto the shore by local water currents – driven by the prevailing southwesterly winds. Once in the water, it drifted on the currents before finally being washed up on the beaches of Devon and Cornwall, UK. Much of the LEGO® looks fresh out of the box – untouched by over 15 years in the sea.

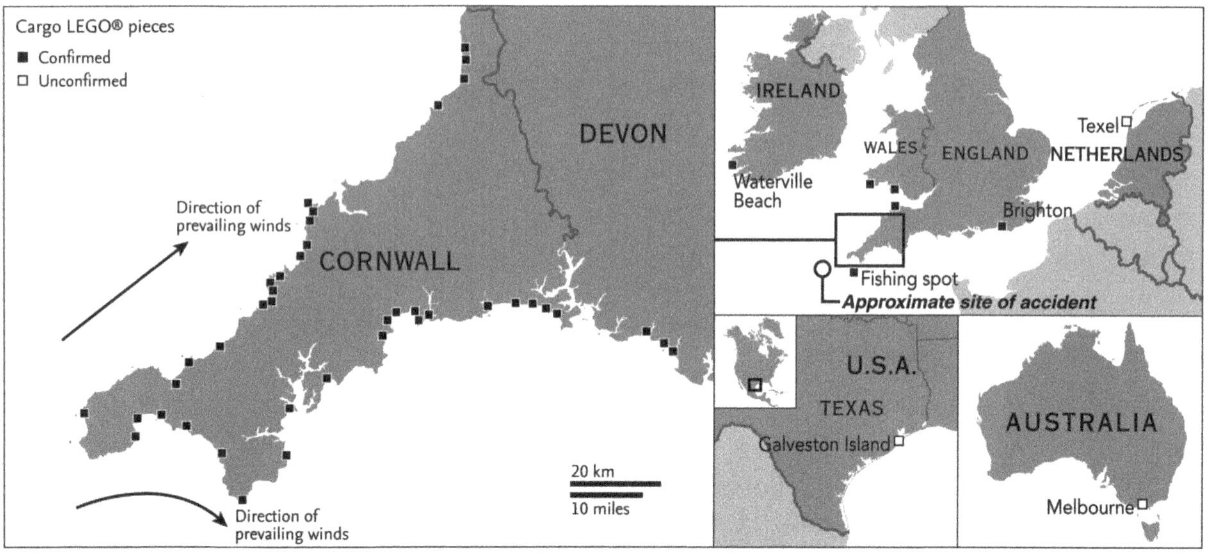

Fig. 5.3 Locations around the world where LEGO® was found washed up on beaches.

Consolidating your thinking

Using the detailed map of warm and cold ocean currents from the Student's Book (Figure 5.9), identify the possible routes taken by the LEGO® pieces on their journey around the world. Further information on the hunt for LEGO® can be found in the links below:

http://m.bbc.com/news/magazine-28367198; **https://www.facebook.com/LegoLostAtSea**; **http://www.bbc.com/news/magazine-28582621**

Fig. 5.4 Dr Curtis Ebbesmeyer.

In 2013, 120 million containers were carried on ships across the globe and some were lost in terrible weather conditions and accidents. Between 2011 and 2013 an average 2600 containers were lost each year. This adds up to a significant amount of material finding its way into the oceans. Some ocean scientists or oceanographers have been taking a particular interest in these container losses as they provide a unique opportunity to study the oceans.

Oceanographer, Dr Curtis Ebbesmeyer became fascinated by the origin of pristine Nike trainers that were washing up on his mother's local beach. So fascinated in fact, that he undertook an amazing global enquiry. In 1990, between Seoul, South Korea and Los Angeles, USA, 21 forty-foot containers were washed from the deck of the Hansa Carrier.

Four split open, spilling 61 820 shoes into the Pacific Ocean. A year later, the shoes began washing up on the west coast of the USA, and Curtis's mother began to collect the local paper reports on this strange phenomenon as he describes in his book, Flotsametrics and the Floating World:

"Hundreds of Nike sneakers, brand new save for some seaweed and barnacles, were washing up along the Pacific coasts of British Columbia, Washington and especially Oregon, Nike's home state [...] The details on how they had gotten there were sketchy, verging on the non existent. 'Isn't this the sort of thing you study?' she asked, assuming as ever that her son the oceanographer knew everything about the sea. 'I'll look into it' I said.

I started looking and never stopped. Seventeen years and many thousands of shoes, bath toys, hockey gloves, human corpses, ancient treasures and other floating objects later, I'm still looking into it."

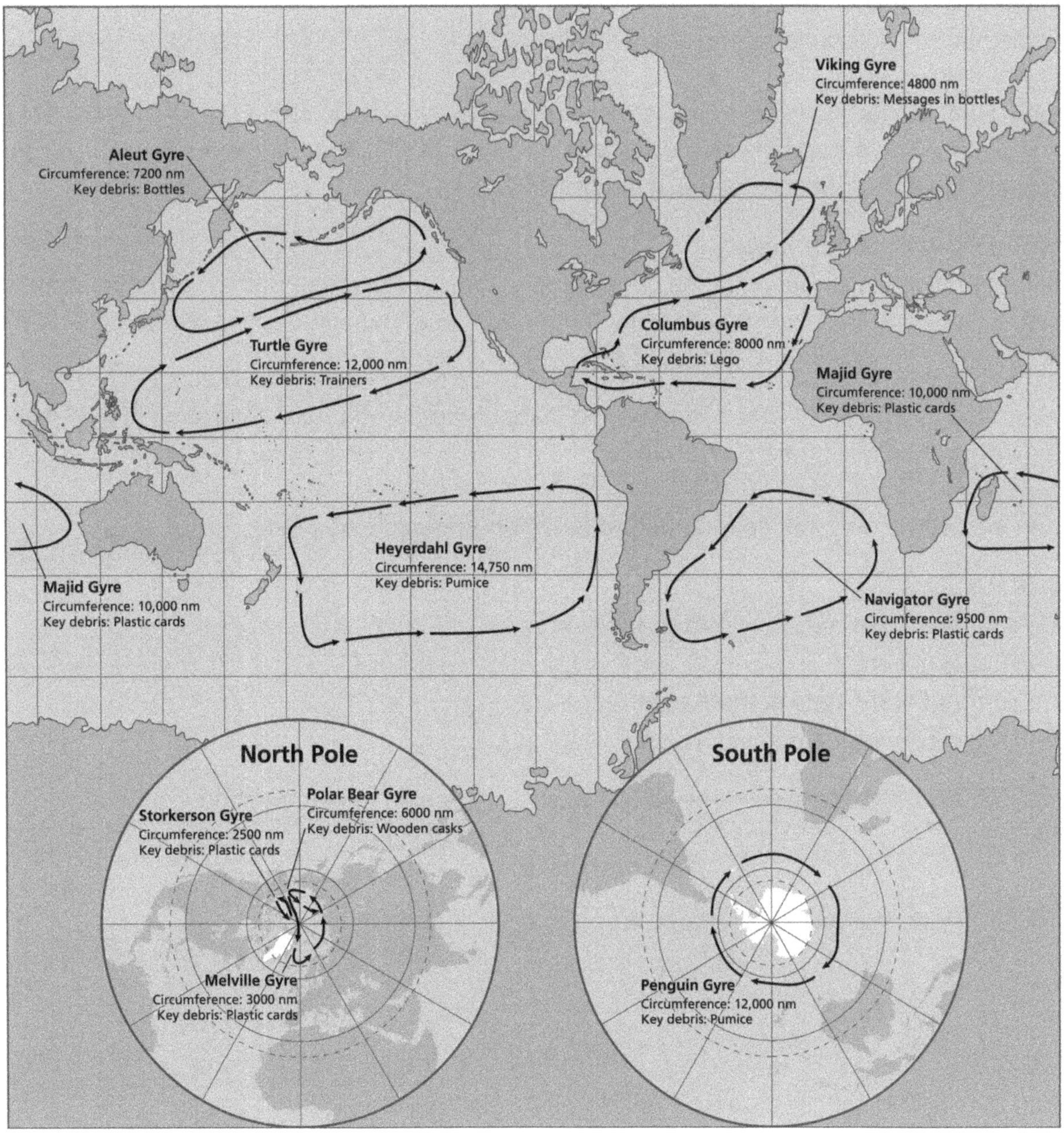

Fig. 5.5 Gyres discovered by Dr Curtis Ebbesmeyer.

Dr Ebbesmeyer began to trace the trainers by their product codes and was able to find out when and where they were lost overboard. As each shoe had a distinct serial number it made the shoes the largest instantaneous release of numbered objects into the ocean at one time. Knowing this, and when and where they were found, enabled him to build accurate maps of ocean currents or gyres. He continued his work for decades – tracking new debris and setting up a worldwide network of beach combers. He discovered new currents and mapped others for the first time with the Ocean Current Surface Simulator (OSCURS) designed by fellow oceanographer, Jim Ingraham. The gyres they discovered are shown on the map in Figure 5.5.

The development of this model of ocean surface currents has been a vital breakthrough in the study of the oceans. Ocean currents play a large role in shaping our world by:

- Influencing weather patterns, for example ENSO in the Pacific. The weather shapes rates of erosion, flooding inland, and drought conditions.
- Transporting nutrients.
- Redistributing pollution and hazardous waste.

The OSCURS model allows us to make more accurate predictions about the strength of ENSO when it occurs. The model was also used extensively to predict the path taken by debris from the missing Malaysian Airlines plane in the Indian Ocean.

Consolidating your thinking

Describe the global distribution of the gyres. Suggest reasons for the pattern of movement seen. Are there any links between the map here and those maps in Section 5 of the Student's Book?

Research the latest ENSO information on the state of temperatures and currents in the Pacific Ocean (**https://www.climate.gov/enso**).

Use the information to produce a group presentation that explains:

- what ENSO is
- the difference between El Niño and La Niña
- the impact of ENSO
- the current ENSO state in the Pacific Ocean
- the predictions for the coming months

Ensure that each slide has less than 60–80 words. You could use embedded videos and animations to help you explain ENSO.

Supplementary case study

The Great Pacific Garbage Patch

Both the example of the Tokio Express and the study of marine debris illustrate the extent to which humans are impacting the oceans. Huge volumes of waste are entering the oceans at an unsustainable rate. Tracking how this waste moves in ocean currents is now possible due to the development of accurate computer models. However, the volume of plastic waste that is accumulating is now a significant environmental management challenge.

Global plastic use has risen exponentially and some expert estimates suggest that 10 per cent of the 100 million tonnes of plastic waste produced annually is ending up in the sea.

Fig. 5.6 A beach after a winter storm.

Fig. 5.7 Accumulated plastic waste on Midway Atoll, Pacific Ocean.

If you walk along almost any beach in the world, you will find evidence of plastic waste, particularly after big storms. This will not **biodegrade** like natural waste but will **photodegrade** instead – where the sun slowly breaks the waste into ever-smaller particles. A single one-litre plastic bottle will eventually break down into enough fragments to put one on every mile of beach in the world. Once in the oceans, it moves around in the large gyres before accumulating in areas in the centre of the currents where the surface moves much more slowly. Observations have now revealed significant accumulation of plastic waste in the Pacific and Atlantic Oceans. One estimate puts the Western Pacific Garbage Patch at around 1 760 000 sq km in size. Not all plastic waste floats, so some will fall to the seabed. Scientists recently discovered 110 pieces of litter for every sq km of the North Sea – a massive 600 000 tonnes in total.

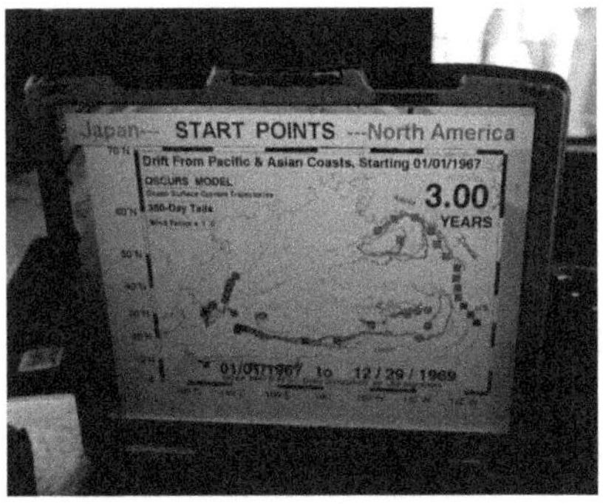

Fig. 5.8 Data from an expedition to the Great Pacific Garbage Patch.

Fig. 5.9 Sample from the Great Pacific Garbage Patch.

Fig. 5.10 Carcass of an albatross containing plastic waste.

Once in the oceans, the plastic is having hugely harmful effects on the marine environment. The photo in Figure 5.10 shows the carcass of an albatross that has eaten a huge amount of floating plastic and died. It is just one of an estimated 1 million seabirds and 100 000 marine mammals killed each year by eating plastic. Huge numbers of fish are ingesting plastic waste and we are eating this fish, so plastic waste is entering the human food chain.

Further research:

http://www.algalita.org/research/gis-mapping/; **http://www.algalita.org/videos/videos/**; **http://marinedebris.noaa.gov/**; **http://theplastiki.com/**; **http://junkraft.org/**; **http://5gyres.org/**

Can we clean up the oceans?

Boyan Slat from the Netherlands was only 16 years old when he was diving in Greece and discovered more plastic bags than fish. He then dedicated himself to researching the problem of plastic waste in the oceans and coming up with viable, sustainable solutions. He founded The Ocean Cleanup Foundation and came up with a passive cleanup concept in 2012. Boyan then led a team to build and trial the concept during a feasibility study. In 2014 the 530 page report, written by 70 scientists and engineers, was published and this indicated that it is possible to clean an area half the size of the Great Pacific Garbage Patch in just 10 years.

Fig. 5.11 Platform in the Pacific Ocean.

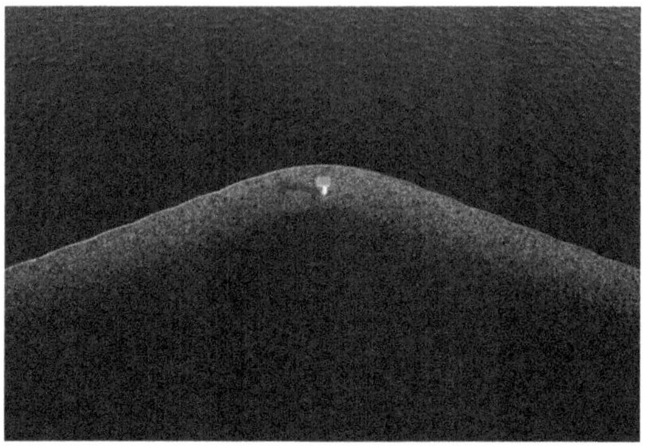

Fig. 5.12 Floating barriers in the Pacific Ocean.

How does it work?

The concept is based on a simple idea: "*Why move through the oceans, if the oceans can move through you?*" By attaching floating barriers and platforms to the seabed, the floating plastic can be concentrated, extracted and then recycled. The platform is solar powered and the whole process is driven by the wind and currents. Nets are not used so the impact on marine life is limited. A completed system would:

- contain two 50 km booms arranged in a V shape with a collection platform in the centre;
- have a platform that would hold 10 000 cubic metres of plastic and would be emptied every 1.5 months;
- be the largest structure ever placed in the ocean;
- remove most of the plastic in the top 3 metres of the ocean where concentrations are highest;
- cost 33 times less than conventional cleaning methods and do this up to 7900 times faster.

Combined with vital action to stop the source of the plastic on land, this method could help turn the tide in the battle to clean up our oceans. The Ocean Cleanup Foundation is now raising funds to build a large-scale working example. You can find out more here: **http://www.theoceancleanup.com/**

Data response and decision making exercises

1. Examine the map of marine species diversity below. This is available in colour in the Student's Book (Figure 5.10).

Fig. 5.13 Marine species diversity.

a) Describe the global distribution of marine species.

....

....

....

....

....

....

....

....

b) Identify three key areas where major concentrations of fish populations are found.

....

....

....

....

....

....

c) Using the map on page 89 and figures 5.11–5.13 in the Student's Book, suggest reasons for the distribution of major marine species.

....

....

....

....

....

....

....

....

....

....

d) What is the global ocean conveyor?

....

....

....

....

....

....

....

e) Describe the oceanic temperature conditions in the Pacific Ocean in an El Niño event. How does this differ from a normal year?

....

....

....

....

....

f) Outline the impact of El Niño on marine fisheries along the western coast of South America.

....

....

....

....

....

....

2. The graph below shows the data of global fish production over time.

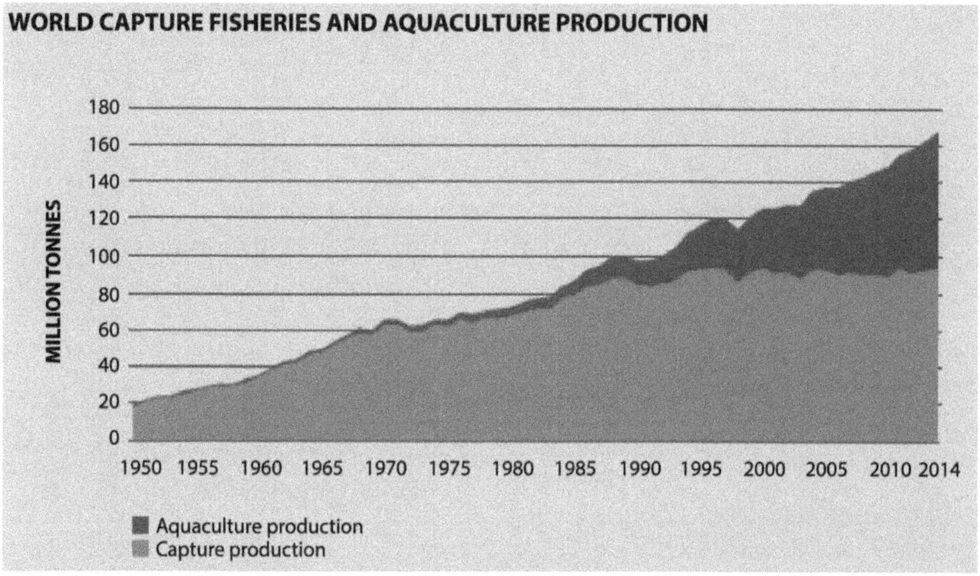

Fig. 5.14 World capture fisheries and aquaculture production.

a) Describe the trend in total fish production over time.

....

....

....

....

....

....

....

b) Suggest reasons for the increase in global fish production over time.

....

....

....

....

....

c) Describe what has happened to production from world capture fisheries since 1980?

....

....

....

....

....

....

....

d) Define the term aquaculture.

....

....

....

....

....

....

Aquaculture is now an important part of global fish production – meeting the dietary needs of millions of people. In 2014, 73.8 million tonnes (or 44.1 per cent of the global total) of fish was produced by aquaculture, with an estimated value of US$160.2 billion. Almost all fish produced from aquaculture are destined for human consumption. Thirty-five countries produced more farmed than wild-caught fish in 2014. This group of countries has a combined population of 3.3 billion, or 45 per cent of the world's population.

e) Outline the advantages and disadvantages of aquaculture production:

Advantages of aquaculture	Disadvantages of aquaculture

f) Suggest reasons for the rapid growth in aquaculture production globally.

....

....

....

....

....

....

....

....

....

....

....

....

....

....

....

3. Just as the human population is not evenly distributed, marine species are found in abundance in some places and are scarce in others. The data below shows the top 10 producer countries that catch the most fish.

Marine capture fisheries: major producer countries					
2012 Ranking	**Country**	**Continent**	**2003 capture in tonnes**	**2012 capture in tonnes**	**% variation 2003–12**
1	China	Asia	12 212 188	13 869 604	13.6
2	Indonesia	Asia	4 275 115	5 420 247	27
3	USA	North America	4 912 627	5 107 559	4
4	Peru	South America	6 053 120	4 807 923	–20.6
5	Russia	Asia/Europe	3 090 798	4 068 850	31.6
6	Japan	Asia	4 626 904	3 611 384	–21.9
7	India	Asia	2 954 796	3 402 405	15.1
8	Chile	South America	3 612 048	2 572 881	–28.8
9	Vietnam	Asia	1 647 133	2 418 700	46.8
10	Myanmar	Asia	1 053 720	2 332 790	121.4

a) Plot the data for % variation over time as a bar graph on the grid below:

b) Describe the pattern of growth or decline in capture fisheries in the top 10 producing countries.

....

....

....

....

....

....

c) Compare and contrast the trend in capture fisheries between Asia and the Americas over time.

....

....

....

....

....

....

....

d) Identify and explain any possible causes of the trends identified above. You will need to draw upon information from more than one section, as well as your own research.

....

....

....

....

....

....

....

....

....

4. The graph below is from the biannual Food and Agriculture Organization of the United Nations report 'The State of World Fisheries and Aquaculture 2016'.

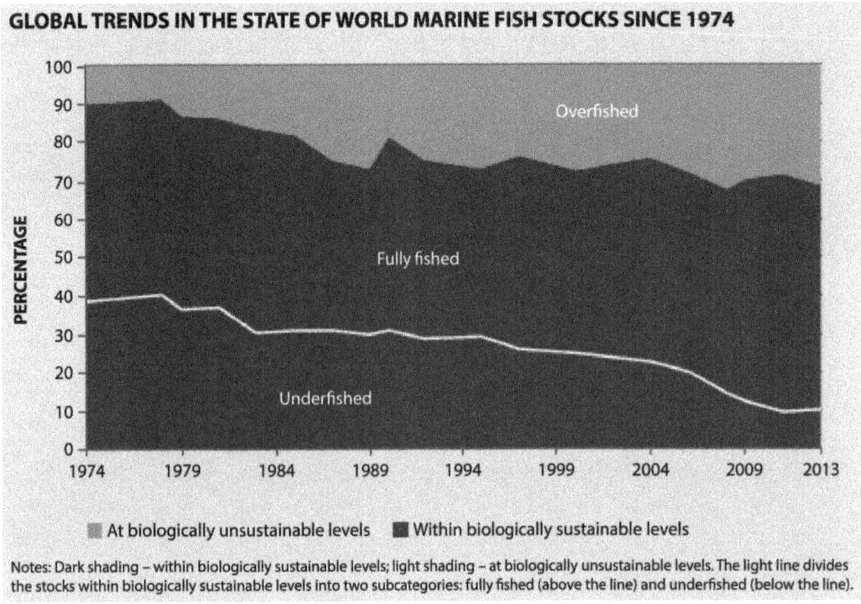

Fig. 5.15 Global trends in the state of world marine fish stocks since 1974.

The comprehensive report examines all of the patterns and trends across the world oceans in terms of fish production. You can access the report at **http://www.fao.org/3/a-i5555e.pdf**. This graph shows an alarming increase in the number of fish stocks globally that are overfished to biologically unsustainable levels. These stocks require management plans to rebuild fish levels. The number of fish stocks that are now fully fished (at the extent of a biologically sustainable level) has grown over time and have no further room for an expansion in catches.

a) Describe and explain how the following practices have contributed to the decline of fish stocks:

i. Overfishing

....

....

....

....

ii. Illegal fishing

....

....

....

....

iii. Overcapacity of global fishing fleet

....

....

....

....

Examine the selection of fishing methods below from the Marine Conservation Society. The league table scores different fishing methods for:

- impact on habitat (how the fishing gear impacts the seabed or coral reefs)
- impact on target species (how selected is the method, what happens to young fish when caught, are they discarded?)
- impact on non-target species (the level of bycatch associated with the method)

Method	**Species targeted**	**Impact on habitat**	**Impact on target species**	**Impact on non target species**	**Overall impact rating**
Pole and line	Tuna	Very low	Very low	Very low	Very low
Pelagic longline	Tuna	Very low	Low	High	Some
Purse seine using FAD	Tuna	Moderate	Low	Moderate	Some
Beam trawl	Plaice, sole, turbot	High	Moderate	High	Moderate
Drift net (high seas)	Tuna, shark	Very low	High	High	High

b) Evaluate the range of fishing methods shown. Consider which are the most sustainable methods. Suggest how higher impact methods can be modified to reduce unwanted effects.

....

....

....

....

....

....

....

5. The government of Vanuatu in the western Pacific Ocean has become increasingly concerned with the level of fishing from foreign-owned vessels inside its Exclusive Economic Zone. The innovative GIS from Global Fishing Watch has allowed the government to clearly identify the areas of highest fishing activity in a four-month period. The government need an action plan to help manage the situation sustainably. They need income from selling fishing licences but need to ensure stocks remain viable in the future.

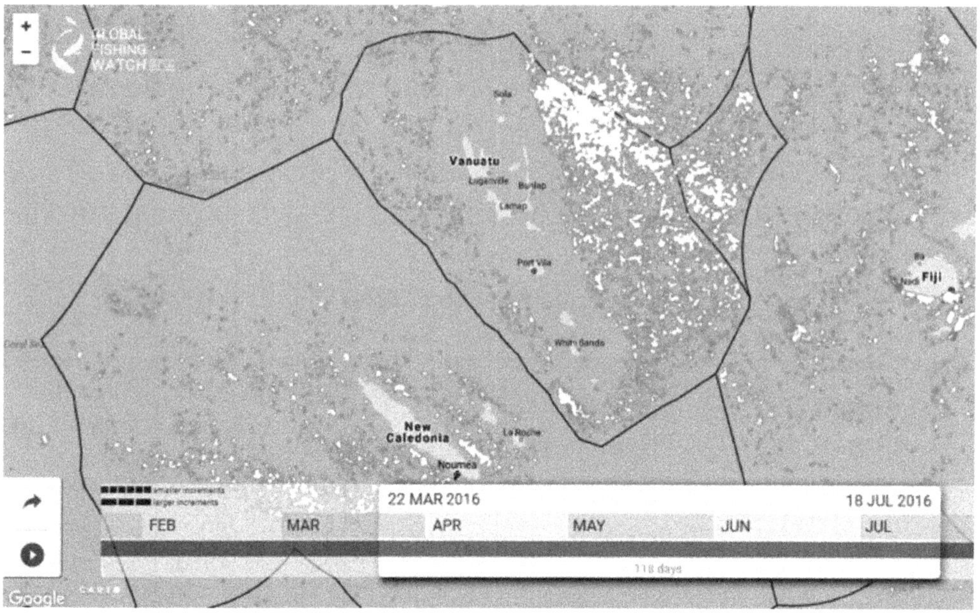

Fig 5.16 Fishing activity in Vanuatu.

Using the PIPA case study from the Student's Book (pages 136–138), plus other parts of the section and your own research, write a detailed action plan for the government of Vanuatu that meets the needs of the people today, without compromising the ability of people in the future to meet their own needs. Some options you might wish to consider recommending:

- a complete ban on all fishing for three years
- sell more fishing licences to maximise short-term income for the country
- develop a 'no take' Marine Protected Area
- develop a restricted-use Marine Protected Area where fishing is restricted at certain times of year
- ban certain types of boat associated with the most destructive fishing methods
- introduce a fishing quota system
- sell cheaper permits to those vessels using the most sustainable methods
- work with Global Fishing Watch to identify, report and ban vessels fishing illegally
- ask environmental charities to support monitoring of fishing vessels
- lobby governments of those vessels found to be illegally fishing to prevent them returning

You might wish to suggest a combination of the ideas as well as some of your own. You must justify why you are selecting certain methods and rejecting others. You might wish to use **http://map.globalfishingwatch.org/** to look at MPA successes in other parts of the world.

....

....

....

....

....

....

....

....

....

....

....

....

....

....

....

....

....

....

....

....

....

....

....

....

....

....

Answers to these questions can be found at **www.collins.co.uk/EnvMgmtIGCSE**

6 Managing natural hazards

Introduction

This section reinforces and extends student learning by:

- Consolidating and developing the factual material in the Student's Book that students will be required to recall and explain (AO1)
- Advancing student thinking through providing more challenging content and activities than those in the Student's Book, which extend some areas of the specification and require the synthesis of information and the application of knowledge and understanding to unfamiliar contexts (AO2)
- Enabling students to grasp that the effective management of environmental issues requires a coherent and holistic approach to problem solving through the principles of sustainable development (AO3)

This is achieved through the provision of:

- Extension content and related activities that secure and progress student knowledge and understanding through tasks that require handling information from a variety of sources to reach conclusions and make judgments
- Supplementary case studies that reinforce and advance key principles and concepts and support evaluative thinking
- A decision making or problem solving exercise that encourages students to appreciate the complexities of environmental management and the pivotal role of the principles of sustainable development in achieving successful outcomes

Links to other chapters

Managing vulnerability to and risk from natural hazards is a key challenge facing countries around the world. Rapid population growth in lower income countries has meant that increasing numbers of people are facing risk from one or multiple natural hazards. The factors that increase or decrease levels of vulnerability are key concepts that are vital to explore with students. The size or scale of a disaster is influenced more by the level of vulnerability of the population than the size of the hazard event. Understanding that humans have little impact on the size and strength of a tectonic hazard or a tropical cyclone is critical, as is recognising the influence of steps taken to reduce the risk by decreasing the level of vulnerability. Each section of the Student's Book contains examples of environmental management challenges that, if not addressed through more sustainable management techniques, will likely result in people facing greater risk from natural hazards. For example, poor agricultural techniques that result in soil erosion and desertification will exacerbate the impact of a drought on a vulnerable population. The capacity of a population to cope with the drought will be worsened by lower crop yield before the drought. Furthermore, deforestation will damage biodiversity in ecosystems and increase soil erosion – increasing the risk of landslides and flooding. Drought and flash flooding are more likely in ENSO years, as is the risk of forest fires in Southeast Asia. These fires lead to regional lowering of air quality – which in turn affects vulnerable populations more adversely.

The threat of climate change, dealt with in terms of extraction of fossil fuels in the rocks and minerals section, consumption in the energy and environment section and explained through the enhanced greenhouse effect in the atmosphere and human activity section is another example of how you can develop the synoptic thinking of students. The cumulative effect of greenhouse gas emissions in the atmosphere and the changing weather patterns associated with warming are likely to increase the number of hydro-meteorological hazards, which in turn will affect more people. Changing weather patterns will cause a decrease in rainfall in some areas and an increase in intense rainfall in others. This will increase the number of droughts and floods that occur. Increasing ocean temperatures will cause sea levels to rise, increasing the risk of coastal flooding generally, as well as increasing the severity of storm surges from tropical cyclones – which are, themselves, likely to become frequent and intense.

Managing natural hazards topic	Links to other subject content	Section
Earthquakes and volcanoes	Formation of rocks Water pollution and its sources Human population distribution and density Ecosystems under threat	1 4 8 9
Tropical cyclones	Managing pollution of fresh water The atmosphere	4 7
Flooding	Causes and impacts of soil erosion The water cycle Ecosystems under threat	3 4 9
Drought	Managing soil erosion Water supply Ecosystems under threat	3 4 9
Opportunities presented by natural hazards	Sustainable use of rocks and minerals Soils for plant growth	1 3

Extension content and related activities

Patterns and trends in natural disasters

A hazard is described as a natural event that has the potential to cause damage, loss of life and disruption, whereas a disaster occurs when the hazard interacts with people. How big a disaster depends on many factors related to the level of vulnerability of the population. For example, a tropical cyclone that passes over an uninhabited island is not a disaster as it does not interact with a vulnerable population. The number of disasters occurring each year are carefully recorded and analysed in the EM-DAT database. Understanding patterns and trends in disasters is important when trying to manage natural hazards. It is very difficult to make plans for a tectonic hazard that occurs every 650 000 years, but by understanding recent patterns, it is possible to plan for events that occur more frequently.

Examine these four graphs. They show graphical representations of disaster data since 1900. Specifically, they show the number of people killed, the number of people affected, the number of disasters reported and the estimated reported damage. To be reported as a disaster, one of the following conditions must be met:

- 10 or more people reported killed
- 100 or more people reported affected
- a declaration of a state of emergency
- a call for international assistance

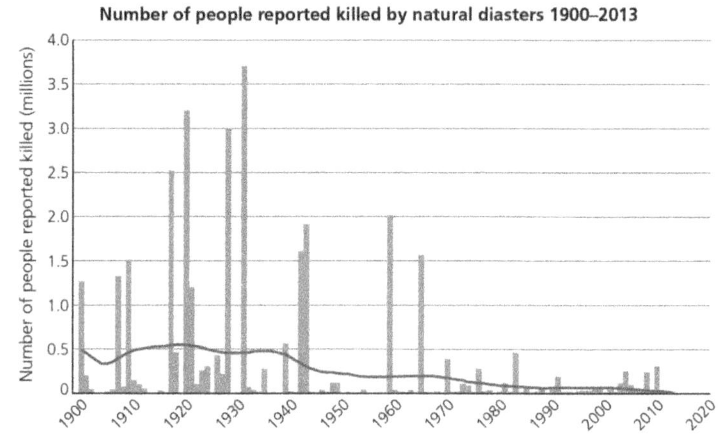

Fig. 6.1 Number of people reported killed by natural disasters 1900-2013.

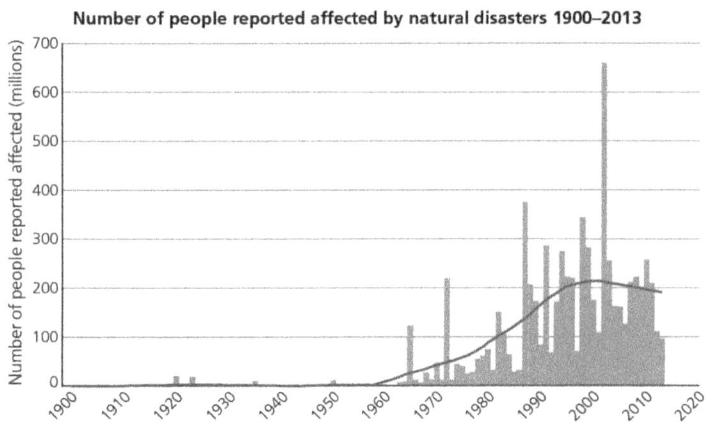

Fig. 6.2 Number of people reported affected by natural disasters 1900–2013.

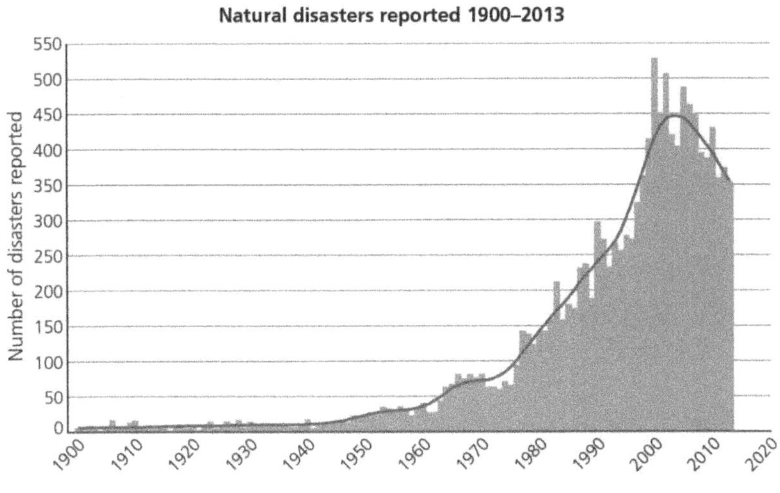

Fig. 6.3 Natural disasters reported 1900-2013.

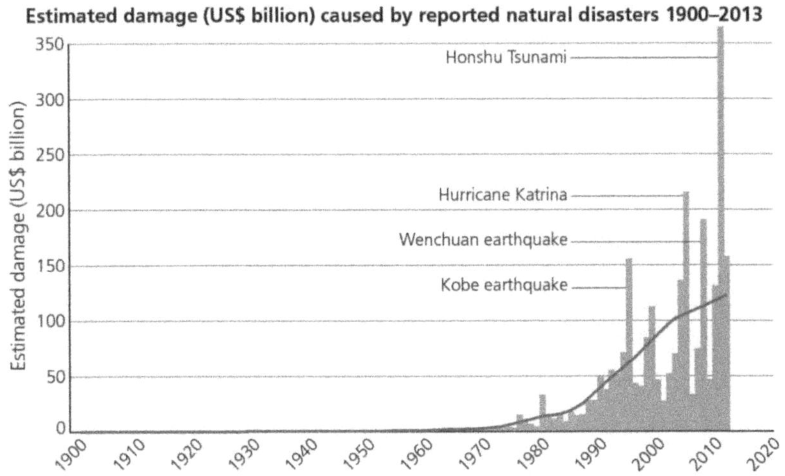

Fig. 6.4 Estimated damage caused by reported natural disasters 1900-2013.

Consolidating your thinking

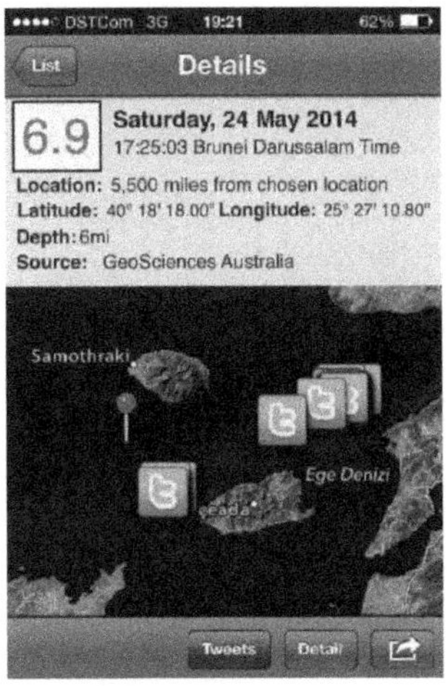

Fig. 6.5 Smartphone app providing earthquake data.

What is the general trend shown in each of the sets of data in the graphs? What could be responsible for each of the trends you have identified? Consider the impact that a rising global population, improvements in recording and reporting, climate change and the role of technology and communication (such as the internet and smartphone apps like Earthquake shown in Figure 6.5) could have had. Use the internet to compile a list of disasters that have occurred globally from 2012 onwards. Does the data you have compiled confirm or contradict the patterns you identified from the graphs above? If not, can you suggest reasons why this might be the case?

Try some real-time earthquake tracking by downloading a smartphone app or checking out the United States Geological Survey – **http://earthquake.usgs.gov/earthquakes/map/**

Risk and vulnerability

Globally, from 2002 to 2011, there were an average of 394 disasters each year, which killed an average of 107 000 people annually. The mean number of people affected by these disasters each year was 268 million and the disasters cost US$143 billion in economic damages. These impacts, however, were not evenly spread across the planet and some places are more likely than others to have higher numbers of fatalities and victims. In some places, smaller earthquakes will do substantially more damage and kill many more people than much stronger earthquakes elsewhere. The same is true for tropical storms where similar scale events in different parts of the world will have substantially different outcomes. Why do you think this is?

The impact of each hazard type is directly affected by the relative level of vulnerability of the local population.

Consolidating your thinking

Working with a partner, make a list of all the reasons why two earthquakes or hurricanes of similar size might have very different consequences depending on where they occur in the world.

For anywhere in the world, there are three important concepts to consider when thinking about the risk from a hazard:

- Probability – how likely it is that a hazard will occur.
- Vulnerability – how exposed the people are in an area to the effects of a hazard.
- The capacity of people to cope – before, during and after the disaster.

For example, Florida, USA has a high probability that hurricanes will occur, but the people there are less vulnerable due to advanced warning systems, education programmes, building codes, compulsory storm insurance, evacuations and disaster management plans. They have a good ability to cope with hurricanes so overall risk is lowered, but, importantly, not eliminated. A hazard here could still become a disaster, but on a smaller scale than if the same event were to hit the Philippines, for example.

Examine the range of factors shown in the spider diagram (right) that affect risk and vulnerability to hazards.

It is key that you recognise that not all hazards become disasters and that it is not simply the size of the physical event that determines the impact of a disaster but a complex interlinked series of human factors. Spend two minutes thinking about each of the factors. Then, with a partner, discuss how each of the factors could impact on how vulnerable people are and how at risk this makes them.

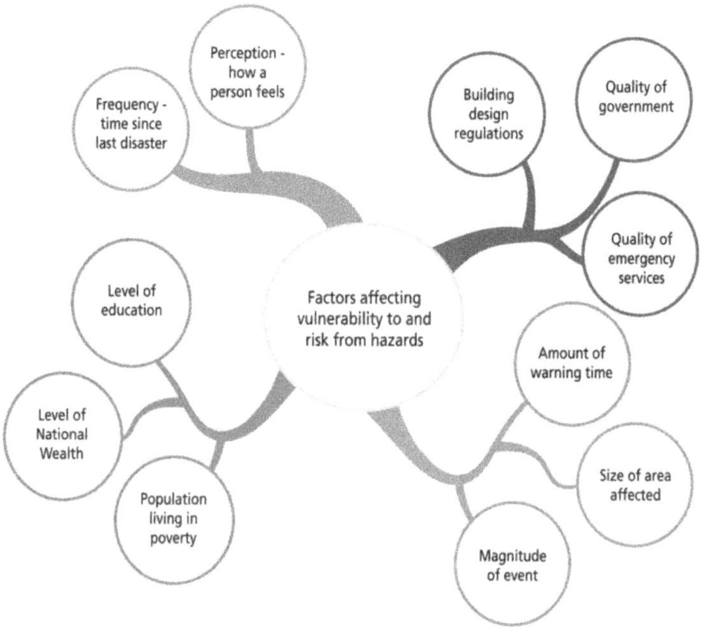

Fig. 6.6 Factors affecting vulnerability to and risk from hazards.

You could split the factors into different categories and you should consider how the factors could increase or decrease vulnerability.

Finally, discuss your ideas with another pair. You should then aim to write about the influence of five factors in detail.

Using this exercise as a basis, analyse the following five images and identify factors that decrease or increase the vulnerability of the local population to natural disasters.

Fig. 6.7 A cyclone shelter in Bangladesh.

Fig. 6.8 Tsunami evacuation sign, Phang Nga, Thailand.

Fig. 6.9 Hillside housing in Peru.

Fig. 6.10 School earthquake drill, Japan.

Fig. 6.11 Earthquake-proof office block, Tokyo, Japan.

Supplementary case study

The Tohoku earthquake and tsunami, Japan, 11 March 2011

Fig. 6.12 Tsunami triggered by an earthquake in northeast Japan.

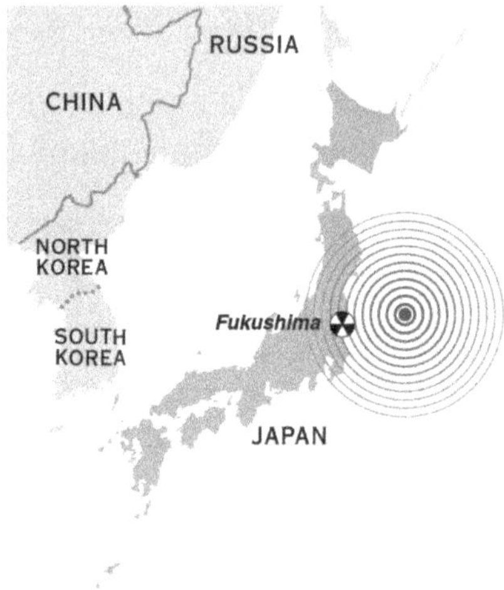

Fig. 6.13 Location of the earthquake, Japan.

The 2011 Tohoku earthquake struck offshore of Japan, along a subduction zone where the Pacific and Eurasian plates meet. It was centred on the seafloor 72 km east of Tohoku, at a depth of 32 km below the surface. The earthquake occurred at 14:46 local time (05:46 UTC) on Friday 11 March, 2011. The shaking lasted about six minutes. The megathrust earthquake, measuring 9.0 on the Richter scale, caused areas of northeastern Japan to shift toward North America by as much as 2.4 m. Areas of the Japanese coast closest to the epicentre experienced the largest shifts with a 400-km stretch of coastline dropping vertically by 0.6 m. The sudden release of hundreds of years of frictional stress caused an upthrust of 6–8 m along a 180-km wide section of seabed 60 km offshore from the east coast of Tohoku. This resulted in a major tsunami that brought destruction along the Pacific coastline of Japan's northern islands.

Less than an hour after the earthquake, the first of many tsunami waves hit Japan's coastline. The tsunami waves reached heights of up to 39 m at Miyako city and travelled inland as far as 10 km in Sendai. The tsunami flooded an estimated area of approximately 561 sq km in Japan.

The waves overtopped and destroyed protective tsunami seawalls at several locations, which had been built in preparation for a smaller water surge. The massive surge destroyed some three-storey buildings where people had gathered for safety. Japan has an extensive network of seismic monitoring stations, which meant immediate tsunami warnings were issued. A study by the Japanese government found that only 58 per cent of people in the affected areas took notice of the warning and headed to higher ground. Of those people that ignored the warning, 49 per cent were hit by water. These people survived to tell the tale, but many did not. In total,15 894 people died with 6152 injured and 2562 people missing. The demographics of this area of Japan meant that older people were disproportionately affected, with 65.2 per cent of the deaths coming from people aged 60 or older and 24 per cent of total victims being in their 70s.

Fig. 6.14 Aerial view of the damage to Wakuya, Japan after the earthquake and tsunami devastated the area.

The damage to buildings and infrastructure was staggering:

- 45 700 buildings were destroyed and 144 300 were damaged.
- 230 000 automobiles and trucks were damaged or destroyed.
- 300 hospitals were damaged with 20 destroyed.
- 25 million tonnes of rubble were created.
- 319 fishing ports were damaged.
- Major ports were damaged and closed.
- Sendai airport was destroyed.
- Irrigation dams were ruptured.
- 1.5 million households lost water supplies.
- Power stations were damaged or taken offline, causing rolling blackouts for months.
- An oil refinery was set on fire.

Perhaps one of the most serious long-term impacts was the destruction of the Fukushima nuclear power station. The reactors were immediately shut down following the earthquake, but the tsunami waves overtopped the sea walls and destroyed diesel powered cooling systems. Three of the reactors went into meltdown and parts of the plant exploded leading to the release of radioactive material into the air and into the Pacific Ocean. Attempts are still being made to access the reactors and to clean up the disaster. This is expected to continue for many years. A radioactive plume has spread across the Pacific toward the USA, although this is not expected to cause long-term effects. Nearer to Japan, the impact of this leak on marine species is still being studied.

Data response and decision making exercises

1. Examine the map below that shows the location of earthquakes and volcanoes around the Pacific Ocean. See Figure 6.3 in the Student's Book for the colour version.

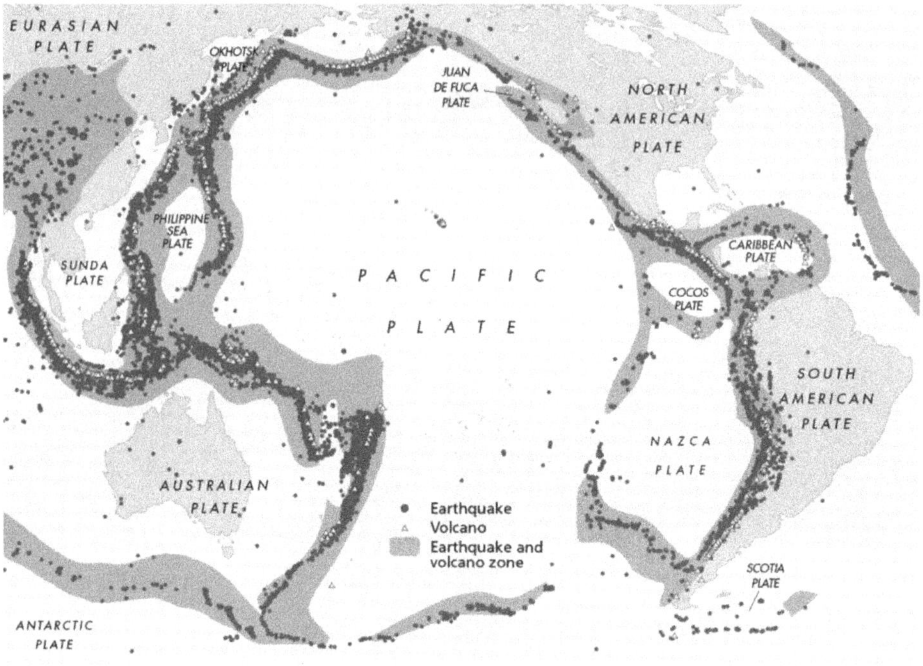

Fig. 6.15 Tectonic activity in the Pacific Ocean.

a) What is an earthquake?

....

....

b) Define the key terms *focus* and *epicentre*.

....

....

....

....

c) Describe the distribution of earthquakes and volcanoes on the map.

....

....

....

d) Suggest reasons for this pattern of earthquakes and volcanoes.

....

....

....

e) Describe the main types of plate boundary.

....

....

....

....

f) Why do tectonic plates move?

....

....

....

....

g) Using diagrams, explain the formation of volcanoes at destructive plate boundaries.

2. The map below shows the plate tectonic setting of New Zealand.

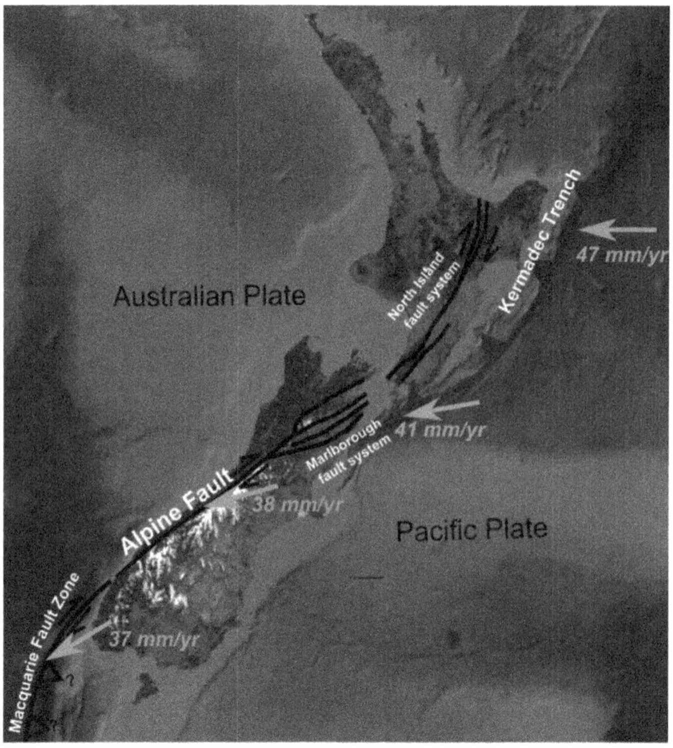

Fig. 6.16 The complex plate boundaries under New Zealand.

New Zealand is highly tectonically active and this creates a dynamic or constantly changing environment. From glaciers in the south to volcanic fields in the north, through dramatic mountains, fault lines and beautiful coastline, New Zealand contains some of the most outstanding landscapes on Earth. Geologically, New Zealand is one of the youngest countries on Earth. However, the plate tectonics that shape the dramatic and beautiful landscapes also create risk from a range of hazards. New Zealand sits on top of an active plate boundary where the Pacific and Australian Plates meet. The resulting geology is complex but developing an understanding of it will help you to explain some of the landscapes and hazards that occur.

a) Using your knowledge of plate boundaries, annotate the map above with diagrams to show the type of faults and plate boundaries occurring in New Zealand.

b) Suggest which tectonic hazards New Zealand is likely to experience and why.

....

....

....

....

....

New Zealand has a comprehensive network of seismic monitoring stations. The maps below show the locations and depth of earthquakes in New Zealand over the past 10 years as well as the location of active volcanoes.

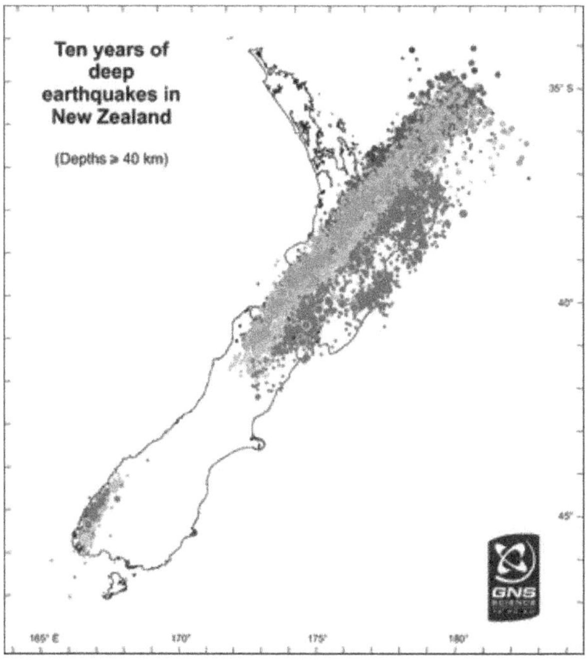

Fig. 6.17 Deep earthquakes in New Zealand.

Fig. 6.18 Shallow earthquakes in New Zealand.

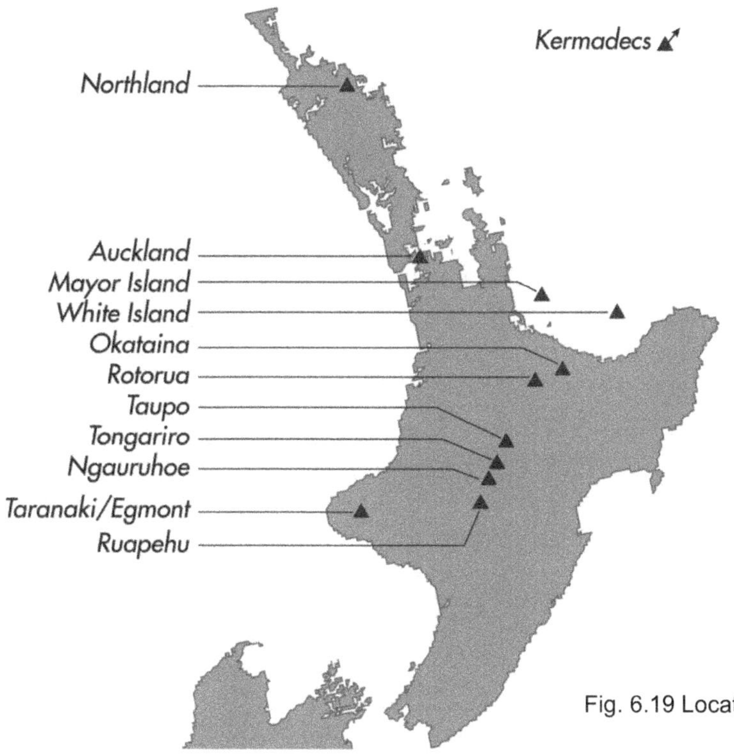

Fig. 6.19 Location of New Zealand's volcanic centres.

c) What is the pattern of deep earthquakes in New Zealand? How does the map in Figure 6.17 link to the plate boundary information?

....

....

....

....

....

....

....

....

....

....

....

d) What is the pattern of shallow earthquakes in New Zealand? How does the map in Figure 6.18 differ from the map of deep earthquakes in Figure 6.17? Suggest reasons for the pattern.

....

....

....

....

....

....

....

....

....

....

....

....

e) The volcano map in Figure 6.19 shows areas of volcanic activity, not just individual volcanoes. For example, The Auckland Volcanic Field is made up of over fifty separate volcanoes scattered across New Zealand's largest city. How does the information in the three maps in Figures 6.17-6.19 help to explain this pattern?

....

....

....

....

....

....

....

....

....

....

....

....

....

....

....

....

....

....

....

....

....

....

....

....

3. Due to the complex tectonic setting, New Zealand is prone to damaging earthquakes. There are stringent building codes, evacuation plans and education in schools. Urban search and rescue teams practise drills regularly. These reduce the vulnerability of the population by decreasing risk and increasing the capacity to cope if a disaster does occur. This was clearly demonstrated in 2010 when an unknown fault line near Christchurch ruptured. The impact of this earthquake is shown below.

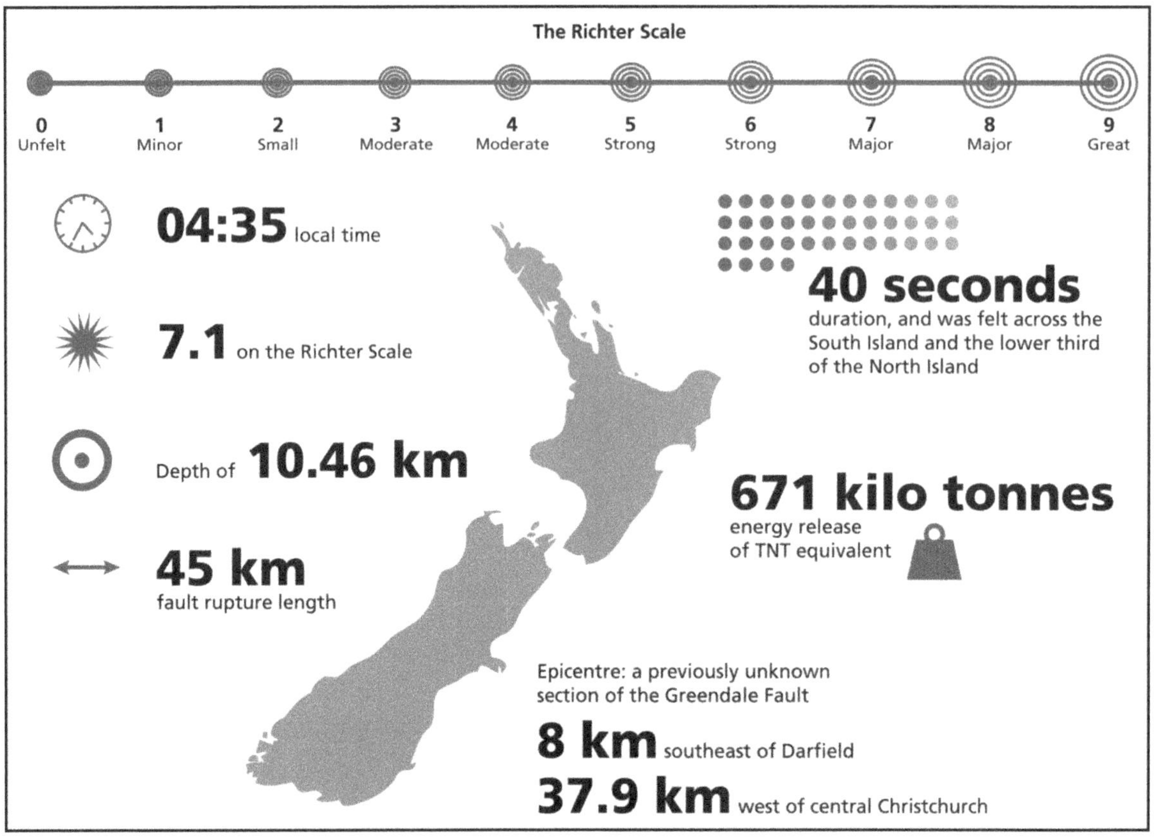

Fig. 6.20 The 2010 Darfield earthquake, 4 September 2010.

Effects of the earthquake

- Across the region, there was widespread damage to infrastructure and housing, and disruption to many businesses. A state of emergency was declared.
- Despite the tremendous damage and the constant aftershocks that made life very challenging, many people felt lucky that there was no loss of life.
- Railway lines buckled and had to be repaired.
- Soil liquefaction caused a lot of problems, with flooding damaging buried pipes and building foundations.
- Because this earthquake happened at night, when most people were in their beds, there were not many people injured by falling buildings or landslides.
- Two people were seriously injured, with approximately 100 injuries in total.

Despite the tremendous power of the quake, many New Zealanders – although shaken – cleaned up, repaired and carried on with life. The fact that there was no loss of life meant people were perhaps lulled into a sense of security about how well they were prepared for an earthquake. They didn't realise that this was to be the first of a sequence of powerful earthquakes over the coming months that would alter the future of the second biggest city in

New Zealand. The Student's Book contains detailed information on the more devastating February 2011 earthquake that struck closer to the city centre.

a) Using the Student's Book, compare and contrast the September 2010 and February 2011 earthquakes.

....

....

....

....

....

....

....

....

....

....

....

....

b) Suggest reasons why the second earthquake was more deadly than the first.

....

....

....

....

....

....

....

....

....

....

....

The map and graph below show the strength and location of the main shocks and huge number of aftershocks.

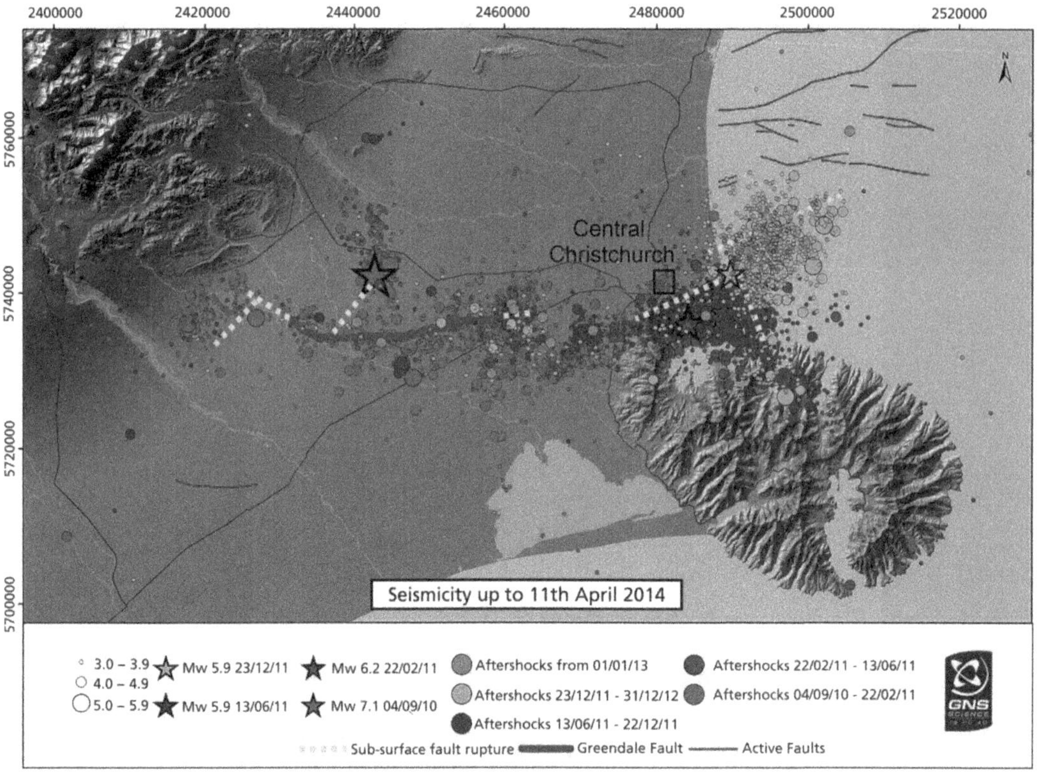

Fig. 6.21 Aftershocks of the Darfield earthquake.

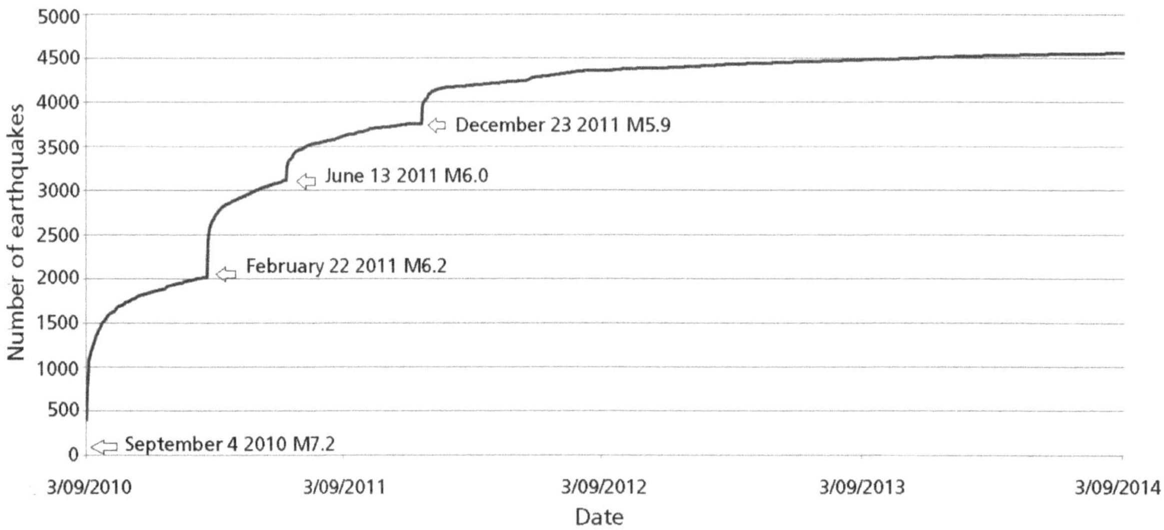

Fig. 6.22 Aftershocks following the Canterbury earthquake in New Zealand, September 2010.

c) Describe the location and strength of aftershocks around Christchurch. What happens to the number of aftershocks after each big quake?

....

....

....

....

....

....

....

How people react to situations such as the quakes that unfolded in Christchurch will depend upon a range of factors. The diagram below helps us to understand how people might respond to hazards.

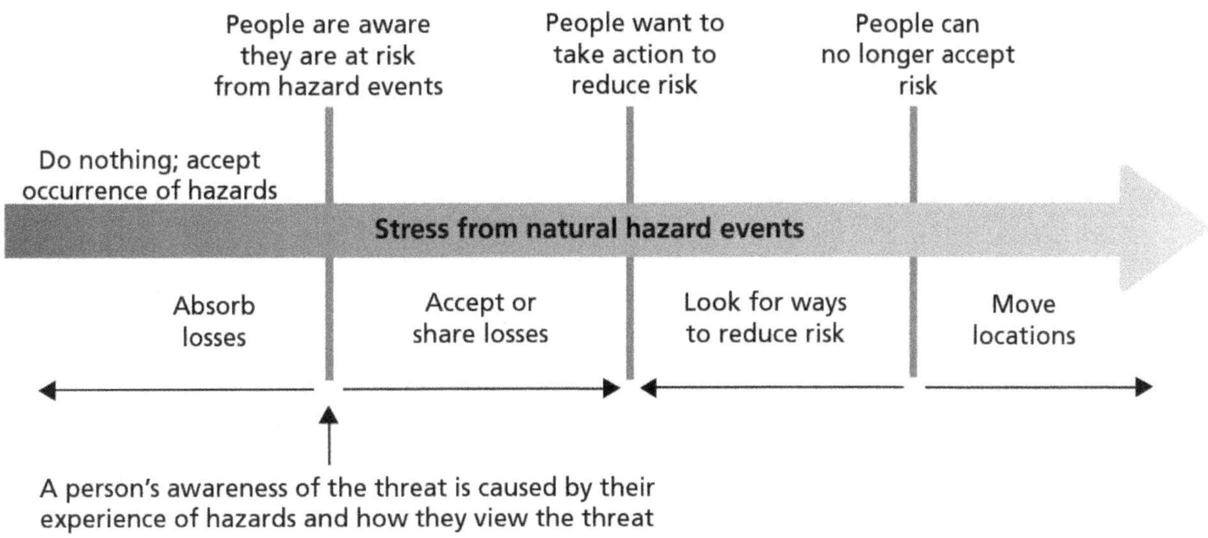

Fig. 6.23 How people may react to natural hazards.

d) Using Figure 6.23, as well as all the information on the two main earthquakes, the damage and the multiple aftershocks, describe how you feel you would react if you were a resident in the city.

....

....

....

....

....

....

....

....

....

....

....

....

....

4. Recovering from a serious earthquake requires significant planning and investment – there are several key stages. These stages are examples from the Christchurch earthquake:
   - The immediate search and rescue operation – hours and days following the earthquake.
   - The demolish, repair, patch-up and planning phase – September 2010 to December 2011.
   - Begin to rebuild, replace and reconstruct – 2012 to 2014.
   - Construct, restore and improve – 2015 to 2020 and beyond.

   A complex and comprehensive recovery plan has been put into place by organisations set up by the New Zealand government. They created CERA (Canterbury Earthquake Recovery Authority) and appointed an earthquake minister to the government to oversee the rebuild, replace and reconstruct phase. CERA has now been disestablished with a shift to more local governance over future projects. The central business district (CBD) of the city was devastated in the second earthquake, so rebuilding this key anchor has been an initial focus. Many of the projects are now constructed. Another significant challenge is what to do with the residential red zone in the city – an area of 6.3 sq km containing 7300 homes along the Avon river, which suffered severe liquefaction and where residential building is no longer allowed.

New Zealand, like many countries, completes a regular census, so has been able to record the social and economic impact of the earthquake. Information on this can be found here: **http://www.stats.govt.nz/Census/2013-census/profile-and-summary-reports/2013-census-infographic-chch.aspx**

Using the information above, the suggested links and your own research, comment in detail on the social and economic short- and medium-term effects of the earthquake, as well as the recovery efforts to date. You should focus on the developments in the CBD as well as the developing plans for the red zone. You might also want to suggest your own plans for the red zone.

....

....

....

....

....

....

....

....

....

....

....

....

....

....

....

....

....

....

....

....

Answers to these questions can be found at **www.collins.co.uk/EnvMgmtIGCSE**

7 The atmosphere and human activities

Introduction

This section reinforces and extends student learning by:

- Consolidating and developing the factual material in the Student's Book that students will be required to recall and explain (AO1)
- Advancing student thinking through providing more challenging content and activities than those in the Student's Book, which extend some areas of the specification and require the synthesis of information and the application of knowledge and understanding to unfamiliar contexts (AO2)
- Enabling students to grasp that the effective management of environmental issues requires a coherent and holistic approach to problem solving through the principles of sustainable development (AO3)

This is achieved through the provision of:

- Extension content and related activities that secure and progress student knowledge and understanding through tasks that require handling information from a variety of sources to reach conclusions and make judgments
- Supplementary case studies that reinforce and advance key principles and concepts and support evaluative thinking
- A decision making or problem solving exercise that encourages students to appreciate the complexities of environmental management and the pivotal role of the principles of sustainable development in achieving successful outcomes

Links to other chapters

Humans are completely dependent upon the atmosphere for the air that we breathe and the greenhouse gases that keep planet Earth at a habitable temperature. The atmosphere also protects us from harmful UV rays from the sun. It is vital that students fully understand the vulnerable nature of the atmosphere to negative human impacts, and this is most clearly illustrated by the air quality in our towns and cities and the enhanced greenhouse effect. Smog and acid rain are clearly visible signs of human impact and the rise in numbers of people affected by poor air quality is something that may impact students in your school. The often transboundary nature of these issues is worth exploring with students when discussing who is responsible for the pollution in Southeast Asia – the farmers burning the rainforest or the consumers of products that contain palm oil – the growth of which is driving the clearing of forest in the first place.

The enhanced greenhouse effect is the greatest environmental management challenge of our time and it is a challenge that is seen impacting upon all sections of the Student's Book. For example, a rising global population living in urban areas demands greater energy consumption, which increases exploitation of fossil fuels and leads to an increase in carbon emissions – enhancing the greenhouse effect. This changes weather patterns and will increase the likelihood of hazardous events such as floods, tropical cyclones and drought. These will, in turn, create more pressure on agricultural land as desertification occurs and this will cause migration from rural to urban areas. The loss of productive land will increase pressure on marine resources as we look to substitute protein sources from meat to fish. A changing climate will also impact biodiversity as species will not adapt quickly enough to rapid changes. Furthermore, growing cities will encroach upon habitats and push certain species toward extinction. Rising temperatures will shrink glaciers – threatening the water supplies of millions of people.

This is one example of the many ways of getting students to make links and it is very easy to focus on the negative. It is equally important to focus on the solutions and the role that the students themselves have to play as agents of change in the future.

Atmosphere and human activities topic	**Links to other subject content**	**Section**
The atmosphere	Tropical cyclones Human population distribution and density	6 8
Atmospheric pollution – causes and impacts	Impact of rock and mineral extraction Water pollution and its sources	1 4
Managing atmospheric pollution	Managing the impact of rock and mineral extraction Management of oil pollution Sustainable agriculture Managing pollution of fresh water	1 2 3 4

Extension content and related activities

Atmospheric pollution and its causes

Tropical forests, like those found on Borneo and in the Amazon Basin, play an important role in regulating the Earth's climate by capturing carbon dioxide (CO_2) as they grow and storing it in plant tissue. All forests store more carbon than other types of land cover, and tropical forests can contain four times more carbon per 0.01 sq km than cropland. These forests are vital in helping to absorb the millions of tonnes of CO_2 that we release each year. They also provide benefits such as rainfall for farming, flood prevention and biodiversity.

However, these forests are under threat as they are being cut down, or deforested at an increasing rate. An area of tropical forest 130 000 sq km in size is cut down and converted to other land uses each year. This is the equivalent of about 8.5 million soccer pitches a year, or 23 483 pitches a day. The photo below shows a landscape destroyed by logging in Borneo.

Fig. 7.1 Land destroyed by logging in Sarawak, Borneo.

The reasons for deforestation are complex. In the past, forests were cut down to provide land to grow crops and to graze cattle for subsistence farming. Today, the land is used increasingly to provide products demanded on world markets, such as soy, palm oil, beef, timber, biofuels, and minerals such as gold, copper and bauxite. Deforestation occurs when it is cheaper to supply products from converted forest land than from other land. Our demand for products like palm oil and beef push the price higher and this leads to more forest being cut down to provide these products. The price of forest land doesn't yet include the value of forests in absorbing carbon from the atmosphere. Until this is added to the price of the land, they will continue to be cut down at increasing rates.

The deforestation is devastating for forest ecosystems. The habitats of animals like orang-utans are being destroyed and they are under threat of extinction. Undiscovered plants might contain valuable medicines that are being lost forever. Forest tribes like the Penan of Borneo, Malaysia are being broken up and are losing the land they have lived in harmony with for generations.

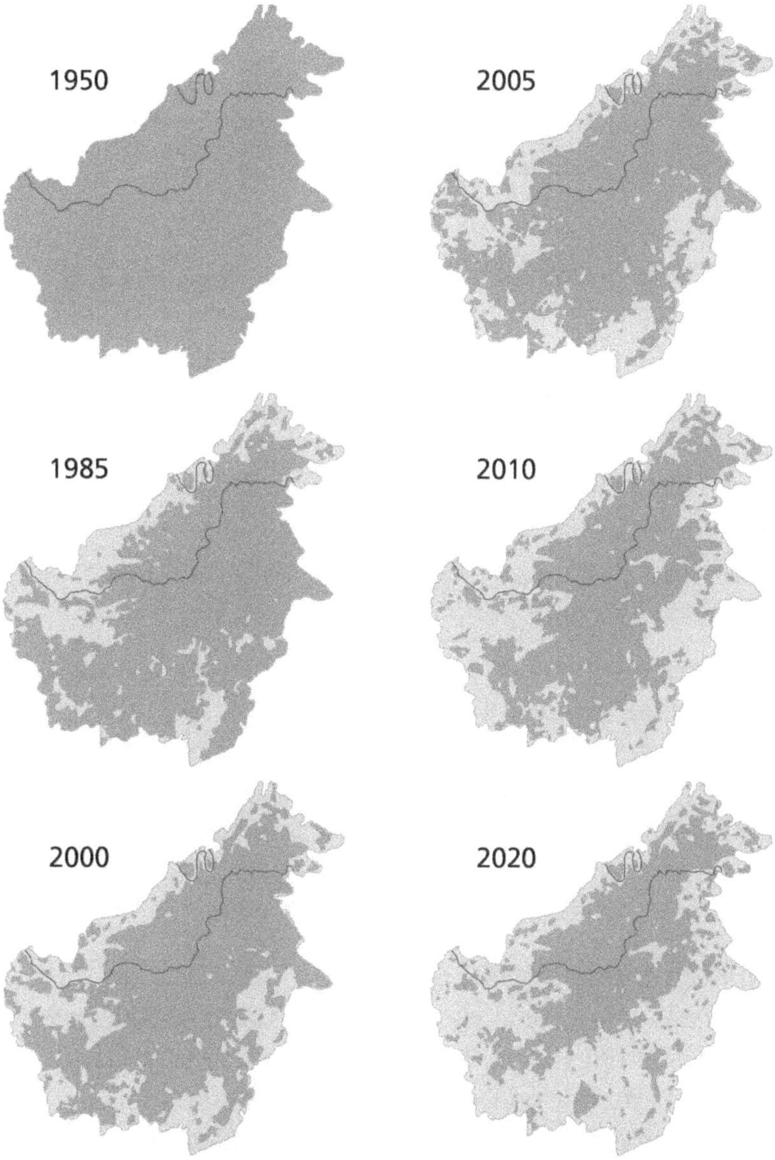

Fig. 7.2 Forest coverage in Borneo 1950–2020; the dark grey represents areas covered by forest.

Furthermore, the forests are often cut and cleared using illegal burning. These fires reverse the CO_2 absorption of the forests and release greenhouse gases into the atmosphere, further accelerating the enhanced greenhouse effect. In addition, fires often burn out of control – exacerbated by drought conditions from El Niño – and cause dramatic reductions in air quality. Many of the fires occur on soil with a high peat content. This soil contains high levels of carbon in partially decomposed plant matter. The burning releases this highly concentrated carbon back into the atmosphere. This has been the case in Southeast Asia in recent years where clearing of forest on Borneo, Java and Sumatra has led to prolonged fires that send a haze over the entire region. A great many of the environmental management challenges facing the world today have been developing over time. Their impacts are increasingly affecting larger areas.

Our knowledge and understanding of what is happening to the environment is greatly enhanced by the use of technology. For example:

- remote sensing data from satellites can pinpoint areas of deforestation
- infrared satellite technology can identify forest fires in time
- GPS trackers can follow the location of fishing boats as they move around the oceans
- earthquakes can be monitored in real time, with warnings issued once the shaking starts
- tropical cyclones can be tracked, allowing evacuations to happen

These are just a few examples, but the key to the success of all of these is the ability of this information to be shared over the internet and to be added to maps to identify patterns and trends over time. Any system of adding layers of information to a base map is known as a Geographical Information System (GIS). Examples include:

http://fires.globalforestwatch.org/home/

http://maps.eyesontheforest.or.id/

http://earthquake.usgs.gov/earthquakes/map/

https://coast.noaa.gov/hurricanes/

http://map.globalfishingwatch.org/

All of these GIS systems are useful for students studying environmental management and learning how to manipulate a GIS is a vital skill for students in the 21st century.

Consolidating your thinking

You will need to use your interpretative skills to analyse the map of Borneo forest loss from 1950 onwards. To analyse a map like the ones in Figure 7.2:

- Describe the pattern of forest loss by using locations like Kalimantan; directions like northeast; use the scale in km and time 1950–2000, 2000–2010 and the projected forest cover in 2020.
- Which area or countries have the most/least forest? Cross reference with an atlas.
- Once you have done this, you are going to focus in on Sarawak, Malaysia and the changes from 2005 to 2010. You will need to download the Google Earth layer from: **http://earth.sarvision.nl/Sarawak_forest_change_2005-2010.kmz**

You should use Google Earth to switch these layers on and off to explore the relationship between forest loss, plantations, parks and reserves and the satellite photos underneath. You can also look at older satellite images to compare the change over time. There is a help sheet available for you below. Take screenshots and paste these into a document with your annotations to build up a picture of what is happening in Sarawak. You can cross-reference the situation in Sarawak with live information on forest fires and haze, as well as the impact on biodiversity, using Global Forest Watch and Eyes on the Forest (linked above).

Using a basic Geographical Information System (GIS)

Environmental scientists use a range of maps and data to view and understand patterns and processes in relation to different places at different scales. A digital map can be used to add different layers of information to see how the information links to the place and how it is changing over time. Google Earth is an example of a GIS. It is very easy to use and once you have found your house, you can begin to add layers of information that are built in, download layers from the internet or even make your own. This user guide will show you how to access the layer of information on forest loss in Sarawak, Malaysia.

- First make sure you have downloaded and installed Google Earth: **http://www.google.co.uk/intl/en_uk/earth/**
- For this exercise, it will work best on a Mac or a PC with a mouse.
- Open Google Earth and explore the basic functions. You can use this link for help: **http://www.google.co.uk/intl/en_uk/earth/learn/beginner.html**
- Download the forest loss information layer (or KMZ file): **http://earth.sarvision.nl/Sarawak_forest_change_2005-2010.kmz**
- Save, then open the file by double clicking on it. It will open Google Earth automatically.

You should use the navigation help guide below to explore this layer. You can switch on and off layers of information that relate to the forest loss between 2005–2010, the location of oil palm plantations, parks and reserves as well as areas of peat. Peat is made of very old decomposing vegetation and is a vital store of carbon dioxide. This CO_2 can be released by deforestation and the burning of forest to make way for oil palm plantations.

To help you navigate these layers, try these tasks:

1. Zoom out to see the whole of Sarawak. Switch on and off the layers that show the peat areas. Repeat this for oil palm areas and the parks. Can you see any patterns emerging? Where is the recent deforestation happening?

2. The oil palm layer shows areas licensed for production, but not always deforested yet. Can you see any places where new forest may be destroyed to make way for oil palm? (Hint: you are looking for peach colours (oil palm areas) on top of green areas (forest).)

3. There is much more to see when you zoom in. Search for Pusa, Sarawak in the search box and zoom in. Again, toggle the layers on and off. The area to the north has very recent deforestation on peat areas, with more to come in the future.

4. Switch the whole 'Sarawak forest change' layer off and you will see the actual satellite image. Zoom in as close as possible with the image still clear. Can you find a dividing line when the oil palm ends and the forest begins? Switch the oil palm layer on. What will happen here in the future?

5. You could drop a place mark here to save the location: **http://www.google.co.uk/intl/en_uk/earth/learn/beginner.html#tab=placemarks-and-tours**

6. You could even switch on historical imagery and use the slider to see any change over time. You should repeat this exercise by exploring and finding different locations where there is evidence of change – dropping place marks and taking photos (screenshots) as you go. Note – the historical imagery is patchy. Why do you think this is?

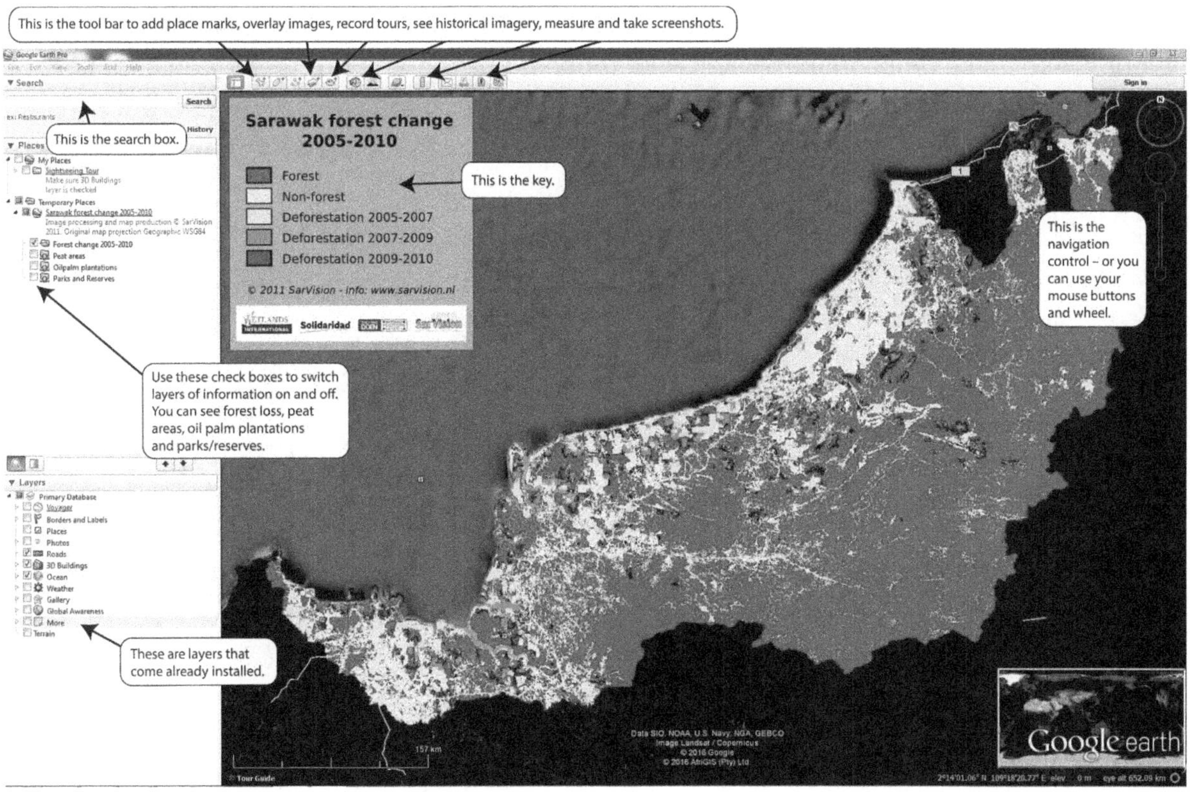

Fig. 7.3 Using a Geographical Information System.

Measuring and reducing your carbon footprint

The 2014 WWF Living Planet Index reported that there has been over a 50 per cent decline in animal population between 1970 and 2010. The report clearly states that "the biggest recorded threat to biodiversity globally comes from the combined impacts of habitat loss and degradation, driven by unsustainable human consumption".

Humans are using ever more of the Earth's resources in a way that means it will affect the quality of life of some people – today and in the future. **Sustainability** is about allowing us to meet our needs today without affecting the chances of people in the future to meet their own needs. Human actions can be seen as **sustainable** or **unsustainable**.

Some facts to consider:

- Sea ice in the Arctic Ocean is melting at 3 per cent every 10 years.
- Since 1980, humans have cut down over 2 250 000 sq km of forest.
- An average person in Mozambique (Africa) uses 4 litres of water per day. In the USA, this figure is an astonishing 575 litres.
- The amount of CO_2 in the atmosphere is higher now than at any point for the last 650 000 years.
- Cutting down 0.01 sq km of rainforest releases 500 tonnes of CO_2 into the atmosphere – the same as driving a car around the equator 28 times!

As levels of wealth grow around the world, global demand for products increases. This rise in consumption is placing increasing pressure on the Earth's resources and this is having an ever more damaging impact on the natural environment. Acting in a more sustainable way allows us to reduce this impact. Humans are using a lot of fossil fuels – these release CO_2 into the atmosphere and contribute to the Greenhouse Effect. The image below represents the ecological footprint of different nations. This is a combination of the land we use for food supply, our energy consumption, our travel and shopping habits and our water consumption. Combined, it shows how many planets we need to live the average lifestyle in different countries. If we all consumed like the USA we would need at least 5 planets. **This is unsustainable.**

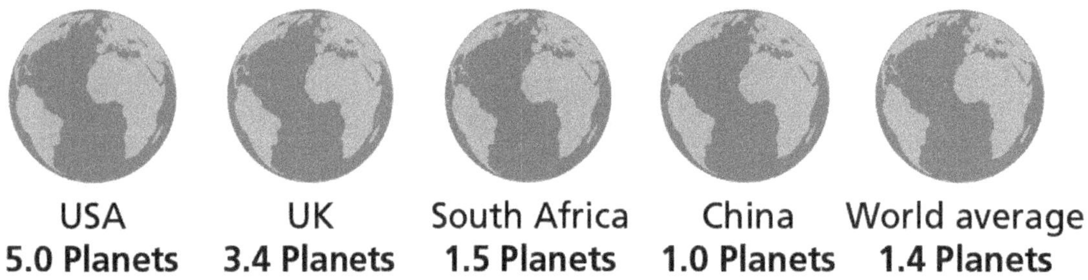

Fig. 7.4 Eco footprints of countries around the world.

Consolidating your thinking

It is vital that people take steps to reduce their ecological impact on the planet. A first step is to calculate the impact that you and your family are having upon the Earth. You can complete a footprint calculator here:

http://www.footprintnetwork.org/en/index.php/GFN/page/calculators/

Having established your footprint, making a plan of how to reduce it will enable small steps to be taken. An example of how you could do this in school is shown below. Schools have lots of buildings and classrooms that need heating/cooling and powering. Increasingly, schools need to reduce their carbon footprint and reduce energy consumption. Doing so is an example of a mitigation strategy to reduce carbon emissions.

You should carry out a simple energy audit of your school using the grid below:

Room number	Teacher name	Class present?	Number of lights on	Computer on/off?	Computer in use?	Projector on/off?	Projector being used?	Heating/cooling on/off?	Window open/closed?	Windows clean?	Doors open/closed?	Other notes

Instructions:

- Spilt into groups and ensure each group goes to a predefined area of the school to audit.
- Complete an audit sheet for each area of the school to identify areas of good and bad energy practice.
- Once the data is collected, each group can discuss the data and present their findings on maps of the school.
- Once the data is presented, make a judgment on which classrooms or teachers were the best/worst energy users or wasters.
- Email the best and worst teachers in the surveyed areas, outlining the results for the room in detail and asking why energy is being wasted or saved. The purpose of this is to bring about behaviour change, so ensure the emails are focused around positive energy saving tips and praise.
- You could follow up with another survey to see if any change has occurred.

Supplementary case study

Sustainable transport strategy in Singapore

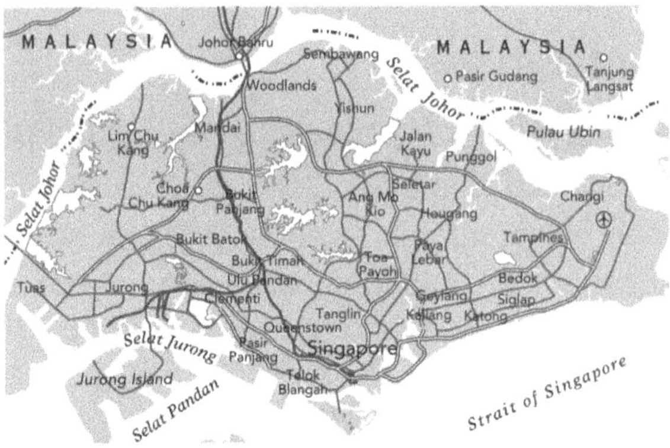

Fig. 7.5 Singapore.

Fig. 7.6 Singapore in the evening.

Singapore has a population of 5 674 472 in a land area of 697 sq km. The small city state has one of the most integrated and cost efficient transport systems in the world. Despite having a population of over 5.6 million, there are only 575 353 cars registered on the road. Cars are heavily taxed and owners are expected to purchase a 10-year certificate of entitlement. The cost of this varies over time, as it is used by the government to decrease the number of cars on the road. Transport accounts for 13 per cent of Singapore's energy consumption and 50 per cent of the fine particle air pollution in the city. Encouraging more sustainable forms of transport is seen as critical for the development of a more sustainable Singapore. Measures taken already include:

- an electronic road pricing (ERP) scheme on busy roads
- a cheap and integrated public transport system that includes a Mass Rapid Transit (MRT), buses and a Light Rail Transit (LRT) system

The system is integrated so that bus interchanges are at MRT and LRT stations – and these are near population centres. 5 308 000 trips are made each day, and at least half of the population utilises it daily. Examples of the integration are shown in these images.

Fig. 7.7 Electronic Road Pricing scheme in operation, Singapore.

Fig. 7.8 Public transport signs in Singapore.

Fig. 7.9 Bus interchanges at MRT and LRT stations in Singapore.

Despite having one of the greenest transport systems in the world, the vision is that by 2030, Singapore will have:

- 8 in 10 households living within a 10 minute walk from a train station
- 85 per cent of public transport journeys (less than 20 km) completed within 60 minutes
- 75 per cent of all journeys in peak hours undertaken on public transport
- a 360-km rail network
- 80 new bus services and 1000 more buses
- more than 200 km of sheltered walkways to transport nodes
- over 700 km of cycling paths, together with enhanced cycling infrastructure and code of conduct for safer cycling

Data response and decision making exercises

1. The graph below shows the data extracted from ice cores in Antarctica. Here, deep ice contains ancient air bubbles that in turn contain isotopes of oxygen and CO_2, allowing us to measure temperature and CO_2 levels in the atmosphere over time.

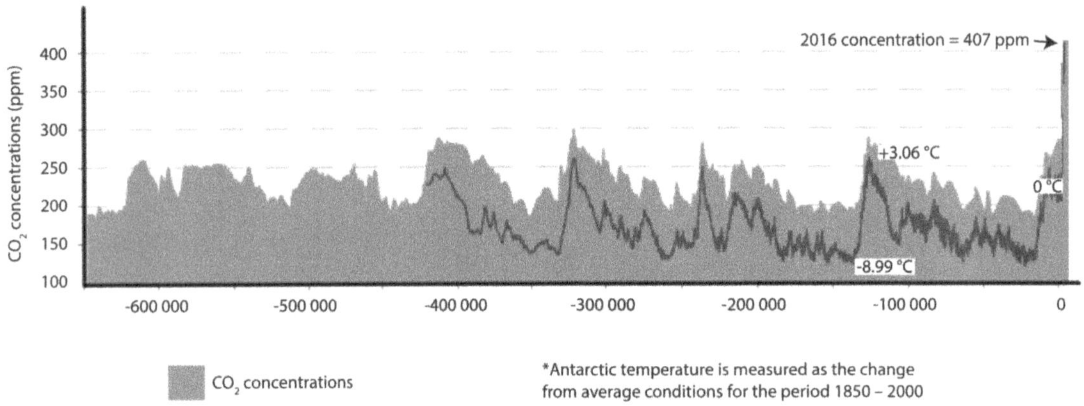

Fig. 7.10 Changes in temperature and CO_2 levels from Antarctic ice cores.

a) Describe the trend in CO_2 concentrations in Antarctica over time.

....

....

....

b) Suggest reasons for the variations in the level of CO_2 in the atmosphere before there was significant human population expansion and industrialisation.

....

....

....

....

c) Describe the observed relationship between CO_2 concentrations and temperature in Antarctica over time.

....

....

....

d) Name two greenhouse gases other than carbon dioxide.

....

....

e) Outline the importance of greenhouse gases to life on Earth.

....

....

....

2. CO_2 concentrations have been recorded in the centre of the Pacific Ocean for many years and these have been compared to global temperatures.

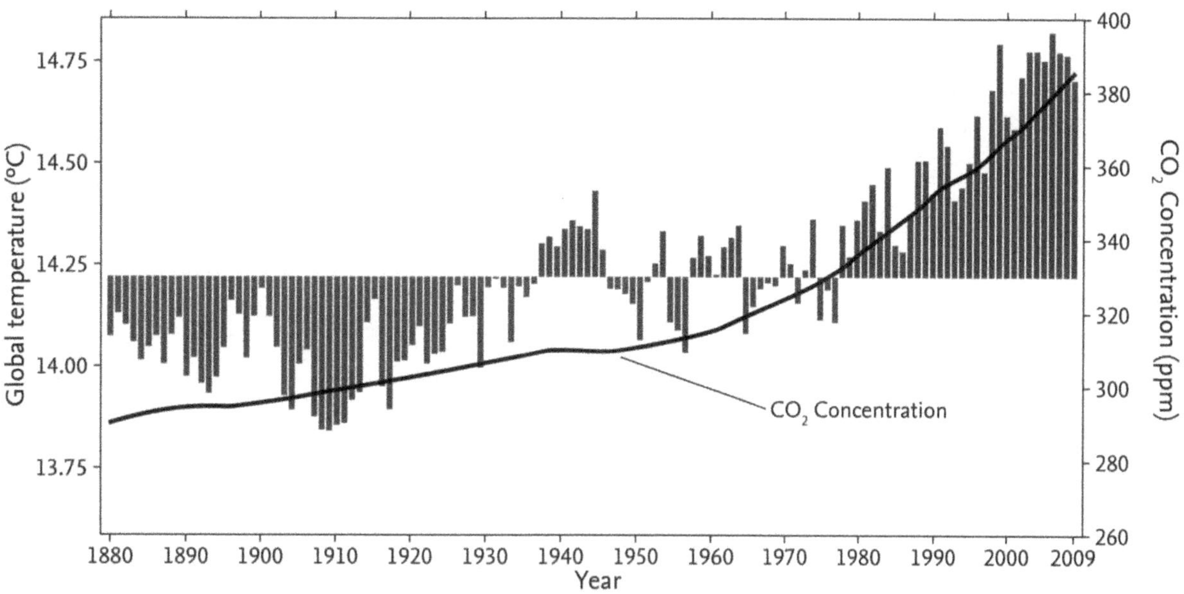

Fig. 7.11 The increase in atmospheric carbon dioxide levels and temperatures from 1880 to the present.

a) Describe the trend in atmospheric CO_2 concentrations and global temperatures since 1880.

....

....

....

....

....

....

b) Using both graphs in Figures 7.10 and 7.11, explain why there was significant global concern about the CO_2 concentration figures – 404 ppm in July 2016.

....

....

....

....

....

....

....

....

....

....

c) Describe and explain the enhanced greenhouse effect.

....

....

....

....

....

....

....

....

....

....

....

....

....

d) Climate change has always and will always occur on planet Earth. Humans are accelerating the rate of change. Outline the human and natural causes of climatic variation.

Natural causes of climate change	Human causes of climate change

3. In 2016, July was the tenth month in a row to break a monthly temperature record and, at this point, it was officially the hottest month since records began in 1880, with the average combined global surface temperature of the planet 1.2 °C higher than the 20th century average. 2015 was the warmest year since records began, beating 2014 and 2013. Temperatures had been pushed higher in part by El Niño, although this had dissipated by July. In Siberia, melting permafrost released anthrax from a deer carcass that had been preserved for years, causing an outbreak of the disease. In Baghdad, the government had to shut down due to extreme temperatures, whilst in Kuwait the temperature reached 54 °C. Temperatures like this are likely to cause significant disruption to human activity in the future. Meanwhile, wildfires in California and floods in Louisiana again added to the weather extremes being experienced. Whilst individual areas of extreme weather cannot be directly linked to climate change they give an indication of the challenges to come in a hotter world.

   The graph below shows predictions for global surface warming up to the year 2100.

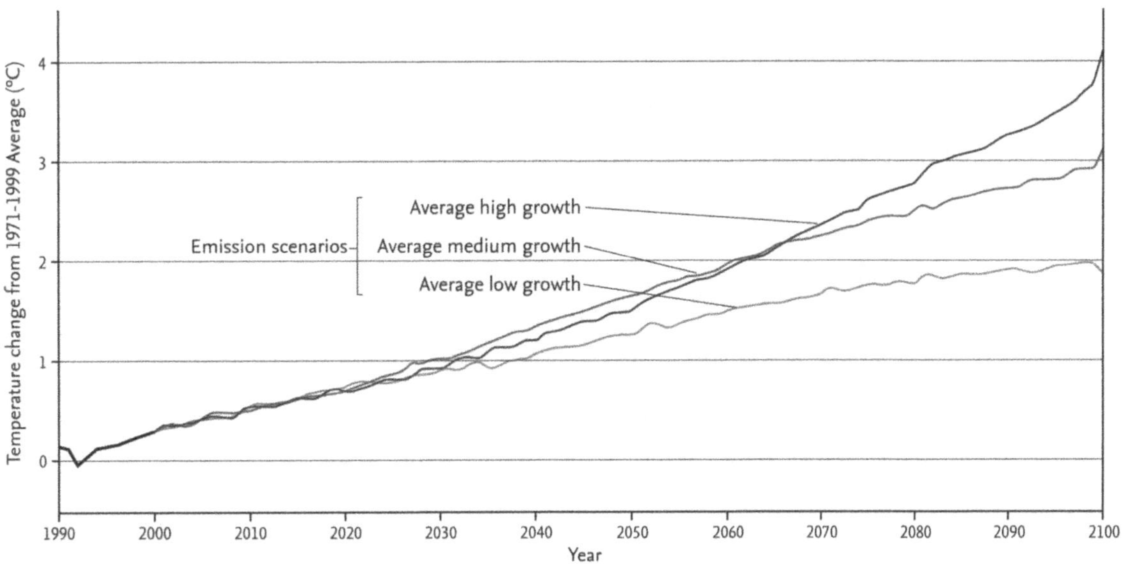

Fig. 7.12 Predictions for global surface warming.

a) Describe the predicted temperature rise by 2100 if carbon emissions continue to grow at the current rate.

....

....

....

b) Suggest reasons why we can't accurately predict the level of surface warming by 2100.

....

....

....

c) Outline the possible effects of a 4 °C increase in global surface temperatures by 2100.

....

....

....

The world map below shows the predicted average mean temperature change (°C) by the year 2080.

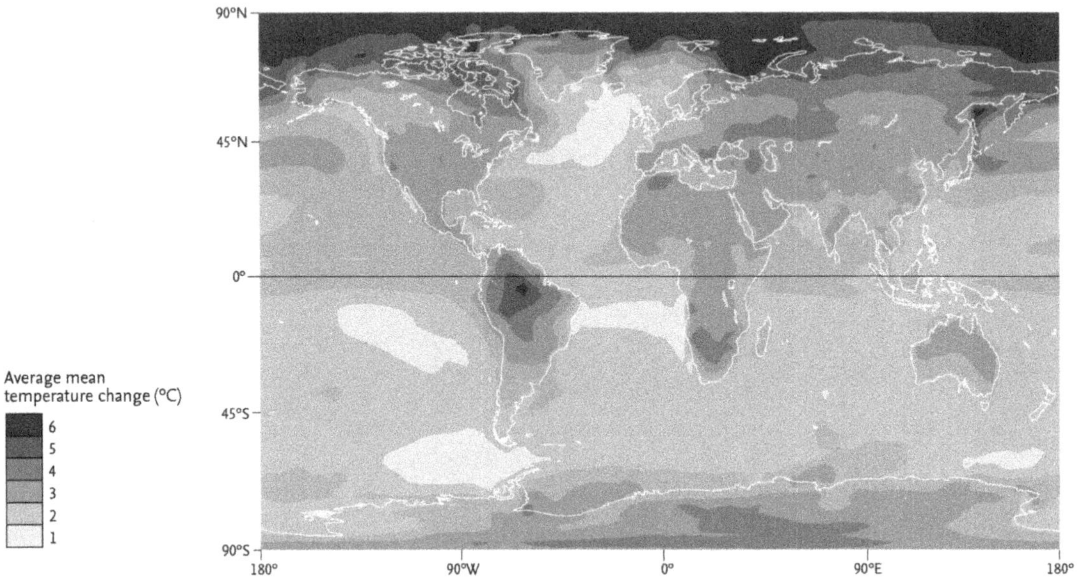

Fig. 7.13 Surface warming is predicted to be unevenly distributed.

d) Describe the pattern of predicted surface warming by 2080. Ensure you use statistics and places/regions to describe the pattern.

e) Temperatures are rising faster at the north and south poles than in other places on Earth. The images below show the reduction in sea ice for the same period between 1984 and 2012. Use these images and the WWF website to identify how climate change is impacting the Arctic Ocean.
http://wwf.panda.org/what_we_do/where_we_work/arctic/what_we_do/climate/

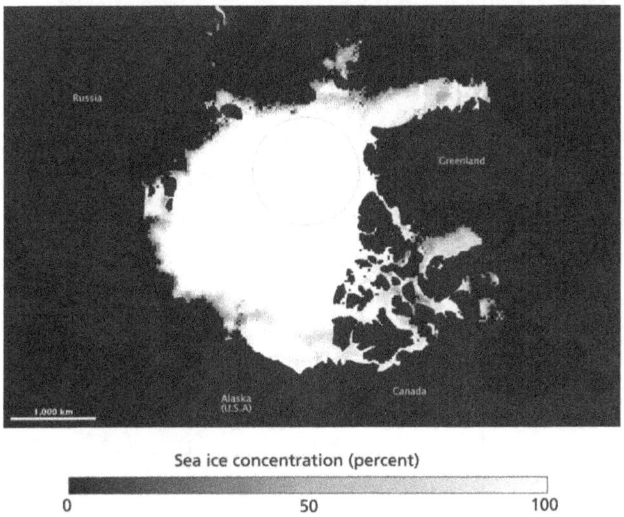

Fig. 7.14 Arctic Ocean ice coverage in September 1984.

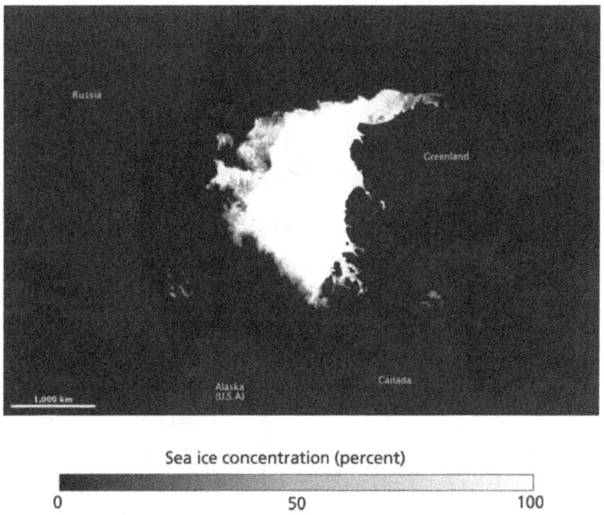

Fig. 7.15 Arctic Ocean ice coverage in September 2012.

4. The image below shows Male, the capital city of the Maldives in the Indian Ocean. The Maldives is a chain of 1200 low-lying coral islands. Male is densely populated and has lost much of its coral reef. A 90 cm rise in sea level will cause 85 per cent of Male to be inundated by water. A metre rise in sea level could see the Maldives – a tourist hotspot, home to a population of 340 000 – disappear completely by 2080.

Fig. 7.16 Location of the Maldives.

Fig. 7.17 Aerial view of Male, the capital of the Maldives.

The Maldives is just one of many small island states that faces a significant risk from rising sea levels. Places like the Kiribati in the Pacific Ocean are also threatened by the highest tides each year. Furthermore, low-lying highly-populated Bangladesh could see 15 million people displaced by rising seas and an increase in storm surges from tropical cyclones.

Examine the data table below.

	1980	1990	2000	2010	2012
China	1448	2269	3165	7389	8106
United States	4776	5041	5864	5580	5270
Canada	457	471	573	548	551
Brazil	186	237	344	461	500
Australia	199	268	356	431	421
Bangladesh	8	15	29	54	63
Maldives	0.01	0.1	0.5	1.1	1.1
Kiribati	0.02	0.02	0.03	0.1	0.1

Table 7.1 Total carbon emissions from the consumption of energy over time (million tonnes).

a) Plot a line graph on the grid on the next page that shows the total carbon emissions over time of Kiribati, Maldives, Bangladesh and three other nations.

b) Compare and contrast the carbon emissions of the selected countries.

....

....

c) It is possible for countries to take steps to reduce the impact of climate change through adaptation, which involves efforts to limit vulnerability to climate change impacts whilst not dealing with the cause. They can also attempt to mitigate the worst effects by reducing their carbon footprint and shifting to more renewable forms of energy. Using research and your own ideas, complete the table below.

Possible steps to adapt to rising sea levels and climate change in low income countries like Bangladesh and the Maldives.	**Possible mitigation steps to reduce the magnitude of sea level rise and climate change.**

d) Countries such as the Maldives and Bangladesh are not responsible for rising sea levels so should not be liable for the cost of taking measures to adapt to rising seas or for reducing their own carbon emissions. To what extent do you agree with this statement?

....

....

....

....

....

....

....

Answers to these questions can be found at **www.collins.co.uk/EnvMgmtIGCSE**

8 Human population

Introduction

This section reinforces and extends student learning by:

- Consolidating and developing the factual material in the Student's Book that students will be required to recall and explain (AO1)
- Advancing student thinking through providing more challenging content and activities than those in the Student's Book, which extend some areas of the specification and require the synthesis of information and the application of knowledge and understanding to unfamiliar contexts (AO2)
- Enabling students to grasp that the effective management of environmental issues requires a coherent and holistic approach to problem solving through the principles of sustainable development (AO3)

This is achieved through the provision of:

- Extension content and related activities that secure and progress student knowledge and understanding through tasks that require handling information from a variety of sources to reach conclusions and make judgments
- Supplementary case studies that reinforce and advance key principles and concepts and support evaluative thinking
- A decision making or problem solving exercise that encourages students to appreciate the complexities of environmental management and the pivotal role of the principles of sustainable development in achieving successful outcomes

Links to other chapters

Population is inextricably associated in one way or another with all of the world's most pressing environmental management challenges. It is important for students to appreciate that the issue is not just one of increasing numbers. Although the net annual increase in global population exceeds 80 million, some regions are experiencing worrying absolute losses whilst other areas expand exponentially. When it comes to the management of the environment per person resource consumption, together with the structure, distribution and density of populations, is arguably of greater significance than sheer weight of numbers. Rapid world population growth combined with a very uneven distribution of people is having serious environmental consequences in some parts of the world. Human activities consume both finite and renewable resources such as minerals, water, forests, fisheries, fibres, fossil fuels and land to maintain and improve standards of living. As a result, wastes such as refuse, sewage, and industrial atmospheric and water pollutants are generated, which can threaten human health. Consumption also uses up non-renewable resources, such as fossil fuels, and seriously depletes renewable resources such as fisheries, forests and soils if they are consumed at a faster rate than they can regenerate. Because there are more people, larger societies tend to consume more resources than smaller ones and are likely therefore to have a more serious impact on the environment.

The human population section cross-references with all other chapters in the Student's Book and the following table highlights the key connections that it would be valuable for students to make. Whilst teaching the syllabus content for human population, students should be encouraged at regular intervals to see the relevance and implications of what they are learning for other areas of the specification. This is crucial to avoid a 'silo approach' to thinking about environmental management and problem solving, which is the antithesis of sustainable development. Supporting students to develop a holistic perspective can be achieved through asking them key questions to investigate from the content of other sections, for example, What do you think are the likely implications of this for…?

Human population topic	Links to other subject content	Section
Human population distribution and density	Energy demand Agriculture types Water quality and availability The atmosphere Ecosystems	2 3 4 7 9
Changes in population size	Managing water-related disease	4
Population structure	Agriculture types	3
Managing human population size	Conservation and management of energy resources	2

Extension content and related activities

Population distribution and density

The choropleth map that shows population distribution and density on page 196 of the Student's Book gives a clear and simple general overall pattern of where people live and do not live, but hides important differences within countries. This was highlighted in the example of Japan in the Student's Book on page 198.

The average population density of China is shown on this map as 101–250 per square kilometre but when we examine a smaller scale map we can see, as with Japan, great variations within the country. Approximately 90 per cent of China's population live in only 30 per cent of its land area, which means that huge areas are uninhabited whilst others have population densities exceeding 2500 people per square kilometre.

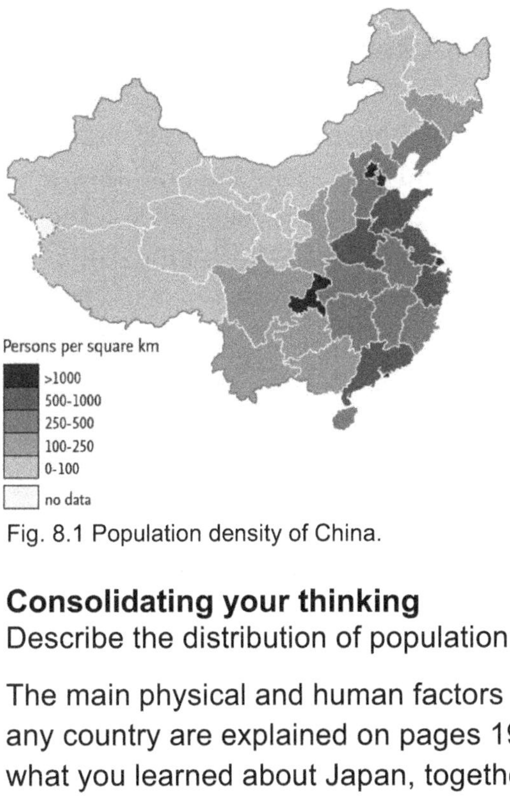

Fig. 8.1 Population density of China.

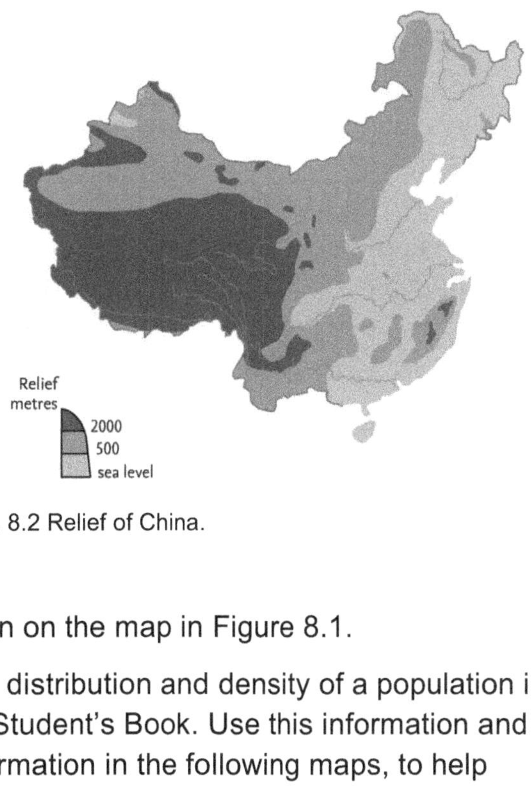

Fig. 8.2 Relief of China.

Consolidating your thinking

Describe the distribution of population in China shown on the map in Figure 8.1.

The main physical and human factors influencing the distribution and density of a population in any country are explained on pages 196–199 of the Student's Book. Use this information and what you learned about Japan, together with the information in the following maps, to help explain the population distribution of China you have described.

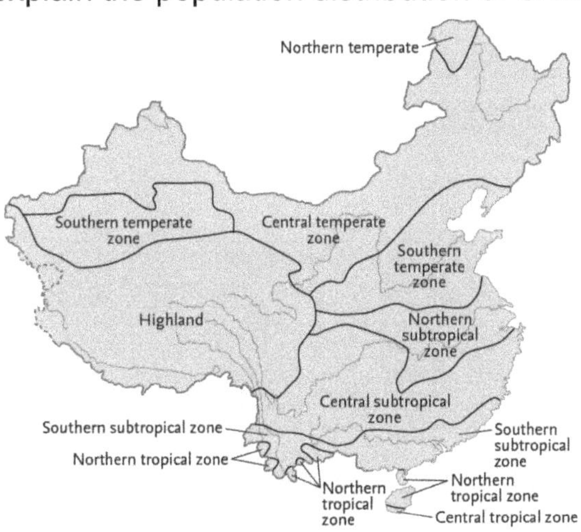

Fig. 8.3 Climate regions of China.

Fig. 8.4 Railway network in China.

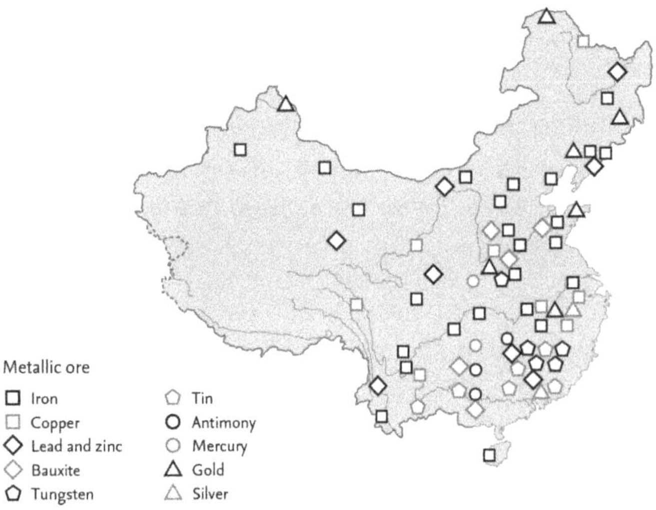

Fig. 8.5 Mineral resources in China.

Fig. 8.6 Coal fields in China.

What this study of China illustrates is that population density increases and is highest in areas where economic opportunities are greatest. The terms 'push' and 'pull' factors are often used in explaining population distributions. Push factors are reasons that may cause a person to leave an area or not move there at all in the first place. Pull factors are things about a place that attract a person to live there and make it unlikely that they will move away again in the short term. Copy the table below and for each of the ten factors that most affect population distributions, write one 'push' and one 'pull' – the first one has been done for you.

Factor	**Push**	**Pull**
Climate	Very hot summers, very cold winters and long dry seasons	Mild temperate climate with evenly distributed rainfall

Changes in population size

In his famous book of 1798, *An Essay on the Principle of Population,* Thomas Robert Malthus said that the population of the world could not go on increasing indefinitely and that eventually mass starvation and disease would occur as the carrying capacity of the world was reached and exceeded. He called this disaster a positive check on numbers in a similar way to that detailed in the decline phase of the growth curve of populations (p.199 of the Student's Book).

Fig. 8.7 Portrait of Thomas Robert Malthus.

Fig. 8.8 Irish potato famine.

Malthus died in 1834 when the population of the world stood at just over one billion. Today it is seven billion and is likely to rise by another three billion by 2100. Using the information in the Student's Book on pages 199–202, and the additional ideas at **http://business.time.com/2011/07/15/was-malthus-right/** and **http://www.forbes.com/sites/williampentland/2011/01/09/thomas-malthus-wrong-yesterday-right-today/#4c3c0bbd2766**, write a letter to Malthus outlining all of the things that have occurred since his death and that he didn't anticipate, which have meant that his prophecy has not come true yet.

Populations change as a result of differences in the birth rate and death rate. Natural increase will occur if the birth rate exceeds the death rate and a natural decrease if the reverse is true. The main factor affecting the birth rate of a country is the fertility level of its population. This is the average number of children born to a woman during her lifetime. In every country of the world, as the level of education of girls and women increases, both fertility and birth rates drop. Quite simply the more years of education a girl receives then the fewer the number of children she will have. The Earth Policy Institute says this:

Female education is especially important. Research consistently shows that women who are empowered through education tend to have fewer children and have them later.

and The New Internationalist says this:

Education of women and girls has been shown to result in the voluntary reduction of fertility rates. Education gives women choices, opportunities and, most importantly, control. Under these conditions, women voluntarily reduce the number of children they bear over their life time.

Make a list of as many reasons as you can to help you explain why more and better education (and particularly being able to read and write) for girls and young women results in them bearing fewer children over their lifetime. Think about:

- getting advice about and understanding family planning and using methods of contraception effectively
- opportunities to find employment and earn an income outside of the home
- being able to progress to study at university, follow a career and marry later in life

Population structure

Newly industrialised countries (NICs) are those experiencing rapid economic growth and industrialisation but that have not yet reached the status of an MEDC (More Economically Developed Country), but are no longer classed as an LEDC (Less Economically Developed Country).

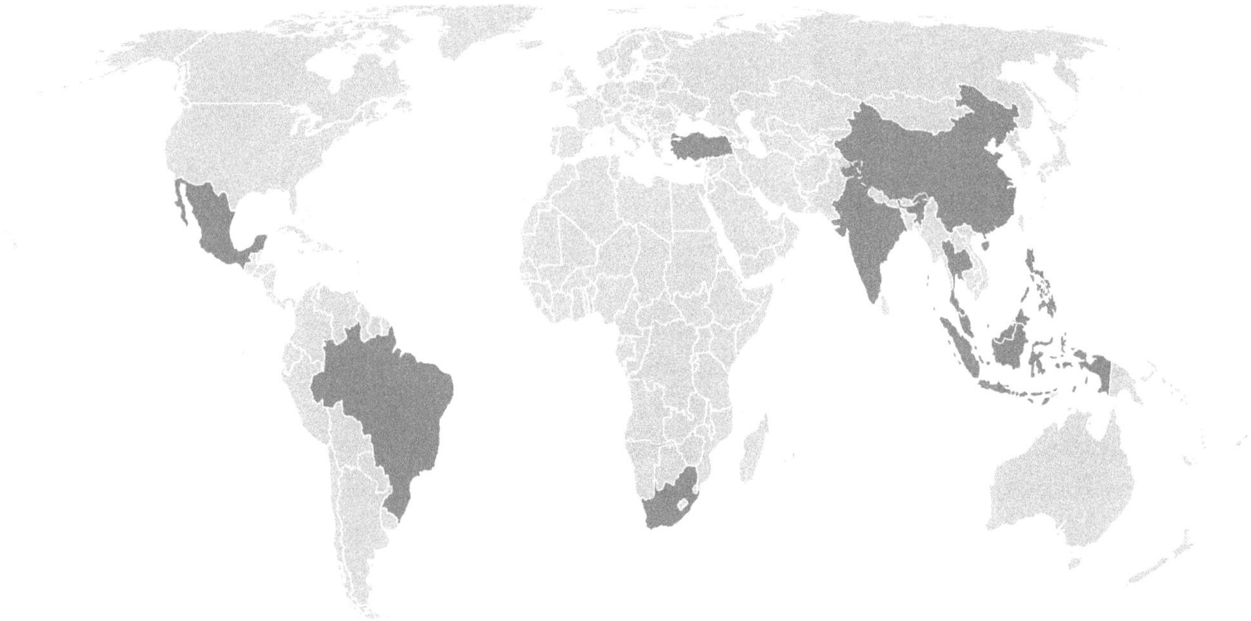

Fig. 8.9 Dark shading shows the newly industrialised countries.

Brazil is an example of an NIC. Compare its population structure shown in the population pyramid below with those of a typical LEDC and a typical MEDC in the Student's Book on page 203. How has its population structure already changed compared to a typical LEDC? How is its population structure not yet the same as a typical MEDC? Try to explain these similarities and differences

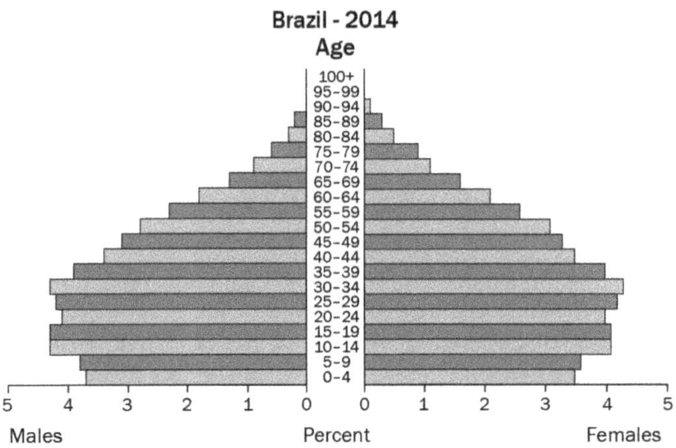

Fig. 8.10 Population pyramid for Brazil, 2014.

Managing population size

With a fertility rate of only 1.41 (2.1 is needed to keep numbers of people stable) the population of Japan is dropping by 1 million a year. Look at the graphs below.

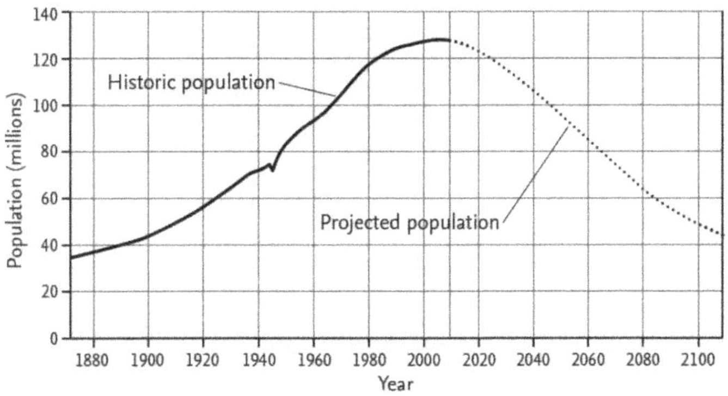

Fig. 8.11 Historic and projected population of Japan.

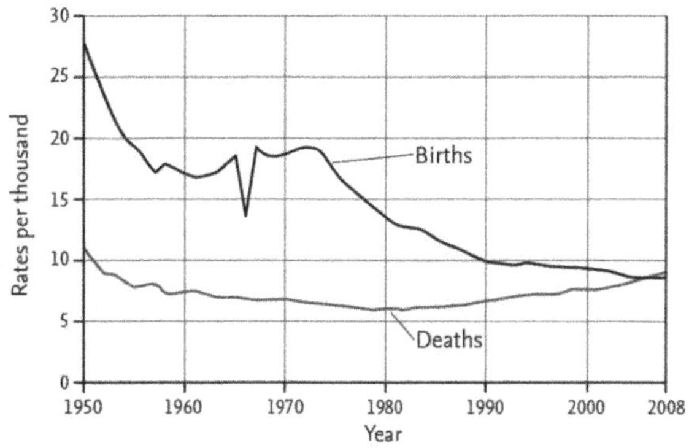

Fig. 8.12 Birth and death rates in Japan.

In which year did the population of Japan begin to decline?

What occurred in that year that made such a decline inevitable?

What will be the estimated total loss of population during the 21st century?

In an attempt to halt the decline and to increase the fertility rate to at least 1.8, the Japanese government has announced emergency plans – known as the New Angel and Plus One policies – to get couples having more children as quickly as possible. The government is providing:

- 50 000 new daycare centres giving free child care to parents
- longer paid paternity leave for fathers to be at home with a new baby for up to six months
- free fertility services for couples finding it difficult to conceive
- US$30 million a year to pay for *konkatsu* parties at which young people can mingle and meet people of the opposite sex
- jobs and housing to 200 000 immigrants from other countries a year

For each of these policies, write down one way in which it might help to solve Japan's population problem and one way that you think it might lead to problems or fail to work.

Connecting the human population topics

Consumption patterns often account for more environmental harm than sheer numbers of people alone. The Ecological Footprint Index is widely used to measure the impact on the environment of people in different countries.

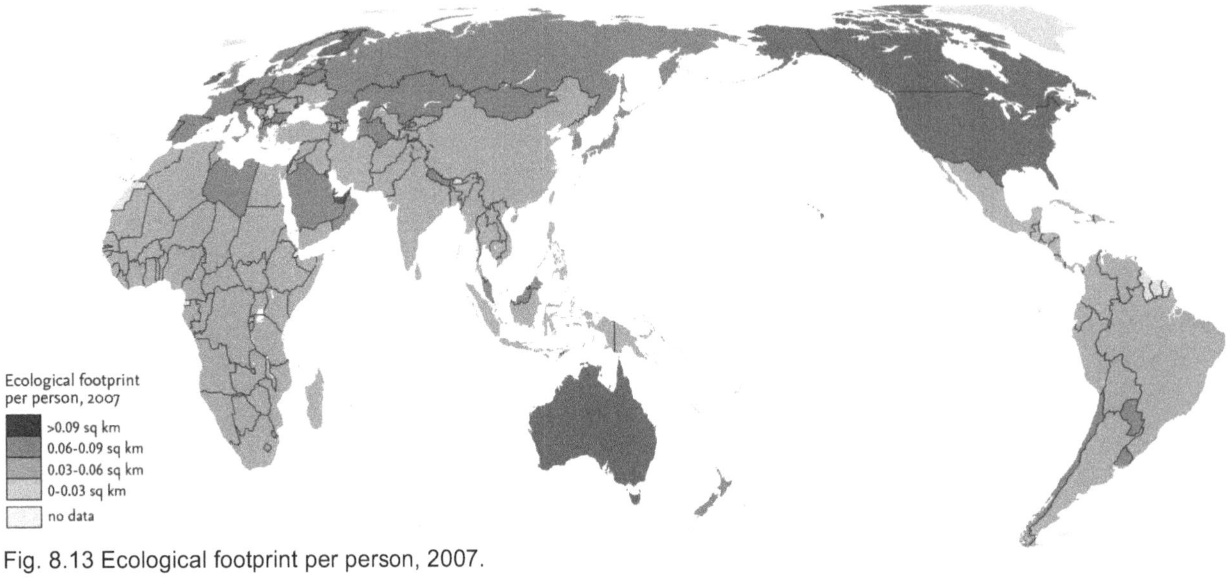

Fig. 8.13 Ecological footprint per person, 2007.

It measures the area of the Earth that is needed to produce the resources a person consumes to maintain their standard of living and to process their waste products. It is a simple measure therefore of human pressure on the planet – the demand individuals place on its natural ecosystems. By dividing the total area of productive land in the world by its population the Index calculates that 0.02 sq km is available to each person to supply their resources and absorb their waste. Consumption at this level by everyone would help ensure environmental sustainability. On average, each person currently requires 0.03 sq km of the environment to meet their needs, and 85 per cent of the world's population is living in countries with biocapacity deficit where the environment can no longer meet levels of resource consumption. In the countries of North America the ecological footprint averages 0.07 sq km per person and in Europe 0.04 sq km, compared with an average of just 0.02 sq km in Asia and 0.01 sq km in Africa. When an isodemographic map of the world is drawn with the area of each country proportional to its ecological footprint such as the one at **www.viewsoftheworld.net/wp-content/uploads/2015/11/EcologicalFootprintMap.jpg** then the difference in resource consumption between MEDCs and LEDCs is clearly evident.

Consolidating your thinking

In order to ensure environmental sustainability, it will be necessary for populations in MEDCs to reduce their resource consumption demands to a level that the planet can support. The Student's Book provides numerous examples of how this could be achieved. In your own words explain three things that could significantly reduce consumption. Areas that you might consider could include:

- Extending the life of existing mineral reserves pages 20–21
- Conservation and management of energy resources pages 38–42
- Management of the harvesting of marine species pages 133–136

Supplementary case study 1

The rise of megacities

One of the greatest changes in the distribution of the world's population over the past fifty years has been the increase in megacities. In 1960 there were just two cities with a population of over 10 million. In 2015 there were more than 25.

A megacity can be a single metropolitan or built up area such as Paris or two or more cities that have converged such as Tokyo-Yokohama. In 2014 the number of people living in urban areas exceeded those in rural locations for the first time. By 2025 there will be an estimated 630 million people living in megacities. Megacities have become centres of great power. They are often the headquarters of multinational corporations, international organisations and financial institutions, as well as the location of a huge number of manufacturing and service industries and cultural and education centres.

In the most modern, technologically advanced industrialised countries, such as Germany and the United States, on average, three out of four people already live in urban areas. As a result the speed of growth in megacities is much less than in countries such as India, with lower levels of industrialisation and where two out of three people still live in rural areas. In megacities such as Mumbai, the opportunity of earning cash, doing jobs in retail or manufacturing, is a huge attraction for poor subsistence farm workers who earn very little money, undertake physically gruelling tasks and regularly have to face challenges such as drought, crop diseases and food shortages.

Fig. 8.14 Dharavi, India.

Fig. 8.15 Indian workers sewing in a clothing factory in Dharavi.

Supplementary case study 2

Voluntary international migration from Mexico to the United States

Figures from the United Nations show that 232 million people, or 3.2 per cent of the world's population, live outside their countries of birth. Migration may be voluntary or forced. If a migrant moves to a new location within their own country then this classifies as internal or domestic migration. Movement to another country is referred to as international migration. The top destination country for international migrants is the United States where 45 million of the total population of 320 million were born overseas. Generally speaking, voluntary international migrants are attracted to or 'pulled' to a different country by a number of economic and social factors. The most significant is the prospect of better employment opportunities and higher wages than are available in their home country. More international migrants tend to be male rather than female as a husband or son may move in order to send regular income back to his family who have remained at home. This money is known as a remittance. Other 'pull' factors may include gaining access to better health care and educational opportunities than those available at home. This is particularly important if an international migrant is travelling with his or her family. International migration has positive and negative effects both for the recipient country (the country to which migrants move) and donor countries (the countries that migrants leave). It is also important to remember that even though a migrant may be leaving their country voluntarily, they may not be entitled to enter the country they propose to move to. As a result they become illegal immigrants and face the prospect of being deported or even imprisoned if discovered. A very good example of this is the attempted migration of over one million people a year from Mexico to the United States. Each year over one million illegal migrants endeavour to cross the border from Mexico to the United States. Over 20 000 agents working for the United States border patrol work to apprehend and return illegal Mexican immigrants. It is estimated that about 10 000 Mexicans try to cross the border each week. One in three is caught. Those that are apprehended and sent back are likely to try again within three months.

Fig. 8.16 Mexican migrant picking grapes on a farm in California, United States.

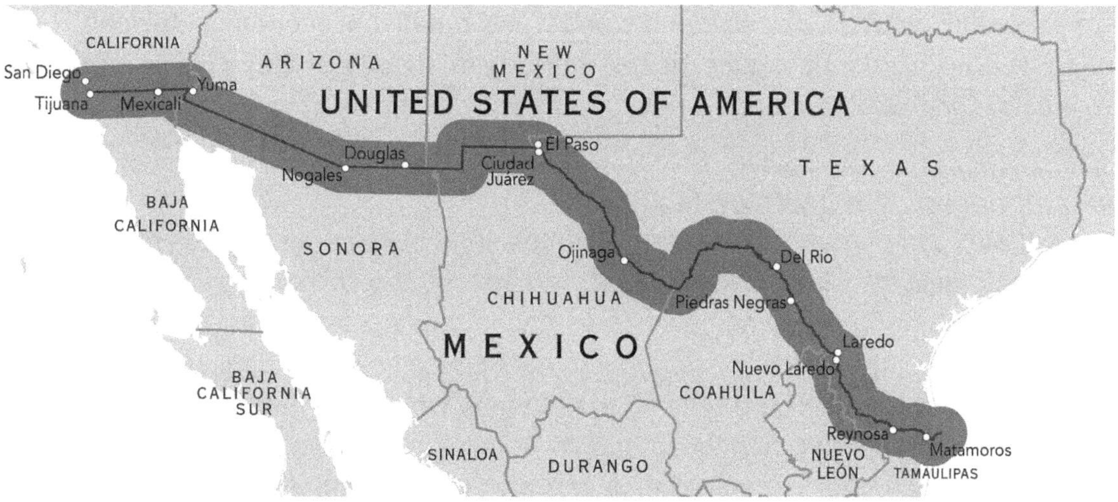

Fig. 8.17 The 2000-km border between Mexico and the United States.

Average annual wages in Mexico stand at US$5800 compared with US$32 000 in the United States. The prospect of obtaining even a low paid job (the minimum wage in the United States is US$7.25 an hour) drives Mexicans to attempt to cross the border into the United States. In rural areas many migrants work as farm labourers, whereas in urban areas they commonly work in construction, landscaping, domestic and retailing trades such as on building sites, garden maintenance, hotels, shops and restaurants. Many will hold down two or more jobs in order to boost income.

Positive and negative impacts on the United States

- Operating the border control service to apprehend illegal migration costs the United States government US$20 billion a year.
- Because immigrants are willing to work for the United States' minimum wage, many Americans argue that businesses deliberately keep wages for jobs as low as possible. For a Mexican immigrant, the minimum hourly wage of US$7.25 represents a massive increase in income compared with Mexico where the minimum wage is US$3.75 a day. For Americans, earning just the minimum hourly wage is a struggle in a country where the cost of living (the prices of things such as food, housing, fuel and clothes) is 165 per cent higher than in Mexico.
- Paying only minimum wages increases the profits of businesses that employ Mexican migrants. This means in turn that they pay more tax to the government, which can use these funds to improve the quality of life for everyone, such as building new schools and medical centres. A successful and profitable business is also more likely to expand, take on more workers and contribute more tax in the future.
- In states such as California (currently housing 11.5 million Mexican migrants) and Texas (8 million), which are very popular destinations for Mexican immigrants, tensions have arisen at times between local people and the newcomers. Sometimes this has been because residents perceive that the immigrants are taking jobs that should rightly be for local people. Other reasons include the feeling that immigrants move in to most of the available housing in communities and put too much pressure on services such as schools and health centres, especially if travelling with their families.

- There is no doubt that as well as being a boost to the national economy, Mexican immigrants have also enriched the United States with aspects of their culture including food, music, dance and language.

Positive and negative impacts on Mexico

- Each year Mexican migrants in the United States send back in remittances over US$10 billion to their families, which is spent improving their quality of life, such as paying school and medical fees or constructing new homes and improving sanitation and water supplies.
- Most migrants leaving Mexico are young and economically active, particularly in the 18–40 age group. As a result Mexico loses millions of those who could be described as its 'brightest and best'. Rather than these people working to improve the economy and social conditions in Mexico, they commit all their energies to benefit the economy of another country. All of the money that Mexico has paid to educate the migrants and to keep them healthy as young people only serves to benefit another country when they leave.
- Many more young men migrate to the United States than women. As a result, many rural communities in Mexico are made up almost entirely of women, children and older men. As a result women find it difficult to find marriage partners and birth rates drop. When the birth rate falls so low that it becomes less than the death rate then the population of such places slowly dies out.
- The United States border patrol estimates that around 250 Mexicans a year die trying to cross the desert and the River Grande that make up the Mexican–United States border.

Fig. 8.18 United States Border Patrol sign in California warning "Caution! Do not expose your life to the elements. It's not worth it!"

Data response and decision making exercises

With a population in 2016 of 187 million, Nigeria contains almost half of the people living in the continent of Africa and is the seventh most populous state in the world. It is situated on the coast of central West Africa and in terms of area is about twice the size of the American state of California. Its capital is Abuja and its largest city and most important economic trading centre is Lagos.

Fig. 8.19 Location of Nigeria.

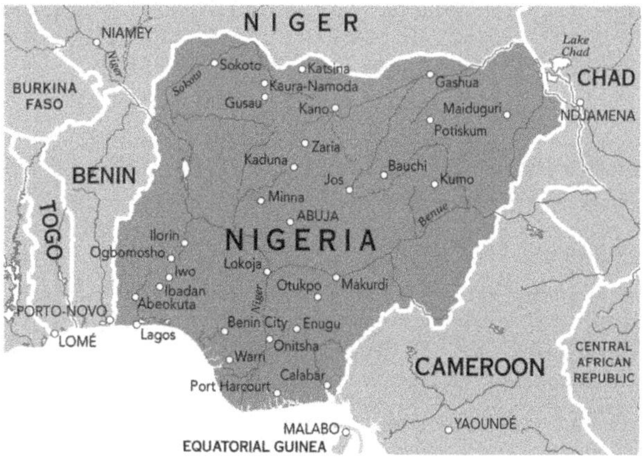

Fig. 8.20 Nigeria.

1. Table 8.1 shows some important information about the population of Nigeria in 2016.

Year	Population	Yearly change	Migrants (net)	Median age (years)	Fertility rate	Density (people per sq km)	Urban population (% of total)	Country's share of world population (%)
2016	186 987 563	4 785 601	–60 000	18	5.67	205	49	2.52

Table 8.1 Population data for Nigeria 2016.

a) What is a 'migrant'?

....

....

b) What is 'fertility rate' a measure of?

....

....

c) What does 'urban' population mean?

....

....

2. Table 8.2 shows how the population of Nigeria is projected to change between 2020 and 2050.

Year	Population	Yearly change	Migrants (net)	Median age (years)	Fertility rate	Density (people per sq km)	Urban population (% of total)	Country's share of world population (% of total)
2020	**206 830 983**	4 925 804	-60 000	18	5.41	227	52.6	2.81
2030	**262 599 107**	5 808 283	-56 000	19	4.74	288	60.6	3.23
2040	**327 405 603**	6 688 076	-60 000	21	4.12	360	67.4	3.7
2050	**398 507 704**	7 222 353	-60 000	23	3.59	438	74.1	4.22

Table 8.2 Projected population change in Nigeria 2020–2050.

a) How many people will be added to the population of Nigeria between 2020 and 2050?

....

b) By how much will the fertility rate drop between 2020 and 2050?

....

c) Suggest a reason why the proportion of 'urban' Nigerians will increase so much by 2050.

....

3. Fig. 8.21 is the population pyramid for the projected population of Nigeria in 2050.

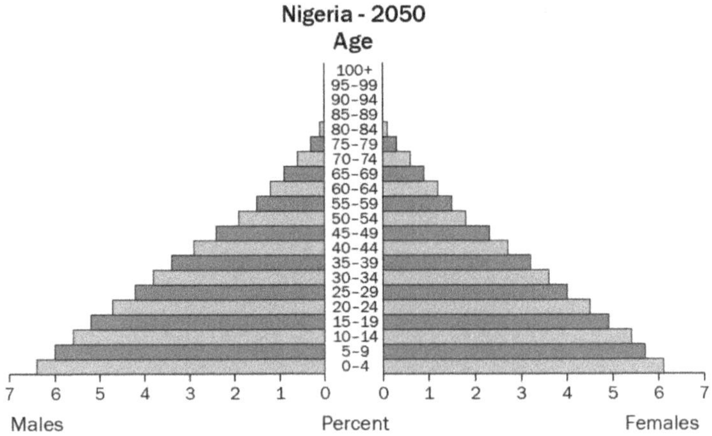

Fig. 8.21 Population pyramid for Nigeria 2050.

a) What percentage of the population will be female and aged 5–9 years in 2050? ....

b) What percentage of the population will be male and aged 50–54 years in 2050? ....

c) Describe three features of the population pyramid that are typical of Less Economically Developing Countries (LEDCs).

i. ....

....

....

ii. ....

....

....

iii. ....

....

....

4.

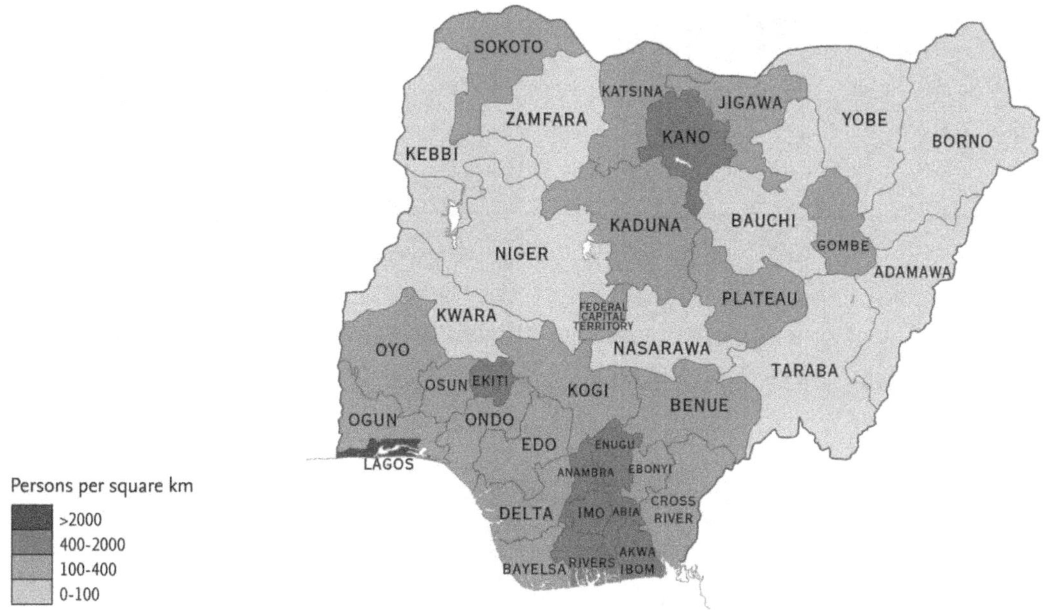

Fig. 8.22 Population density within Nigeria.

Figure 8.22 shows that population density within Nigeria varies a great deal between different districts. Suggest three reasons that might help to explain why the population density of the district of Kano is so much greater than that of the district of Niger.

a) ....

....

....

....

b) ....

....

....

....

c) ....

....

....

....

5. The rate of urbanisation in Nigeria is one the fastest of any country in the world. This increase is already causing a number of serious environmental problems as shown in Figures 8.23–26.

Fig. 8.23 Goats and chickens searching in street rubbish in Kano, Nigeria.

Fig. 8.24 Slum in Lagos, Nigeria.

Fig. 8.25 Deforestation in Nigeria.

Fig. 8.26 A water kiosk in Nigeria.

Describe and explain the causes and effects of each of the environmental problems shown in the images.

6. According to the World Bank, only 28 per cent of Nigerians have access to improved sanitation and this is a major reason explaining why life expectancy is low at 52 years and infant mortality high at 117 deaths per 1000 live births by the age of five years. This compares for example with a life expectancy of 82 years and an infant mortality rate of 3 in Sweden.

   Explain what 'improved sanitation' is and, using examples that you have studied from elsewhere in the world, describe the kind of things that could be done in an LEDC such as Nigeria to improve the sanitary conditions in which people live.

7. In 1956 the government of Nigeria discovered oil in Ogoniland, which covers approximately 1000 sq km in Rivers State in the southern Niger Delta region of the country. Ogoniland forms part of the third largest mangrove forest ecosystem in the world and is home to over one million indigenous Ogoni people.

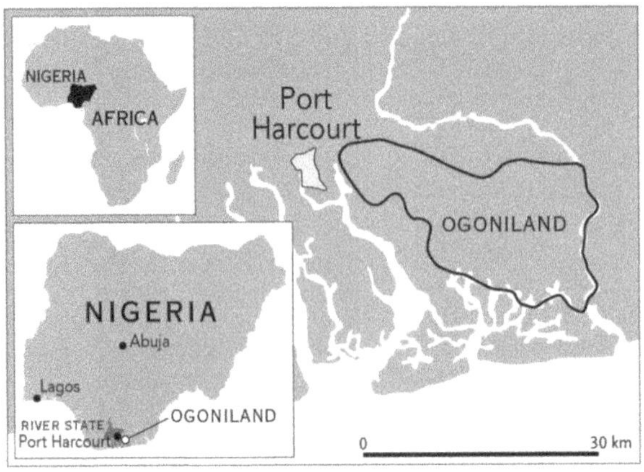

Fig. 8.27 Location of Ogoniland.

Fig. 8.28 Mangrove forest.

Fig. 8.29 An Ogoni woman catching fish in the mangrove forests of the Niger Delta.

a) Why would the government of Nigeria have wanted to extract as much oil as possible from Ogoniland?

....

....

....

....

....

....

Read the following extract, which is from a report by the United Nations Environment Programme (UNEP) about the impact of oil exploitation in Ogoniland.

While oil exploration and production in the Niger Delta began in the late 1950s, operations were suspended in Ogoniland in the early 1990s due to disruptions from local public unrest. The oilfields and installations have since largely remained dormant. However, major oil pipelines still cross through Ogoniland and oil spills continue to affect the region, due to such factors as a lack of maintenance and vandalism to oil infrastructure and facilities.

Environmental contamination in Ogoniland from oil spills remains untreated, or only partially remediated, today.

Fig. 8.30 A boy stands next to a danger sign in an oil contaminated area of Ogoniland, Nigeria.

Fig. 8.31 An oil pipeline crossing a mangrove forest in Ogoniland, Nigeria.

b) Describe the impacts that oil pollution can have on marine ecosystems.

Mangrove forests are considered one of the most threatened tropical ecosystems. At least 35% of the world's mangroves have already disappeared. In India, the Philippines and Vietnam, this figure reaches as high as 50%, and in the Americas, mangroves are being cleared more quickly than tropical rainforests.

There are many threats to mangrove forests and their habitats – pollution is a major one. Pesticides, fertilisers and other man-made toxic chemicals carried along by rivers from upstream sources can seriously harm and kill animals that live in mangrove forests. Furthermore, oil pollution smothers mangrove roots and results in the suffocation of trees.

c) Drawing on examples that you have studied, outline other causes of forest destruction apart from pollution, around the world.

....

....

....

....

....

....

....

....

....

....

....

UNEP estimates that restoring the degraded mangrove forest ecosystem of the Ogoniland is likely to take at least thirty years and become the world's most wide-ranging and long-term oil clean-up exercise ever undertaken.

d) Using other examples that you have studied, describe how oil pollution of the Ogoniland region might be managed in a way that could mean that the environment there might eventually be restored.

....

....

....

....

....

....

....

....

....

....

....

Answers to these questions can be found at **www.collins.co.uk/EnvMgmtIGCSE**

9 Natural ecosystems and human activities

Introduction

This section reinforces and extends student learning by:

- Consolidating and developing the factual material in the Student's Book that students will be required to recall and explain (AO1)
- Advancing student thinking through providing more challenging content and activities than those in the Student's Book, which extend some areas of the specification and require the synthesis of information and the application of knowledge and understanding to unfamiliar contexts (AO2)
- Enabling students to grasp that the effective management of environmental issues requires a coherent and holistic approach to problem solving through the principles of sustainable development (AO3)

This is achieved through the provision of:

- Extension content and related activities that secure and progress student knowledge and understanding through tasks that require handling information from a variety of sources to reach conclusions and make judgments
- Supplementary case studies that reinforce and advance key principles and concepts and support evaluative thinking
- A decision making or problem solving exercise that encourages students to appreciate the complexities of environmental management and the pivotal role of the principles of sustainable development in achieving successful outcomes

Links to other chapters

All animal, plant and human life depends on the healthy functioning of terrestrial and aquatic natural ecosystems. The effective management of environmental issues arising from human activities relies therefore upon a thorough knowledge and understanding of the structure and operation of ecosystems and particularly their inherent fragility. In the past, scant regard has been paid to the potential impact on ecosystems and the communities of living organisms that they support, by the wholesale and unregulated exploitation of natural resources. As a consequence, the extraction and processing of rocks and minerals including fossil fuels, the indiscriminate exploitation of the Earth's surface and oceans by intensive commercial operations, and the pollution that has accompanied it, have left many pressing environmental problems for current generations to manage. The spread of the world's deserts through the human-driven process of desertification, the unsustainable consumption of groundwater reserves, acid rain and the accumulation of anthropomorphically generated greenhouse gases in the atmosphere are just a few examples of this legacy. The number and variety of living things continues to decline rapidly as a consequence of habitat loss, resulting from short-term and poorly-managed human activities. However, whilst every section highlights one or more negative impacts of human activities on ecosystems, it also looks to the future and illustrates how it is possible for healthy functioning habitats and their communities to coexist alongside the sustainable exploitation of natural resources. The concept of sustainable development – that which enables economic growth and improvements in living standards for all to occur whilst conserving and enhancing the natural ecosystems on which all material, social, spiritual and cultural prosperity relies – is emphasised in all other sections. This management principle will enable another three billion people to be supported in a viable way by the end of the century. It will underpin strategies to conserve the life of rocks and minerals, prevent and manage soil erosion and the overexploitation of freshwater, and reduce pollution. Above all it is about understanding the benefits that natural ecosystems provide and ensuring that they are conserved when natural resources are exploited. Underlying all of the resources humans consume are ecosystem processes – the biological, chemical and physical interactions between the living and non-living components within habitats – that will continue to provide huge benefits to humans if they are recognised and managed appropriately.

Natural ecosystems and human activities topic	Links to other subject content	Section
Ecosystems	Soils for plant growth World fisheries Human population distribution and density	3 5 8
Ecosystems under threat	Flooding Drought Earthquakes and volcanoes	6 6 6
Deforestation	Conservation and management of energy resources Impact of agriculture Causes and impacts of soil erosion	2 3 3
Managing forests	Managing soil erosion	3
Measuring and managing biodiversity	Sustainable agriculture Management of the harvesting of marine species	3 5

Extension content and related activities

Ecosystems under threat

Habitats are lost through actions such as clear felling forests, draining wetlands, mining rocks, minerals and energy supplies, water extraction from lakes and rivers, building major engineering projects such as dams, planting out commercial forests, expanding towns, cities and transport routes, pollution from farms and factories and the dumping of domestic and industrial waste. One quarter of the Earth's land area is now agricultural land of one kind or another and the conversion of land to farmland is the planet's main cause of habitat loss.

The cheetah is Africa's most endangered big cat. According to the Cheetah Conservation Fund, over 100 000 roamed across the continent in 1900. Today there are less than 10 000 living in a habitat range that has been reduced by 77 per cent in the past one hundred years. It is now extinct in twenty African countries where it existed in 1900. It requires vast areas of tropical grassland in order to find suitable prey, cover and water supplies. As savannah is ploughed up for crop production or commercial livestock herds are introduced, the wildlife carrying capacity of the remaining grassland is reduced drastically. Cheetah numbers decline as a result. This situation is made worse by the fact that cheetahs do not do well in protected areas such as national parks or wildlife reserves. These often contain high densities of larger predators such as lions, leopards and hyenas, which not only compete for the same prey as cheetahs, but also kill cheetah cubs in large numbers. As a result, most cheetahs choose to live outside protected areas on private farmland. Conflict with humans is inevitable when cheetahs kill farm animals, and this regularly leads to them being killed by farmers. Unlike most big cats in Africa, cheetahs do the majority of their hunting during the day, making them highly visible (and at risk) at times, especially when on the lookout from small hills or trees.

Fig. 9.1 Cheetahs require very large hunting ranges.

Fig. 9.2 Commercial farmland in Tanzania.

As a consequence, the genetic diversity of remaining cheetah populations is very low. It is estimated that only a very small number of cheetahs survived the great Pleistocene extinction event of 12 000 years ago when 75 per cent of the world's largest mammals were wiped out. Generations of inbreeding has resulted, and this is being made worse now because isolated populations in fragmented habitats are unable to interact and mate. As the rate of inbreeding within smaller isolated populations increases, there is even more reduction in genetic diversity and abnormalities are becoming apparent. Lower molar teeth infection is endemic, kinked tails have developed, and the sperm quality of male cheetahs is very low. According to the

International Cheetah Studbook, numbers are now approaching a critical point of no return or what is termed a statistically irrecoverable extinction.

The Cheetah Conservation Fund (**http://www.cheetah.org**) is the world's leading organisation dedicated to the conservation of the cheetah in the wild. Summarise in your own words how it is attempting to achieve this under the following headings: *research, human wildlife conflict, habitat restoration* and *education*.

Managing forests

Karura Forest Reserve is located in the northern part of Nairobi city in Kenya. With an area of over 10 sq km, it is one of the largest city forests in the world. It is managed by the Kenya Forest Service and a community-based group called the Friends of Karura Forest Association. Living within the forest are 605 species of plants and animals, including two hundred species of birds and three types of antelopes.

Fig. 9.3 Karura Forest, Kenya.

Fig. 9.4 Waterfall in Karura Forest, Nairobi, Kenya.

Karura is a very good example of the development of ecotourism in a woodland area. The forest has been managed sustainably since the 1990s to ensure that:

- it is protected from development for housing and business in a city of three million people
- residents of Nairobi can visit and enjoy the forest
- the natural ecosystem of the forest is restored and conserved for the future
- local people, especially in the Huruma shanty town that surrounds much of the forest, see the value of preserving the forest and work to protect it

Fig. 9.5 Kibera slum in Nairobi, Kenya.

Every year an average of 200 000 paying visitors enter the forest to enjoy its wildlife and other attractions including caves, waterfalls and rivers. Facilities like picnic sites and walking and cycling trails have been laid out in the forest. Although a security fence has been built around the forest, the most important reason why the forest has survived is that people in the local community now have an incentive to protect it. For example, over one hundred local people earn income from jobs connected to the forest such as wildlife scouts and rangers, administration officers, tree minders and general labourers who clear bush and plant out native plants and trees. On two days a week, local people are allowed to enter the forest and collect naturally fallen wood for use in their homes. Schoolchildren and their teachers from nearby schools are given free entry to the forest to learn about forests and conservation at any time.

Because Karura Forest is situated only two kilometres from Nairobi city centre and within a city of three million people, the government is constantly under a lot of pressure from developers to allow the forest to be cut down for housing and industry. Currently the government is considering whether to allow 0.05 sq km of the forest to be felled to make way for a luxury six star hotel. The proposed development will include a spa and horse riding school, among other amenities.

The developer who proposes to build the hotel stresses that only 1.5 per cent of the forest will be lost and that the luxury hotel will benefit the local area in many ways. Make a list of how the local area and its people could benefit from the development.

What counter-arguments to the development is the government likely to receive from the Friends of Karura Forest Association?

Measuring and managing biodiversity

Restoring the world's blanket bogs

There are only about 150 000 sq km of blanket bog remaining in the world. Blanket bog consists of a mixture of rushes, mosses and heather growing in thick wet layers or 'blanket' of peat. They form in areas with a cool wet climate where rainfall exceeds evapotranspiration. The UK contains about 15 per cent of the world's blanket bog in upland areas where:

Fig. 9.6 Blanket bog in the Scottish Highlands.

- annual rainfall is high, exceeding 1000 mm
- there are more than 160 'wet days' a year (at least 1 mm of rain falling each day)
- where the average temperature of the warmest month is less than 15 °C
- levels of evapotranspiration are low

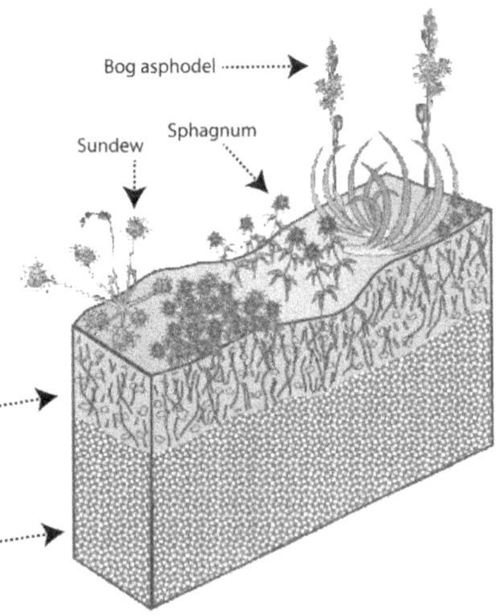

Fig. 9.7 Structure of a blanket bog.

Peat is the partially decomposed remains of plant material. Within a blanket bog, peat accumulates very slowly in a nutrient poor and acidic environment (approximately 1 mm a year under optimum conditions) because the decomposition of plant material (especially sphagnum moss) occurs in a cool, anaerobic (without air) and waterlogged environment. Over thousands of years, large areas of undulating ground in upland Britain have gradually been covered under a 'blanket of peat' including 30 sq km on Exmoor in the southwest of the UK. The typical structure of a blanket bog is shown in the diagram on the left. Over five thousand years, a specialised ecosystem has developed on the blanket bogs of Exmoor consisting of animals and plants, such as the carnivorous sundew, that have adapted to living in a very acidic and waterlogged environment with low levels of nutrients. In addition, the blanket bogs function as important reservoirs of fresh water for human consumption and act as massive carbon stores. Healthy growing peat absorbs carbon dioxide, one of the most potent greenhouse gases, from the atmosphere.

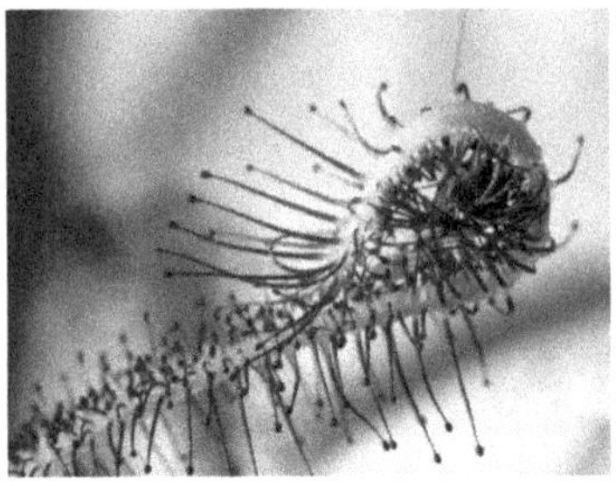

Fig. 9.8 A sundew plant.

Fig. 9.9 Peat cutting.

Fig. 9.10 Restoring blanket bogs using wooden dams.

During the past two hundred years on Exmoor, much of the peat in its blanket bogs has been cut for fuel or drained to create drier land for grazing livestock. Today, the blanket bogs and the ecosystems they support are heavily degraded.

The Exmoor Mire Restoration Project is aiming to restore over 10 sq km of blanket bog in the next three years. This is being achieved through a process of 'rewetting' the peatland by blocking up old peat cuttings, farm drains and ditches with wooden, peat and heather bale dams. This allows the rainwater to accumulate on the surface and percolate down into the peat below.

Go to **http://www.exmoormires.org.uk/** and click on *Exmoor Mires Partnership.* From the *Why are we doing it?* page, summarise in bullet points the main benefits of managing the peatland like this in the future.

Captive breeding programmes

Captive breeding involves mating wild animals to produce offspring within controlled environments such as zoos and wildlife parks. It has been used around the world since the 1960s as a means of both saving animals from extinction and of reintroducing animals back into the wild to boost dwindling populations. One of the first successful captive breeding projects involved the reintroduction of the Arabian oryx, which was hunted to extinction in the wild in 1972. In 1962, Phoenix Zoo in Arizona, United States began a captive breeding programme of oryx, and from nine individuals, over two hundred young were bred. These oryx were then distributed to zoos around the world, resulting in many more herds being started in captivity. In 1982, the first oryx was reintroduced to the world in Oman. There are now also reintroduced herds in Saudi Arabia and Israel, and the total global wild population stands at 1100 animals.

Fig. 9.11 Arabian oryx.

Fig. 9.12 Californian condor.

More recent captive breeding successes include the Californian condor. In the 1970s, ecologists found that only a few dozen condors remained in the wild, and in 1980, a major conservation project was started to try to prevent the birds becoming extinct. This included collecting the eggs of wild birds and artificially incubating them at Los Angeles Zoo and San Diego Wild Animal Park. The resulting chicks were then released back into the wild when they became adults. However, this did not halt the continued decline in the number of wild birds and so the decision was taken to capture all of the remaining condors and house them in zoos. In 1987, the last wild condor was captured and the entire world population in that year amounted to just twenty-seven. The first captive condor chick hatched in 1988 and by 1999 the population had grown to 161 birds. Two captive bred birds were released back into the wild in 1992. The condor population has continued to increase and by 2015 there were over 125 wild condors in California.

Despite successes such as these, captive breeding programmes have been criticised for a number of reasons:

- They draw attention (and a great deal of money) away from the issue of protecting habitats, which can mean that the captive bred animals have no suitable location in the wild to return to. The substantial costs of captive breeding (the California condor programme has already cost US$35 million) could be used more effectively to protect these wild species and habitats.
- Because captive breeding only involves relatively small numbers of animals or birds, serious genetic problems caused by interbreeding can occur. Breeding from such a narrow gene pool can lead to genetic changes in offspring that make them less able to survive when they return to the wild.
- The environment in which captive breeding occurs is often very different from the wild habitats to which captive bred animals will eventually be returned. The geographical knowledge therefore of the best places to find food, water or shelter, and predators and hazards to avoid in their wild habitats, cannot be transferred in captivity. This makes the released captive animals much more at risk in the wild. For example, many reintroduced California condors have been killed in collisions with overhead power lines.
- Animals bred in captivity do not build up a natural resistance to pests and diseases found in the wild, which places them at greater risk when eventually released. In addition, captive bred birds and animals can carry diseases contracted whilst in captivity into the wild and transmit them to wild species that have no resistance to them.

Connecting the natural ecosystems and human activities topics

Ecosystems have an immeasurable ecological value as the home of billions of communities of living organisms interacting with each other and the environment around them. All human life depends on these interactions. In recent years ecologists have been trying to calculate exactly how 'valuable' ecosystems are to people. In doing this they have considered the word 'value' in its very widest sense. We often associate value with only how much something is worth in monetary terms (its price or cost), but 'value' means much more than that. The true meaning of the word value is 'the worth of something' or its importance and the overall benefits that it brings to people. So ecologists are investigating the question: *How much are ecosystems worth to people?*

The full range of benefits that ecosystems bring to people is known as **ecosystem services**. For any ecosystem, large or small, ecologists try to work out its value in terms of the benefits gained from:

Previsioning services – the value of what the ecosystem supplies in meeting human physical, economic and material needs such as food, water, timber, rocks and minerals, employment, and the generation of monetary wealth.

Cultural services – the value of the ecosystem in terms of its contribution to the spiritual and emotional wellbeing of people, together with the potential health benefits it provides.

Support services – the value of the ecosystem in terms of maintaining life on Earth through things such as oxygen generation, storing or 'fixing' carbon, and nutrient recycling.

The photographs opposite show four ecosystems – *coral reef*, *river*, *tundra* and *temperate forest*. Consider each from the perspective of the different 'value' or 'benefits' that they are likely to offer people using a copy of the table opposite to make some notes. The table provides some suggestions on what you might consider for each ecosystem.

Fig. 9.13 Coral reef.

Fig. 9.14 Ganges river and the Himalayas in India.

Fig. 9.15 Arctic tundra in Alaska, US.

Fig. 9.16 Beech forest in Poland.

Ecosystem service	Possible benefits
How does this ecosystem help to meet the physical and material needs of people and contribute to increasing wealth and prosperity?	
How does this ecosystem help to improve the wellbeing of people such as their health and contribute to their spiritual and emotional happiness?	
How does this environment provide essential support services upon which all human life depends?	

Supplementary case study

Conservation of the orang-utan in Borneo

There are two species of orang-utan in the world. The Sumatran orang-utan is found only in the far north of the Indonesian island of Sumatra, and the Bornean species is confined to the island of Borneo (Indonesia and Malaysia). A hundred years ago there was an estimated 230 000 orang-utans in the wild, ranging in habitats from southern China to Java. Today, the Sumatran orang-utan is classified as 'critically endangered', with only 6600 remaining in the wild, and the Bornean species as 'endangered' with 54 000 individuals.

Fig. 9.17 The distribution of orang-utans in Sumatra and Borneo.

Fig. 9.18 A Sumatran orang-utan.

The orang-utan's habitat is lowland tropical forest, and they play a vital role in maintaining the health of this ecosystem, especially the way they contribute to widespread seed dispersal. The Sumatran orang-utan is entirely boreal (does not descend from the trees) but the male of the Bornean species regularly climbs down to the forest floor.

The main cause of the population decline of orang-utans is habitat loss. Throughout Sumatra and Borneo, huge areas of forest are being cleared for farming and for palm oil plantations in particular. This is leading to orang-utans having to inhabit ever smaller parcels of fragmented forest that are separated from each other by commercial farms. The international conservation organisation WWF reports that the Sumatran orang-utan population has now been fragmented into thirteen populations living in twenty-one separate forest blocks. It is probable that only six of these populations are large enough to have sufficient genetic diversity to ensure the group will have a viable future.

Fig. 9.19 Forest being cleared for a palm oil plantation, Borneo.

Fig. 9.20 Young palm trees planted on cleared forest land.

Fig. 9.21 Oil palm fruitlets.

Orang-utan numbers are also falling because young animals are captured in the wild for the international pet trade. Very often their mothers are shot and killed to gain access to the young who live with their mothers for up to eleven years. Orang-utans are also killed as bush meat and frequently shot or trapped when they encroach onto farmland in an effort to move from one fragmented block of forest to another. Forest fires, which are often set deliberately in order to clear the land for farming, are another cause of orang-utan mortality. In 1997–1998, a huge forest fire burned uncontrollably in Borneo during the draining and clearing of the peat swamp forest. By the time it was under control, it had killed at least 8000 orang-utans.

A number of international conservation organisations such as the WWF and the Orang-utan Foundation work in partnership with the Indonesian and Malaysian governments and local communities in Borneo in an effort to conserve the orang-utan and ensure its long-term survival in the wild. The Orang-utan Foundation is working particularly in the central Kalimantan region of Borneo where the largest groups of wild orang-utans live.

Go to **http://www.orangutan.org.uk/** and the pages on orang-utan conservation. Summarise in your own words the key things that the foundation are doing to conserve the orang-utan under the following headings:

- Habitat protection and reforestation
- Translocation and release
- Capacity building and sustainable livelihoods
- Education and awareness
- Scientific research

Data response and decision making exercises

1. St Lucia is a small island country of 617 sq km located in the Lesser Antilles chain of islands of the eastern Caribbean Sea. Table 9.1 shows a range of economic, social and environmental information about St Lucia.

Fig. 9.22 Location of St Lucia.

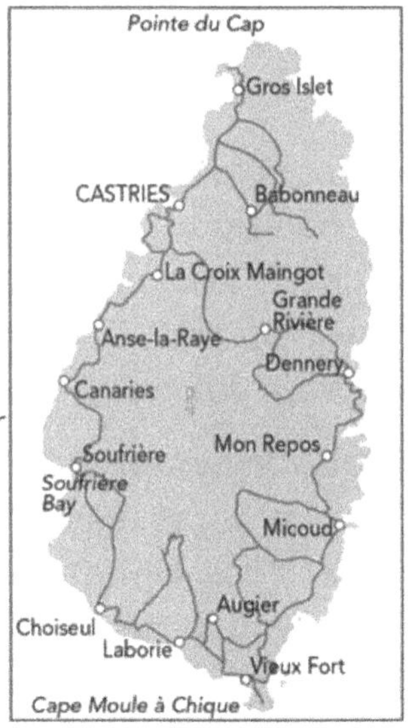

Fig. 9.23 St Lucia.

Fig. 9.24 Mountains from Edmund Forest, St Lucia.

Fig. 9.25 Hotel with pool, St Lucia.

Population	164 000
Population density	270 per sq km (world: 54 per sq km)
Population density world ranking	43/244
Annual population growth rate	0.74%
Population doubling time	95 years
Life expectancy	77.6 years
Literacy rate	90%
Population with access to improved sanitation	91%
Population with access to improved water	96%
Infant mortality rate	11.45 per 1000 people
Land area covered by forest	77%
Main employment provider	Tourism (54%)
Main income provider	Tourism (65%)

Table 9.1: St Lucia – selected economic, social and environmental indicators.

What do each of the following indicators measure?

a) Literacy rate

....

....

....

....

b) Population with access to improved sanitation

....

....

....

....

c) Infant mortality rate

....

....

....

....

2. A recent report by the United Nations Environment Programme (UNEP) identified deforestation particularly in the drier northern part of St Lucia as a major cause of land degradation. Loss of biodiversity, soil erosion and the sedimentation of rivers and coastal coral ecosystems and a reduction in the quality of both drinking and recreational water quality were all recognised as consequences of tree removal.

a) From the information in Table 9.1, suggest one reason for the removal of forest cover in St Lucia.

....

....

....

....

....

b) Draw a labelled diagram in the box below to show how sedimentation of rivers and coral ecosystems around the coast is likely to be caused.

c) Why would it be likely that sedimentation of drinking water sources would lead to consumers in St Lucia having to pay more for their supplies?

....

....

....

3. Over thirty species of bird are resident in St Lucia. Of these, five are endemic species that can be found only on the island. One of these is the St Lucia parrot. Its habitat is tropical forest and with an estimated population of just 350–500 individuals, the bird is classified as 'vulnerable to endangered'. Loss of habitat through deforestation followed by illegal collecting for the pet trade, are the two main causes of the bird's decline from at least 1000 at the beginning of the 1950s. When the estimated number of parrots dropped to just 150 in the late 1970s, the Durrell Wildlife Conservation Trust supported by the St Lucian government began a captive breeding programme. The first pair of captive bred parrots was returned to the wild in 1989.

Fig. 9.26 St Lucia parrot.

a) Captive breeding and release programmes are sometimes criticised as a means of protecting and restoring biodiversity in the wild. Using examples you have studied, explain why this is.

....

....

....

....

....

....

....

....

....

....

b) The Durrell Wildlife Conservation Trust together with the St Lucia Forestry Department are now planning new surveys to obtain a more accurate count of parrot numbers. They do not have the resources to survey the entire remaining forest. How would you advise them to go about estimating parrot numbers on the island using a random sampling method?

....

....

....

....

....

c) One of the rarest endemic plants on St Lucia is *Bernardia laurentii* a small shrub found only on the rocky summit of the volcanic cone Petit Piton. It is not found anywhere else in the world and is classified as being under the threat of extinction.

Fig. 9.27 *Bernardia laurentii* plant.

Fig. 9.28 Petit Piton in St Lucia.

Explain how an ecologist might go about estimating numbers of the shrub using a quadrat or line transect. Suggest two things that might affect the reliability of your results.

....

....

....

....

....

....

....

....

....

....

....

....

....

....

....

....

....

4. Rainforest Adventures is a company offering fun and educational excursions for tourists and visitors to St Lucia. It aims to *'promote environmental consciousness and conservation awareness while striving to provide world class eco tourism'*. It offers activities such as riding forest canopy zip wires, leisure hiking along forest ecosystem nature trails, waterfall climbing, birdwatching and abseiling.

9.29 Hiking at Des Cartiers Rainforest Trail, St Lucia.

Explain what ecotourism is and why it might be considered a sustainable way of exploiting the forest of St Lucia that will ensure its long-term existence.

....

....

....

....

....

....

5. Around the coast of St Lucia there are 90 sq km of unique coral reefs that grow on volcanic rocks. They are particularly extensive off the south and southwest coasts close to Soufrière Bay.

Fig. 9.30 Coral reef in St Lucia.

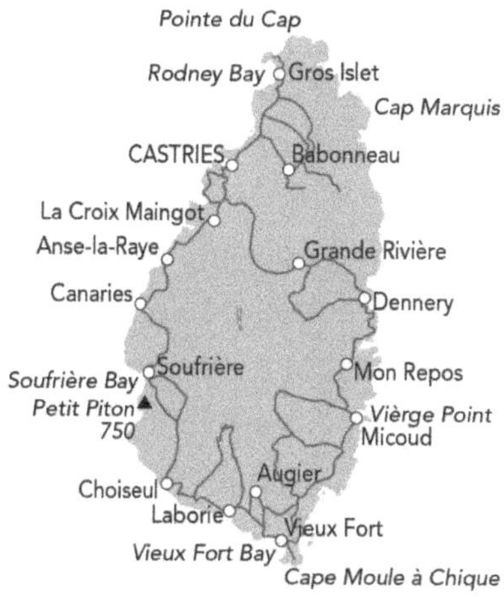

Fig. 9.31 Location of Soufrière Bay.

Sedimentation caused by eroded soil from the land that ends up in the ocean, where it reduces water quality, 'smothers' the coral and deprives it of light is a major threat to the coral ecosystem of St Lucia. The main natural cause of sedimentation of coral reefs is hurricanes and tropical storms, which impact the island regularly. The most serious human cause is the development of the coastline for hotels, villas and apartments. Suggest how both hurricanes and human coastal development can cause sedimentation of coral reefs in and around Soufrière Bay.

....

....

....

....

....

....

....

....

....

....

....

....

6. During the 1980s and early 1990s, pressure built up on the coral reefs around Soufrière Bay as both the resident population and the number of tourists visiting the south and southwest of the island increased rapidly. By 1990, there were over 150 commercial fishermen working the bay and two large holiday resorts, together with four smaller hotels and a number of guesthouses and restaurants right on the seashore, had been built. In addition, growing numbers of day charter boats and water taxis provided day excursions to the bay for people staying in hotels in the more developed north of the island.

   This pressure created a number of environmental problems including:

   - pollution of coastal waters by sewage, chemical fertilisers and solid domestic waste, especially plastics
   - serious depletion of near shore fish stocks
   - yacht anchor damage to reefs
   - sedimentation of the reefs caused by soil erosion run-off from the land
   - unregulated tourist activities such as diving causing damage to the coral reefs

   These problems led to growing conflicts between different interest groups or stakeholders using the resources of the bay, particularly the following:

- disagreements between fishermen and dive operators who were trying to work the same areas
- disputes between yacht owners and fishermen when boats were anchored in fishing areas
- hostility between local residents and hotel and resort operators over which beaches tourists would be given exclusive access to
- arguments between fishermen and hoteliers and resort owners over which beaches would be used for commercial fishing activities such as processing and packing and which would have only recreational and tourism activities such as swimming and sunbathing

To solve these environmental problems and conflicts, in 1995 the government of St Lucia authorised the setting-up of the Soufrière Marine Management Association (SMMA) in order to conserve the natural marine environment and ensure its sustainable development in the future.

a) What do you understand by the term 'sustainable development'?

....

....

....

....

....

b) Why is plastic waste a serious marine pollutant?

....

....

....

....

....

c) Suggest how yacht anchors might damage coral reefs, particularly in stormy weather.

....

....

....

....

d) One of the first things that the SMMA did was to draw up a code of conduct for people diving onto the coral reefs to adhere to. Suggest three things that they might have included.

....

....

....

....

....

....

....

....

7. The map below shows what the SMMA did to ensure the sustainable development of the marine ecosystem of Soufrière Bay in the future.

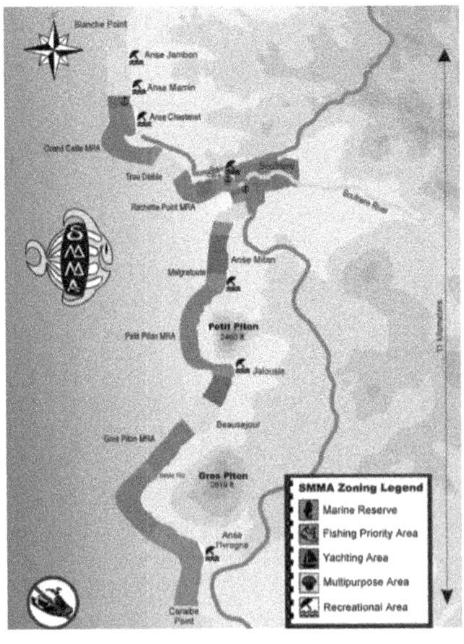

9.32 SMMA marine zones.

a) Explain in your own words the action that the SMMA has taken.

....

....

....

....

....

b) Why might this not necessarily end conflict between different users of the bay?

....

....

....

....

....

8. St Lucia is a relatively poor country by world standards. Gross national income per person (at purchasing power parity) stands at US$10 290 compared with US$38 530 per person in France. Each year the government of St Lucia earns US$2 billion. In comparison the government of France earns US$2544 billion a year. St Lucia is ranked by the World Bank as the 96th wealthiest country in the world (out of 186) and France is ranked 25th.

a) Imagine a foreign developer approached the government to seek permission to build a huge resort that would accommodate at least 20 000 foreign tourists every year along a section of the coast designated as a marine reserve. Why might the government be persuaded to allow such a development?

....

....

....

....

....

b) If you were an environmental manager, how might you convince them to hold to the SMMA sustainable development plan and not allow the development?

....

....

....

....

....

....

Answers to these questions can be found at **www.collins.co.uk/EnvMgmtIGCSE**

Answers

The answers given in this section have been written by the authors and are not taken from examination mark schemes.

1 Rocks and minerals and their exploitation: answers to Student's Book questions (pages 238-240)

1. Rock is the solid and naturally occurring material that forms the Earth's hard outer layer or crust. Rock is almost always made up of a mixture of grains of different chemical substances called minerals.
2. Igneous rocks such as granite are formed when magma solidifies either within the Earth's crust (intrusive) or on the surface of the Earth (extrusive). Sedimentary rocks like chalk are formed of the remains of plants and animals combined with particles of rocks and minerals that have been compressed together through cementation to form layers of hard rock. When igneous or sedimentary rocks are heated up under pressure, they can sometimes form new or metamorphosed rocks. For example, limestone can be metamorphosed into marble.
3. The diagram explains how rocks are constantly being formed, broken down by the forces of weathering and erosion, and then reformed again in a cyclical process. As soon as a rock has been formed it comes under attack from agents of weathering, like heat and cold, and forces of erosion including the wind and rain. As a result, rocks are broken down into smaller particles called sediments. These are transported by rivers and run-off to the oceans where they build up in hollows on the sea floor. Increasing pressure and cementation here then turns the sediment back into 'new' layers of sedimentary rock. As soon as these new sedimentary rocks, together with new igneous rocks cooling from magma, are exposed on the surface of the Earth, the rock cycle begins again.
4. All soil is formed from rock of one kind or another and everyone depends on soils as crops are grown in it and animals feed on the grass that grows in it. We use millions of tonnes of rocks and stone every year to construct buildings and lay out roads. Rocks contain essential ores and minerals such as iron ore, bauxite and hydrocarbons (oil, gas and coal) that humans process to make industrial metals and fuels like steel, aluminium and diesel.
5. Geologists use a range of techniques, including taking remote-sensing images of the underlying rock structure from satellites. These images are often used in conjunction with seismic maps of the rock structure generated by small explosions on the surface that send shock waves underground. Geologists also look for signs of radiation or variations in magnetic fields as possible indications of mineral deposits.
6. The photograph with the bucket excavator shows surface mining. This method of mining is used when the rocks containing the desired mineral (known as the ore body) are found close to the Earth's surface. Large excavators and drag lines are used to remove the overlying material (known as the overburden) to reach the ore below, which is then excavated and processed. The image with the miners shows subsurface mining, which is used when the mineral ore is deep underground. It is reached by tunnels and shafts, and the excavated ore is then brought to the surface by trucks or lifts.
7. Mining will only go ahead if it is certain that the income from selling the mineral over the lifetime of the mine will be greater than all of the costs involved in extracting, processing and transporting it to customers. There are also costs to consider for restoring mine workings when a mine is exhausted. Four important things that have a big influence on whether a mine will begin operating are:
   - How expensive it will be to extract the mineral. For example, if the ore is close to the surface then cheaper surface mining techniques could be used compared with much more expensive deep mining involving digging tunnels and shafts if the mineral is a long way underground.
   - The grade of the ore, which means how much of the mineral is made up of the chemical element required. The greater the proportion of the element, the more worthwhile it will be to extract it. Ores with little mineral content will likely cost more to extract than the processed mineral will sell for.
   - Whether financial support in the way of grants and loans (called incentives) are available from local or national governments. These will help to reduce costs and improve profit margins.
   - How attractive the location is for mining. A location that is easily accessible by road and rail, and presents few physical problems to overcome, will be much less expensive to mine than a remote location, with poor communications, in a mountainous or heavily forested area.
8. Economic benefits include things that will contribute to increasing wealth and improving incomes and living conditions for people in a place. For example, when a mine opens, many new jobs will be created for people in the local area. They will spend their wages buying homes, cars, food and enjoying leisure time. This means that other indirect jobs in places such as shops, sports centres, schools and hospitals will be created. This is known as the multiplier effect. The government will also receive tax from the profits the mine makes and from the wages of the direct and indirect workers. They will likely spend some of this on improving living conditions for people such as constructing new roads, medical centres and sports facilities.
9.

Possible social benefits	Possible social problems
The mine company may sponsor community development projects such as a new swimming pool or library in the local community from which everyone will benefit.	The mine may cause pollution. Freshwater supplies may become contaminated with metals such as mercury, and air pollution by particulate matter may cause an increase in respiratory conditions such as asthma.
New roads and railways built to service the mine also make transport much easier to access places that were once difficult for everyone to reach.	Some indigenous people or communities may have to be moved from the land that is to be mined. This may cause resentment and sometimes conflict, especially if people feel they have not been adequately compensated for their loss.
Regular jobs and salaries improve prospects for the families of mine employees, for example, being able to pay school and college fees for their children.	Although new jobs are created, other people such as small-scale independent miners and farmers on the land to be mined may lose their livelihoods.

Career and training programmes provided by the mine will offer employment opportunities for young people that may not have existed before.	The arrival of people with different values and lifestyles from outside of the community may lead to changes in local cultural traditions and ways of life, especially amongst the young.

10. Three other potential impacts are water pollution, soil erosion and sedimentation, and visual and noise pollution. Water contaminated with heavy metals, such as mercury, used in processing ores at mines can leak into nearby streams, rivers and lakes. Here it can be toxic to wildlife, and a health risk to humans, who consume the water. Topsoil and overburden removed to reach the ore below and piled up around the mine can be easily eroded by the wind and rain. Soil carried in solution by rainwater can form layers of sediment in rivers. This makes them shallower and more likely to flood. Finally, mines that operate twenty-four hours a day can be very noisy and floodlighting may mean that the local area never becomes dark at night.

11.

	What it involves	Example
Remediation	Doing things that ensure the mine workings and surrounding environment are made safe.	• Demolishing buildings • Back-filling mine shafts • Removing processing machinery • Removing toxic waste
Restoration	Returning the mine area to its pre-mine use, for example, open countryside or farmland.	• Planting native trees • Replacing top soil • Seeding with native flowers and shrubs
Reuse	Using the mine or quarry for something else that will benefit the local community economically and socially.	• Landfill site • Visitor attractions such as fishing lakes • Nature reserves

12. a)

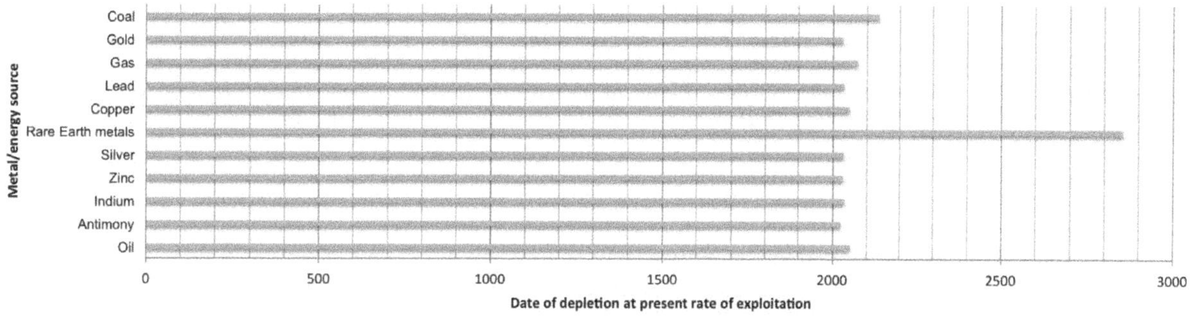

b)

Metal/energy source	Years before depletion (base year 2017)	Metal/energy source (continued)	Years before depletion (base year 2017) (continued)
Antimony	7	Copper	32
Gold	13	Oil	34
Zinc	14	Gas	56
Lead	15	Coal	119
Silver	16	Rare Earth	839
Indium	18		

c) Oil, coal and gas.

d) Rather than mining new mineral resources, priority could be given to reprocessing waste ores and tailings discarded over hundreds of years at existing mines. This waste rock often contains enough ore to make processing using modern technology profitable. As minerals become rarer, their price goes up and so it is possible now to make a profit from deposits that previously were considered too expensive to mine. Increasing the amount of minerals that are recovered through recycling materials such as scrap metal will also help mineral reserves in the ground last longer. Obtaining metals from new reserves such as mineral nodules is another way of increasing the lifespan of precious metals such as those in the table. Mineral nodules are relatively small lumps of rock containing valuable minerals such as nickel and copper. They are found on seabeds and ocean floors at depths of 4000 to 5000 metres and so are both difficult and expensive to collect. However, rising mineral prices and continuing technological developments will make it easier to exploit them in the future.

2 Energy and the environment: answers to Student's Book questions (pages 241-243)

1. a) Fossil fuels are non-renewable organic energy resources such as oil, gas and coal, which are hydrocarbon based.
   b) Non-renewable energy sources are a naturally occurring source of energy such as coal, which can only be used once for energy generation and cannot be used again.
   c) Renewable energy sources are energy sources such as wind that are not depleted when used.
2. Renewable: solar, hydroelectric, biomass, geothermal, tidal, wind
   Non-renewable: coal, gas, nuclear, oil
3. Fossil fuels are an abundant energy source that are found across the planet. Humans have been able to harness fossil fuels to develop transport, industry and agriculture. The globalised modern world is built upon use of cheap fossil fuel based energy.

4. There are several stages involved in the formation of coal:
   - Decomposing vegetation is buried under sediment, forming peat.
   - Peat is compressed over time and heats up to form lignite.
   - With further time, pressure and heat, bituminous coal is formed.
   - Finally, anthracite is formed at the greatest pressures and temperatures over time.
5. Oil and gas were created from organisms that lived in the water. They are often found together in sedimentary rocks. Organisms such as plankton fell to the bottom of the sea and were buried by layers of mud. Due to the lack of oxygen, they did not decay completely and accumulated in a layer of mud rich with organic matter. High temperatures and pressure cook the organic matter and turn it into oil and gas, which is trapped in porous rocks.
6. The increase in demand over time has led to an increase in exploitation of these resources. This has had an environmental impact on the places where extraction occurs. This has also led to increases in the transport of oil and gas, which has increased the risk of spills. The increase in demand has increased job opportunities for people in the oil and gas sector, which has, in turn, led to economic growth for countries that have oil and gas reserves. However, the use of fossil fuels releases carbon dioxide in the atmosphere, which is creating an enhanced greenhouse effect, leading to an increase in global average temperatures.
7. Thermal power stations use heat to turn water to steam. The steam is then used to turn turbines that generate electricity. The heat can be generated by burning oil, coal or gas. Nuclear power stations use uranium fuel rods to heat the water into steam.
8. Countries that are energy secure are not reliant on other countries for imports of energy. They can meet their own energy demand and can ensure that there is a secure supply. This protects them from price shocks or sudden interruptions in supply.
9. See Table 2.2 in the Student's Book.
10. The greatest energy use is seen in North America, Europe, East Asia and Oceania. The largest consumers of energy are the US and China, who use over 1000 Mtoe. Sub-Saharan Africa has the least energy use with countries using between 0 and 0.9 Mtoe. The Pacific coast countries of South America are using less energy than Brazil.
11. **Domestic demand** – Domestic demand is increasing due to the increase in the number of devices, goods and fittings that require power. As levels of income increase, our energy consumption will increase.
    Industrial demand – Industrial demand uses 50 per cent of all the energy consumed each year. Rising income leads to rising demand for consumer products, which in turn leads to greater demand for energy by industry.
    Transport – Demand for energy used in transport has doubled since 1970 with the majority of this coming from individual cars and trucks on the road. Globally, there are now over 1 billion cars on the road.
    Wealth and development – Increasing levels of wealth leads to greater personal consumption, which in turn leads to increases in demand for electricity. As countries develop, they will build the infrastructure to meet the growing demand for services, which all require more energy.
    Climate – Weather and climate can have a significant impact on the demand for energy. In colder countries, demand for energy for heating will increase in colder periods. In warmer countries, the use of air-conditioning in buildings is now a significant part of the rising demand for energy.
12. Answers will vary depending on the country chosen.
13. The importance of different energy sources has shifted over time. Due to rising atmospheric pollution and the emission of carbon dioxide from fossil fuels, countries that are reliant on coal, oil and gas are looking to reduce the reliance on non-renewable polluting sources of energy in favour of more sustainable methods. Countries need to plan for the shift in energy mix as they need to ensure security of supplies, whilst moving to more renewable energy sources.
14. Households can reduce demand for energy by changing behaviour and installing more energy efficient technologies. For example:
    - turning off lights when not in use
    - adjusting the temperature to reduce energy use – or adding/removing layers of clothing rather than turning on the heating or air-conditioning
    - using energy-saving lightbulbs
    - installing a smart meter to monitor energy use in real time
    - installing solar water heaters or solar panels to generate electricity
15. Educating consumers about strategies to reduce consumption by changing behaviour can lead to dramatic reductions in energy consumption. Many schools and companies around the world are working towards reducing energy use by conducting energy audits and identifying areas that can be addressed. Educating people from a young age about the need to save energy will help transform behaviours and ultimately lead to a reduction in energy use.
16. There are many different developments underway to reduce the reliance on fossil fuels for transportation. Increasingly we are seeing electric cars on the streets of our cities. Electric cars have batteries that drive the power train. These cars produce no carbon emissions when running. However, they do require regular charging as the battery life can run out. Battery technology is rapidly developing, as is the number of car makers developing electric versions of cars. There is now a FIA motor racing series for electric racing cars. Of course, the real challenge is to ensure that the electricity they are using is generated using non fossil fuel energy sources. Other technologies being developed include hybrid cars that have both a petrol engine and an electric system – increasing fuel economy. These will be further advanced by developments in energy recovery systems. These have been developed in Formula One, where cars harvest the energy from braking and from the exhaust gases and reuse this for acceleration. This technology is now appearing in passenger vehicles. Many manufacturers are now looking toward developing hydrogen powered cars. This abundant gas could be harnessed in fuel cells. However, many people feel that this technology will take a long time to develop and that electric vehicles are a more immediate way of reducing fossil fuel consumption by vehicles.
17. Both Singapore and London have introduced schemes to reduce the number of vehicles on the road. London has a well-developed public transport infrastructure that includes an underground and overground rail system, a light railway and thousands of famous red buses. A congestion charge was introduced in 2003 that charges vehicles for entering the city at peak times. Charges increase for larger or more polluting vehicles. Whilst initially successful in reducing cars entering the city and in reducing air pollution, by 2007, numbers of cars had increased back to pre-introduction levels. However, the rate of growth is lower and there are now more people using public transport. Singapore introduced the first road pricing in 1975 and updated this to a system of electronic road pricing in 1998. Charges vary throughout the day depending on congestion. As the city has grown over the past 50 years, the

government has developed an integrated public transport system with MRT, LRT and bus system. The government has also introduced expensive taxes on new car purchases. The combined efforts of these have reduced the number of cars on the road as well as increased revenue from the pricing.

18. Both fracking and tar sands are highly controversial methods of extracting fossil fuels. The fundamental arguments should focus upon whether it is appropriate to be investing in yet more fossil fuel source development rather than low carbon alternatives. Arguments for and against fracking are shown below:

For	**Against**
These resources could improve the future energy security of countries by reducing the need for imports.	Shale oil and gas are still finite, non-renewable fossil fuels that release CO_2 into the atmosphere. They will not help meet targets for carbon emission reduction.
Gas is seen as 'greener' than coal as it produces less CO_2, so supporters argue that fracking helps reduce CO_2 emissions.	There are concerns over the chemical waste water and contamination of water supplies by the fracking fluid and gas.
Fracking could provide thousands of new energy jobs in the countries where shale gas is found.	Sites will see an increase in traffic that will disrupt communities.
These resources could also reduce the energy bills for households. The USA saw a 70 per cent decrease in gas prices.	There is concern that money for fracking will take money away from investment in renewable energy.
Fracking companies have proposed community benefits such as payments when the wells are started.	Fracking has caused minor localised earthquakes. This caused the UK government to stop drilling while investigations take place.
As technology develops, more oil and gas could be recovered in the future.	There are concerns about methane leaking from the drilling sites.

19. The tar sands production facility has severely impacted the environment in the photo. The topsoil has been removed completely, along with the trees. The facility also appears to be releasing gases into the atmosphere, which could be impacting local air quality.
20. a) Offshore extraction of oil can lead to difficult-to-contain spills. Leaks can occur if equipment is poorly maintained or old. Rigs are also vulnerable to strong winds. Oil can also be spilled when being transferred to other ships.
    b) Oil pipelines are the most common method of transporting oil on land. Pipes can become corroded and the welding joins can fail. They are also vulnerable to attack and accidental collision.
    c) Oil spills from ships can occur if ships get into trouble in bad weather, collide with other ships or run aground through navigational errors. When these accidents occur they can be devastating to the local environment.
21. See Figure 2.21 in the Student's Book.
22. MARPOL now regulates the discharge of oil from ships into the sea. It was an important marine treaty that has banned the discharge of oil waste and introduced tracking of ships to monitor oil discharges.
23.

Strategy for reducing and managing oil spills	**Evaluation**
Double hulled tankers	Reduce chances of spills if an accident does occur with a ship. Oil is also restricted from the front section of the ship. This had significant costs as new ships needed to be built, but the changes were phased in. Single hulled oil tankers have now been phased out.
GPS monitoring	Use of GPS allows ships to navigate accurately – reducing the risk of running aground. The risk is not completely eliminated however.
Booms	These floating barriers contain oil spills behind the booms. These are much less effective in large waves, as the oil can escape.
Chemical dispersants	These are effective at breaking the oil down into smaller particles, which then biodegrade. However, adding chemicals to the water is harmful to the marine environment.
Skimmers	These boats can collect oil from the sea. They are effective at saving the oil so it can actually be reused. However, large numbers are needed to clear up large spills. They are less effective in large seas and bad weather.
Sorbents	Effective at cleaning up smaller spills, sorbents can also be deployed with skimmers. They are often made of organic material, but they do also absorb water and can sink.

Burning	This process is effective at removing oil contained by booms. However, this is only possible after extensive collection and works in calm weather.
Vacuum trucks	The trucks are effective at small-scale clean-ups on beaches. However, problems of access in some places and the scale of spill mean that trucks are of no use, or many are needed.

24. Answers will vary.

3 Agriculture and the environment: answers to Student's Book questions (pages 244-246)

1. Inorganic mineral particles, from the weathering and erosion of rocks that are slowly broken down into smaller particles of different sizes.
   Organic matter of living plants, animals and microorganisms and their decaying remains, called humus.
   Water from precipitation, such as rain or snow, which drains into it.
   Air that tends to be rich in carbon dioxide and poor in oxygen.
2.

Mineral ion	Mineral element	How it is used in plants
Nitrate NO_3^-	Nitrogen (N)	Combines with glucose to form amino acids, which in turn bond together to create proteins required for cell
Phosphate PO_4^{3-}	Phosphorous (P)	Important component of DNA and cell membranes and required for respiration and growth.
Potassium K^+	Potassium (K)	Must be present for the enzymes required for photosynthesis and respiration to function effectively.
Magnesium Mg^{2+}	Magnesium (Mg)	For manufacturing chlorophyll (each chlorophyll cell contains one magnesium atom) without which photosynthesis would not occur.

3. Organic matter consists of decomposed plant and animal material in the soil and is very important for a number of reasons. Firstly it is a store of nutrients, such as phosphorous, which are constantly released into the soil. Secondly, it is a store of water, which is released into the soil gradually over the course of the year. Thirdly, it helps to improve soil structure by binding or clumping smaller soil particles together and this enables it to absorb more water and to allow water to flow through it easily. Finally, because organic matter contributes to anchoring the soil in place and encourages plants to grow long, strong roots, it helps to prevent soil erosion.
4. The larger particles of sand help plant roots to move easily through the soil and this means that water tends to drain quickly as well. Whilst this can be a good thing during heavy rain because it prevents waterlogging, sandy soils do dry out very quickly in times of low rainfall. Adding organic matter (which holds water) to sandy soils helps to prevent this drying out. When water drains too quickly (called leaching) through sandy soils, they can become acidic and infertile. Because sandy soils have a fine texture, they can be easily ploughed and warm up quickly in early summer.
   Clay soils have very small particles, which can make it difficult for plants to develop long and strong roots. Because clay is a thick, heavy soil, it is much more challenging to plough than sandy soil. Clay has poor drainage, which means it easily becomes waterlogged when rainfall is heavy but then dries out and cracks during dry periods. However, clay is naturally more fertile than sandy-based soils as nutrients get trapped in the small spaces between its small particles, although organic matter is often required to help release these nutrients for plant uptake.
5. Subsistence farming, such as shifting cultivation or slash and burn in places such as the Amazon Basin, involves the farmer producing only enough crops or livestock meat for family consumption. There is little or nothing remaining to sell or trade. Commercial farming, on the other hand, involves farmers producing crops and livestock for profit. It often involves the intensive use of machinery and technology, with relatively few manual workers, and achieves high yields as a result. Almost all farming in MEDCs, such as cereal-crop growing in the prairies of Canada, is commercial.
6. The agricultural yield or productivity of a farm refers to the volume of crop or weight of meat that farmers obtain from every 10 000 square metres of land. Farmers are always seeking to increase their crop and animal yields and use things such as fertilisers, GPS tracking, modern machinery and irrigation to help them achieve this.
7. Rotation involves regularly alternating the crop that farmers grow in each field or area of their farms to ensure that the soil does not become depleted of specific nutrients. This is because crops tend to use different nutrients in the soil and so regularly changing them to an agreed sequence keeps the soil as fertile as possible without having to add chemical supplements. A farmer may choose to include a nitrogen-fixing crop in their rotation, which has the benefit of actually adding nutrients to the soil through its root nodules.
8. A fertiliser is any natural or synthetic substance that is added to soils to supply one or more nutrients removed by growing crops. It could be natural animal manure or a chemical compound produced by a pharmaceutical company. The purpose of using all fertilisers is to increase agricultural yields and farm productivity. This means assisting farmers to increase the volume of crop or weight of animal meat they are able to obtain from every 10 000 square metres of farmland year on year.
9. The problem here is called eutrophication. It is usually caused when chemical fertilisers rich in nutrients such as phosphates get washed from fields by heavy rainfall into nearby streams, rivers and lakes. The build-up of nutrients, especially in still waters such as ponds, causes an explosive growth in algae that quickly grows to cover the entire surface of the water as shown in the photograph. These are known as algal blooms. It has serious environmental consequences as often the water becomes deoxygenated, leading to the death of fish, water plants and insects.
10. Irrigation is the artificial supply of water to farmland in order to help the farmer increase yields and productivity on their land. Surface irrigation is commonly used and involves flooding whole fields, such as rice paddies in countries such as India, with water. This method tends to be inefficient because much of the water will be evaporated, particularly in hot climates. Localised irrigation

such as drip irrigation, which delivers small droplets of water to the roots of individual plants through rubber tubes, involves much less wastage of water through evaporation. A third method commonly used in MEDCs is sprinkler irrigation, where water is piped through a hose to a central location in a field, and sprayed as a fine mist over the crop. This method is most like natural rainfall.

11. Synthetic chemicals that are produced to kill weeds, insects or bacteria and viruses are known as pesticides. Most often they are sprayed on growing crops. Fungicides destroy diseases caused by fungi such as rust. Herbicides are sprayed on weeds, which absorb the toxin and die. Insecticides kill insects that feed on or attack crop plants.
12. Bioaccumulation is a serious ecological problem that particularly affects top or apex consumers in food chains such as the peregrine falcon. It is the gradual build-up of toxins at higher concentrations through the trophic levels of the food chain. The use of DDT is a good example of bioaccumulation. When farmers spray plants with DDT, it is absorbed by the plant's leaves and stem. Insects that eat the plants are poisoned but do not die straight away. Many of these poisoned insects are eaten by birds, which then build up higher levels of DDT in their bodies. Peregrine falcons, which eat many birds, are worse affected as they accumulate the highest concentrations of DDT of all. The big effect that DDT had on peregrine falcons was to make the shell of their eggs so thin that when the adult birds tried to incubate them, the eggs were crushed by their weight.
13. Organic farming is a form of sustainable agriculture that seeks to achieve a balance between achieving the highest possible yields and conserving the natural ecosystems on which all life depends. As a result, organic farms avoid using synthetic fertilisers and pesticides and rely on natural manure and the biocontrol of pests. Many organic farmers also have strong ethical beliefs and ensure that high standards of animal welfare and safe and fair working conditions for people exist on their farms. This is different from many intensive farms that are often very intensive businesses that use high levels of technology and machinery together with chemical pesticides and fertilisers to maximise the profits they make from the land.
14. This involves the natural crossbreeding of animals or plants on mostly intensive commercial farms. For example, farmers may select only cows with high milk yields to breed with a bull. This will make sure that in the future, their herds of dairy cows will only be made up of high milk yielders. Arable farmers might crossbreed a variety of wheat that produces a large amount of grain with a variety that has strong disease resistance. The new variety formed (called a hybrid) will have the genetic makeup of both and therefore be high yielding and disease resistant. Crossbreeding is used to increase yields of meat and grain for every 10 000 square metres on commercial intensive farms and therefore raise profits as a result.
15. Genetic modification occurs in a laboratory and involves swapping genes between animals and plants of different species. Genes can be swapped from one plant to another, from a plant to an animal and from a microorganism to a plant. The objective of genetic modification is the same as for selective breeding – to create animals and crops that will yield more from every 10 000 square metres of farmland. Almost all maize grown in the world is now resistant to the herbicide glyphosate, which is sprayed on crops to kill weeds. The gene that makes most maize plants resistant was discovered in a wild grass and then introduced into the maize plants to provide protection when the weed killer was sprayed on it.
16. In some MEDCs, commercial farms often produce more food than people require. The United Nations estimates that a massive one-third of all the food produced each year in the world is never consumed by people. The governments of some countries offer farmers guaranteed prices for their crops and meat, no matter how much they produce. This encourages overproduction because farmers know that the government will always step in to buy what they produce no matter how much. In many MEDCs where farms are very intensive and high yielding, populations are not growing or even declining. As a result, there is not enough demand to consume everything that is produced. Finally, huge amounts of perfectly good and nutritious food are wasted each year because supermarkets reject fruit and vegetables with minor defects such as blemishes or because they are the wrong shape or colour.
17. A cash crop is a product such as cocoa or coffee that a commercial farmer grows in order to sell for profit. This is different from subsistence farming, where farmers work hard to be self-sufficient, producing only enough for their family needs. Converting from subsistence to cash crops can have many disadvantages for the farmer. Firstly, cash crop farmers have no control over the price they will be offered for their products. This means it is very difficult for farmers to predict exactly what they are going to earn each year. Most cash crops grown in LEDCs, such as sugar or tea, are exported to MEDCs. If demand drops for cash crops in MEDCs then prices paid to the farmer may be less than the cost of growing it in the first place. If farmers' incomes fall, they may not then have enough money to buy their family enough food or cover the costs of clothing or education. Many cash crops are more costly to grow than subsistence crops as they often require more water and fertilisers and this will also reduce profits.
18. Erosion occurs when top soil is washed or blown away by heavy rain or strong winds. This is serious because it means that precious nutrients are removed from the land. As erosion continues, the land can become so degraded that it comes to resemble a natural desert such as the Atacama or Gobi. The water table drops, surface water, such as lakes and rivers, disappears and the remaining soil often becomes contaminated by salts. This is caused salinisation. Changes such as this to the environment are known as desertification. A very important cause of desertification is overgrazing in regions of the world such as the Sahel in Africa. As the population grows, there are more farmers keeping animals such as cows and goats. In the past, these herds used to roam over large areas, but now they tend to be fenced into smaller areas. As a result, all the vegetation is eaten, plant roots die and the soil is no longer anchored in place. Erosion by wind and rain begins the process, which can lead to the creation of a desert as described above.

19.

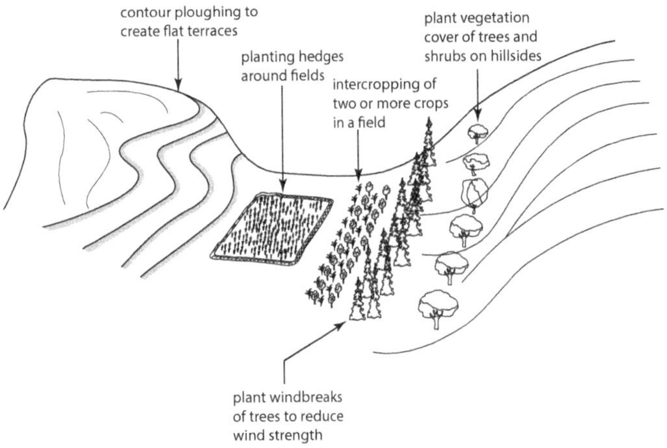

20. Sustainable agriculture is farming that seeks to balance making as much profit as possible through high yields and productivity with conserving the ecosystems on which all life depends. They seek to farm in balance with the environment and as a result, are more likely to use natural ways to fertilise the soils and to control pests and diseases. This approach is sometimes called stewardship rather than the exploitation of the land. Sustainable farms will also be more likely to have ethical welfare standards to ensure, for example, that animals are well cared for and that workers are treated fairly and not exploited. Above all, sustainable farmers work in a way that will not harm the environment and will enable future generations of farmers to do the same.
21. Biocontrol is often used on sustainable farms as a way of combatting pests and diseases without using synthetic chemicals, which are potentially harmful to the environment. For example, rather than spraying aphids with an insecticide, a farmer may encourage large populations of ladybirds to live on the farm. Ladybirds are a natural predator of aphids. Providing suitable habitats for owls and birds of prey will naturally control the numbers of vermin such as rats and mice on the farm.
22. a)

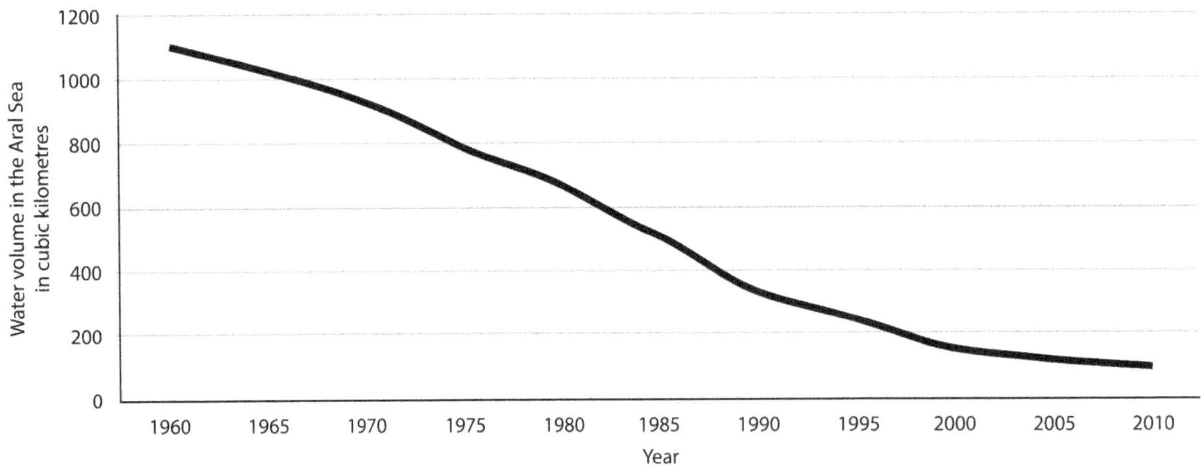

b) 91.03 per cent
c) 1985–1990 (175 cubic kilometres)
d) 1995–2000 (37.7 per cent)
e) The Aral Sea in Kazakhstan and Uzbekistan was once one of the largest inland areas of water in the world. Beginning in 1960, water was diverted away from its tributary rivers to irrigate 80 000 square kilometres of cotton and other crops in the dry regions surrounding the sea. By 2007, its area had shrunk by 90 per cent.

4 Water and its management: answers to Student's Book questions (pages 247-250)

1. Most of the Earth's surface water is locked up in ground ice and permafrost with lakes being the next largest store. Smaller quantities are held in rivers, the atmosphere and the soil.
2. It describes the constant movement of water between the oceans, land and the atmosphere. Because the hydrological cycle is such an efficient system, the volume of water circulating on Earth has remained very much the same for billions of years.

3.

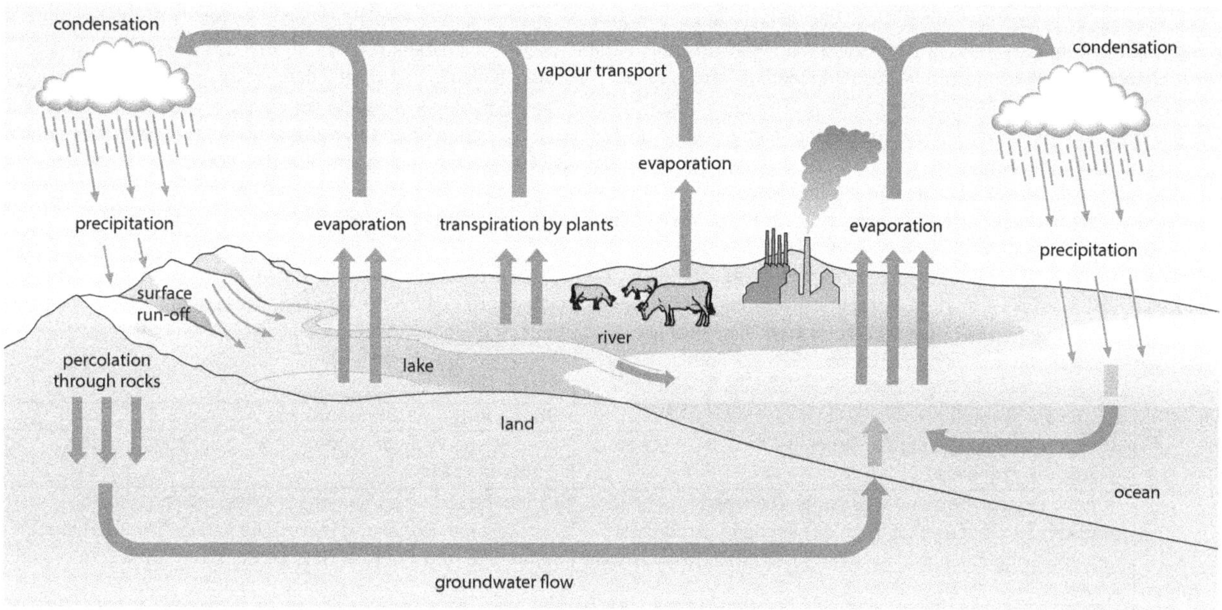

4. An aquifer is a layer of rock, like sandstone, below the Earth's surface that absorbs and stores groundwater. Rocks that form good aquifers are those with a loose granular structure with relatively large air gaps between the rock particles. Water is extracted from aquifers by creating an artesian well. As shown in the diagram on page 86 of the Student's Book, a pipe is drilled down from the surface until the aquifer is reached. Often the pressure in the aquifer is high enough for the water to move up through the pipe to the surface without the need for pumps. Where this happens, the well is called a flowing artesian well.
5. Water is held in underground layers of rock that absorb water – these are known as aquifers – and they are the world's most important source of freshwater. When water is pumped out of these aquifers at a faster rate than rainwater replaces it, they become depleted. This means that the amount of water they hold decreases each year. The main reason for depletion is population pressure and the fact that in some parts of the world there is little control over how much water people can extract from the ground. This has been the case in Bundelkhand in India. Here the water table has dropped and many hand pumps, tanks and ponds used for drinking have dried up. The result has been that farmers have not had enough water to grow crops, leading to food shortages for local people. This situation has been made worse by the fact that rainfall has been less than expected in Bundelkhand in recent years, causing a drought in some places.
6. Las Vegas obtains most of the water it requires for its two million residents and forty million visitors a year from surface water supplies. The River Colorado has been dammed to create the Lake Mead reservoir. Water is piped from Lake Mead to the city. Today, the reservoir is shrinking because more water is being extracted than is being replaced by rainfall carried into the lake by rivers. The causes of this have been an increasing population, leading to more demand for freshwater in homes and hotels, as well as for irrigating gardens and golf courses. The situation has been made worse by a long drought, which has meant that the city has not received as much rainfall as expected. To help the situation, the city government is working to a water conservation plan that aims to reduce its water consumption by 30 per cent by 2023.
7. Desalination involves removing soluble salts from seawater and brackish water to make it suitable for drinking. At the moment, it is used mainly in countries and regions such as Saudi Arabia or Israel where there is virtually no surface water like lakes, or where the groundwater reserves have been exhausted or are running low. It is a very expensive process compared with exploiting surface and groundwater supplies because of the amount of energy required to remove the salt and the size of the processing plants that are needed. This means that most countries with surface water and groundwater reserves are unlikely to use it until it becomes a much cheaper process.
8. The most important reason explaining how much water is consumed in agriculture, industry and in homes (called domestic use) is the level of economic development of a country. In most LEDCs such as Zambia, the majority of people work in farming, often using less efficient systems of irrigation such as surface flooding. There tends to be less use by industry because most manufacturing at the moment happens in small workshops or at home rather than in large modern factories. Compared with agriculture, there is much less water consumed in the home. This is because many rural areas in LEDCs still do not have piped water, which means that it has to be collected by hand from rivers and wells. This tends to reduce the amount of water used in the home and little is wasted. Living standards in LEDCs are generally lower than in MEDCs, so there are far fewer modern water-consuming appliances such as washing machines in homes. In industrialised countries such as Belgium, income is earned mainly from manufacturing industries and services rather than farming. Farming in MEDCs is intensive and irrigation is much more efficient, for example by using drip systems. Manufacturing industries, on the other hand, such as food processing and steel making, require massive amounts of water compared with farming. Water use in the home is also much higher than in LEDCs such as Zambia. This is not only because most homes have more domestic appliances such as dishwashers and washing machines but also because many homes have more than one bathroom or toilet. Water is also used to water gardens, fill ponds and wash vehicles.
9. A physical water shortage happens in those places where all available reserves of water such as lakes and rivers are being exploited to their maximum but demand for water from people, agriculture and industry is still rising. An economic shortage of water occurs in places where there are ample reserves of water such as in underground aquifers but the country does not have the technology or sufficient money to cover the cost of extracting it.

10. Trachoma is an infection of the eye caused by bacteria often found in drinking water contaminated with human faeces. Over 150 million people are blind or have serious vision problems as a result of this disease. It is thought that at least 1.5 million people a year die from the effects of consuming pathogens in contaminated water, which cause diseases such as cholera. The most common illness contracted from contaminated water is in fact diarrhoea, which is particularly dangerous for babies and young children because it dehydrates the body. The main cause of water-borne diseases is people not having improved sanitation in their homes and communities. This means that human waste often comes into contact with the water supplies people use for drinking, washing and bathing. Over two billion people in the poorest regions of the world, such as many of the countries of the Sahel region of Africa, still do not have improved sanitation.
11. A dam is a barrier constructed across a river to control its flow of water for different purposes. As well as generating hydroelectricity, other common reasons for building dams include creating reservoirs of water that can be used to irrigate farmland or to supply people in towns and cities with freshwater. Forty per cent of the world's crops are grown on irrigated land. Dams are also built to create a store of water that industries require to manufacture products. For example manufacturing an average sized family car consumes 177 000 litres of water. Dams are also built to help prevent flooding in places where rivers can rise very quickly during periods of heavy rainfall.
12.

Economic benefits	**Social and environmental costs**
Jobs are created both to construct the dam and to operate it once it is complete.	Homes and livelihoods are lost when land is flooded to create reservoirs.
Irrigation water allows nearby farms to expand into new areas and increase yields from existing land. Profits will rise and living standards for farmers and their families will improve.	Damming a river can have a serious impact on local ecosystems. For example, fish like salmon may no longer be able to move upstream to breed.
The availability of electricity will make the location of the dam attractive to new businesses, which will move to the area. New factories will employ local people and others who move in from other places around the country.	High concentrations of pollutants such as fertilisers may accumulate in reservoirs causing eutrophication and deoxygenation. This can lead to the death of many types of organisms like insects and crustaceans.
People with new jobs and increased incomes will pay tax to the local and national government. Some of this will be spent improving amenities and services, such as schools and medical centres, in the local area.	Once the dam is built, the flow of the river downstream is reduced greatly, particularly during dry spells. People who rely on the river for things like fish farming or leisure boat cruises for visitors may be forced out of business.

13.

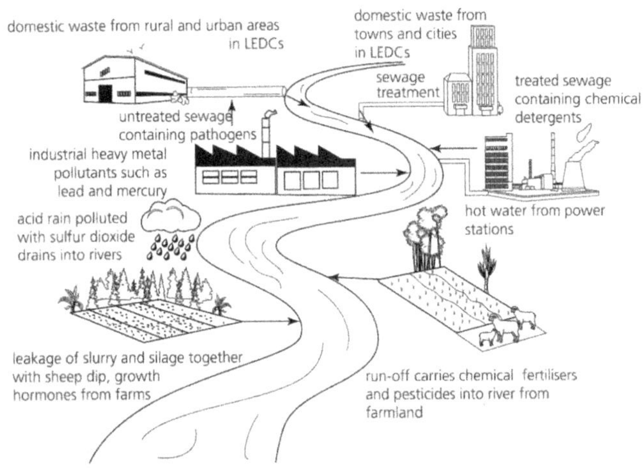

14. Improved sanitation means that the waste or faeces that people produce is carried away and disposed of in a way that ensures it never has contact with their freshwater supplies. The United Nations estimates that at the moment there are 2.5 billion people in the world living without this kind of sanitation. Almost all are living in rural areas of the poorest countries of the world such as Burkina Faso in the Sahel region of Africa. These countries are unable to afford the modern systems of sanitation found in most MEDCs and so tend to work with aid agencies to design improved sanitation appropriate to their level of economic development. In Kenya, Oxfam have been introducing into homes 'fresh life' toilets, which separate solid and liquid waste into two containers. These are then collected by local companies to create dried biofuel pellets for heat and fertiliser for vegetable gardens. Another Non-Government Organisation (NGO) called Practical Action working with the government of Bangladesh has introduced solar-powered sludge beds on which solid human waste can be dried and then composted into fertiliser for farms.
15. Malaria is a blood infection caused by a parasite spread by a female Anopheles mosquito, which feeds on the blood of both animals and humans in tropical and sub-tropical areas of the world. Each year there are about 200 million cases of malaria leading to around 400 000 deaths, particularly amongst babies and children. The mosquito tends to feed on humans at dusk and during the night. If it feeds on someone whose blood contains the parasite then it is likely to suck up the parasite together with a small amount of blood into its body. When it moves on to bite its next victim it can inject the parasite it is carrying into their bloodstream. When the parasite is in the bloodstream it tends to move to the liver. Some infected people may show the signs of malaria right away whilst in others the parasite may remain dormant for many years.
16. Many of the tropical and semi-tropical countries where malaria occurs are amongst the poorest in the world. They simply cannot afford the antimalarial drugs or prophylaxis that offer up to 90 per cent protection from infection. Vector control using bed nets treated with insecticide, which have to be replaced every five years, is also expensive, and many people in the poorest LEDCs

cannot afford it. Aid agencies based in MEDCs tend to donate these nets. However, only the very smallest gap in a net will allow a mosquito in to a body underneath. It is difficult therefore for everyone to remain covered all the time, especially if toilets are outside of the home or people have to rise early before daybreak for work. The main reason, however, why malaria is so hard to eradicate is that both the Anopheles mosquito and the parasite it carries are quickly able to build up resistance to both drugs and insecticide sprays through genetic changes or mutations. Another reason why eradication is difficult is the cost involved. The Gates Foundation estimates that at least US$120 million will be needed to completely eradicate the disease in the future. Much of this will need to be spent on trying to identify an effective vaccine. Countries where it occurs are going to have to rely on the goodwill of richer MEDCs where malaria does not occur to provide almost all of this money.

17. Cholera is another very serious water-borne disease caused by consuming water or food contaminated by bacteria. It affects the small intestine and symptoms include severe diarrhoea, stomach cramps and vomiting. Without treatment, serious dehydration can occur, which can lead to a massive drop in blood pressure and death. One of the main ways in which the disease spreads is through people drinking or cooking with water contaminated with the faeces of an infected person. Places such as refugee camps where people live at very high densities and where there are often poor sanitation facilities such as open latrines rather than self-contained toilets, can allow cholera to spread quickly. In these conditions, it is easy for drinking and cooking water to become accidently contaminated with faeces, especially if there are no opportunities for people to wash their hands regularly with antibacterial soaps or liquids.

18. a)

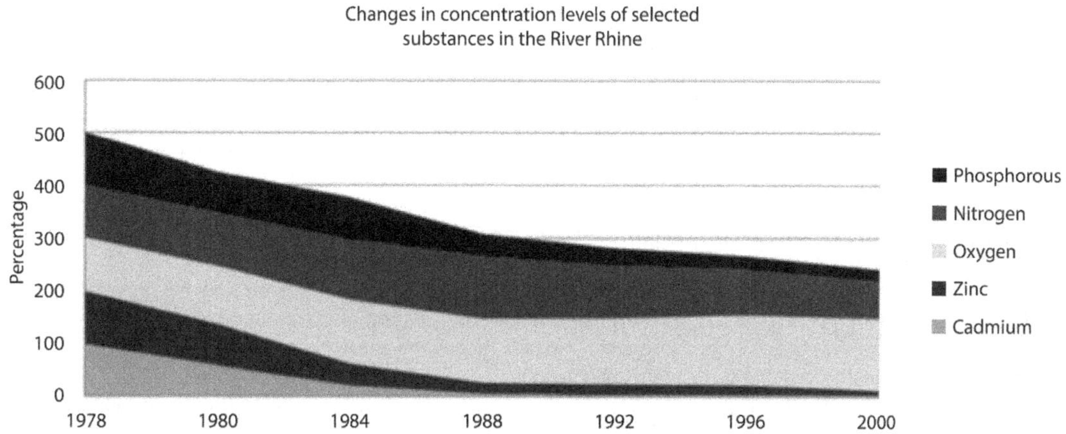

b) Nitrogen

c) Nitrogen is frequently used in artificial fertilisers, which are spread either as a liquid or nodules over farmland to increase nutrient levels for uptake by crops. However, during periods of heavy rain, nitrogen capsules can be washed off the land into nearby streams and rivers. Here the sudden increase in nutrients can cause an explosion of algal and plant growth and the deoxygenation of river water through a process known as eutrophication.

d) After the disaster, a number of laws were passed and countries adjoining the River Rhine agreed to take action to prevent such an event occurring again and to clean up the river. One example of joint working is The Rhine International Warning and Alarm System called 'Rhine Alarm'. This has been introduced at eight locations along the course of the River Rhine, which includes places in all the countries through which it flows. Water quality is constantly monitored at these sites so that information about pollution events can be communicated to all countries immediately as they happen. Regulations have also been passed requiring all major industries that use hazardous chemicals that are located along the river to have large retention basins where polluted run-off water can collect in the event of an accident rather than flowing into the river. Water pollution of the River Rhine as a result of industrial accidents has decreased by 99 per cent since the passing of these laws in 1991.

5 Oceans and fisheries: answers to Student's Book questions (pages 251-253)

1. Use the information on pages 122 and 126 in the Student's Book to create the annotated map and factfile.
2. The oceans are a valuable resource base for humans. They provide climate services such as the absorption of carbon dioxide as well as food supplies, energy, transport, building materials, tourism and are a potential source of fresh water.
3. Ocean transport is vital to the global economy. In 2013, 9.93 billion tonnes of freight was transported by sea. This has grown significantly over time with the development of large container ships.
   The oceans also have potential as a source of drinking water. Currently desalination of salt water is expensive and energy intensive. Only 1 per cent of all freshwater is obtained this way. However, with increasing water scarcity and climate change, this is likely to change in the future.
4. An ocean current is the movement of water in oceans from one location to another. These are driven by tides, wind and thermohaline circulation.
5. a) A gyre is a circular system of ocean currents rotating clockwise in the northern hemisphere and anticlockwise in the southern hemisphere.
   b) Thermohaline circulation is the oceanic circulation system driven by variation in ocean temperature and salinity.
   c) Upwelling is a process in which deep, cold, nutrient-rich water rises towards the surface.
6. Upwelling causes nutrient-rich water to rise to the surface. This stimulates food chains and webs leading to higher biodiversity in the regions where this occurs. This is particularly the case on the west coast of South America where upwelling leads to the abundance of Peruvian anchoveta – which in turn has led to one of the largest fishing industries on the planet.
7. The oceans do not have uniform temperature and salinity, so when the warm water reaches polar regions, it cools, becomes saltier and more dense, and then sinks down. These cold, deep water currents move along the seabed back towards the equator. The

warm and cold ocean currents combine to create a massive global conveyor belt of water. It is estimated that water takes 1000 years to complete one whole circuit around the conveyor.

8. The highest concentrations of marine biodiversity are found in the warmer shallower waters of the Western Pacific Ocean and around the Philippines, Borneo and northern Australia. There are also concentrations of biodiversity around island chains in the Pacific and Indian Oceans. Areas of the continental shelf also have higher concentrations of biodiversity. Lower diversity of marine species is found in the centre of ocean current gyres and in colder water at the North and South Pole.
9. Ocean currents move the surface water and create areas of upwelling off the coast. The combination of nutrient-rich water and surface movements encourages the development of food webs. Smaller fish are attracted in huge numbers to the nutrients. This in turn attracts larger predatory fish and marine mammals.
10. Areas of upwelling appear to occur on continental margins where the water is shallow. The upwelling is linked to the movement of surface currents that pull up cold, nutrient-rich water, which attracts concentrations of marine species. An example of this is off the coast of Peru in the eastern Pacific Ocean.
11. ENSO is a climate phenomenon that causes a reversal of surface winds and ocean currents in the eastern Pacific Ocean. In an El Niño year, the easterly trade wind weakens and the warmer water of the western Pacific Ocean moves eastwards. This causes sea levels to rise on the Pacific coast of South America. ENSO changes weather patterns – causing drought in the western Pacific region and East Asia and flooding in South America.
12. When El Niño occurs, the warm water of the western Pacific Ocean moves east. The arrival of the water means that upwelling normally caused by easterly trade winds will stop.
13. The impact of ENSO on the west coast of South America:

Environmental	**Economic**	**Social**
The warming of the eastern Pacific Ocean means the cold Humboldt current that moves up the coast of South America is overwhelmed by the warm ocean current. The sea temperatures become between 4 °C and 8 °C warmer than normal. This reduces the upwelling of cold water, which reduces the productivity of the ecosystems and causes fish to reproduce in fewer numbers or migrate elsewhere.	The loss of fish has a devastating effect on the economies of countries along the coast. There have been a number of occasions where overfishing off the coast of Peru during an El Niño event has caused fish stocks of Peruvian anchoveta to completely collapse – with reduction in the catch of up to 80 per cent. In Peru, an El Niño year often reduces gross national income by 5 per cent.	The economic downturn has significant impacts on coastal communities. Food supplies are threatened. People have reduced income so cannot afford education and healthcare. Some fishermen cannot afford to pay loans so have to sell boats and migrate toward larger urban areas.

14. Overfishing occurs when more fish are caught than the population can replace through natural reproduction. When fish are caught using certain commercial techniques, there are significant numbers of unwanted fish and other marine creatures trapped by the nets. These are often discarded dead back into the sea. This is a significant environmental management challenge as it is putting marine species under significant pressure. There has been a 39 per cent decline in marine catches between 1970 and 2010, with overfishing and bycatch the primary cause.
15. Overfishing occurs when more fish are taken from the ocean than the species can cope with. When the young smaller fish are taken, the species numbers can collapse quickly. When this occurs it is described as being fished beyond its maximum sustainable yield. There are many causes:

a) catching of vulnerable species
b) destructive fishing methods
c) unselective fishing methods that create wasteful bycatch
d) illegal or pirate fishing
e) overcapacity of the global fishing fleet
f) a lack of management
g) ever-larger fishing vessels using technology to find fish

16. Overfishing is having a devastating impact on global fish stocks, with 28.8 per cent of fish stocks fished at a biologically unsustainable level and 61.3 per cent of fish stocks fished at capacity with no room for further growth in production. The 10 most productive species are either fully fished or overfished.
17. Banning certain fishing nets, such as drift nets, is an effective way of reducing bycatch. Scientists are also looking at ways of using known fish behaviours to design fishing nets that reduce bycatch. Some nets use separators to allow certain species to escape, whereas other designs include diamond shaped panels at parts of the net that allow smaller fish to swim out. This allows the non-target or smaller species to escape.
18. The European Union has been using quotas to manage fish stocks for many years. The combined governments of the EU member states have agreed to strict limits being placed on the total allowable catches of certain species – usually a number of tonnes of a certain species from a certain region, for example, North Sea cod. These quotas reduce the number of fish caught and ban the catching of other endangered species. By limiting catches, more fish are left to breed, allowing the population to slowly recover. However, the quotas have some undesired effects. Sometimes fishermen catch many more fish than the quota allows, so select the most valuable sized fish, discarding the rest of the dead fish into the sea. Furthermore, fishing vessels might catch fish that are not the target species and that might have already reached the quota placed on numbers. Fishing vessels are forced to discard perfectly good fish to avoid fines. The quota system sometimes means that vessels sit in port, being paid not to fish.
In contrast to the EU, the government of Mozambique in Africa has enforced a closed season where fishing of certain species is

banned at key times of year. This allows fish species to be protected during the breeding season. Shallow water shrimp in Mozambique are now protected for 5 months each year.

19. Marine protected areas (MPAs) are a key part of the sustainable environmental management of fisheries. These areas ban the removal of any resources, including fish, as well restrict movement of shipping. However, illegal fishing does take place and enforcement requires innovative monitoring and use of GIS. Networks of MPAs are growing globally in response to overfishing and degrading of the marine environment through pollution. The Phoenix Islands Protected Area has been successful at reducing fishing around the islands. This has been effectively monitored by Global Fishing Watch. Since the designation as a MPA, there has been an almost total lack of fishing boat traffic in the area, allowing fish stocks to recover and spill over into surrounding areas.
20.

Advantages of salmon farming in Scotland	Disadvantages of salmon farming in Scotland
• Employment is generated in coastal aquaculture areas, creating 1700 jobs in Scotland. • Large profits stimulate the local economy – often rural areas that suffer a lack of investment. The industry was worth US$1 billion in 2014. • Controlled water quality and protection against predators ensures stocks survive. • Regular feeding and selective breeding can lead to more rapid growth than wild fisheries.	• Every 1kg of salmon produced requires on average two to three times their weight of wild-caught fish. • Waste from fish cages is deposited on the seafloor causing seafloor pollution and a reduction in water quality – if unmanaged. This can impact on sensitive habitats and species in polluted areas. • Salmon are more closely packed than in the wild, so diseases can spread more easily. • Open water systems can lead to fish escapes and interaction with endangered wild species.

21. Answers will vary depending on students' choice of topic and investigative focus. See Section 5 of the Student's Book and the supplementary case studies in the Teacher's Guide for more information. See also www.collins.co.uk/EnvMgmtIGCSE

6 Managing natural hazards: answers to Student's Book questions (pages 254-256)

1. The layers of the Earth can be divided into the crust, mantle and core. The crust is the outermost layer of the Earth and is solid. It varies in thickness from 5 km to 70 km and can be classified as oceanic or continental crust.
2. Earthquakes are found on plate boundaries around the world. They are concentrated in narrow bands around the Pacific Ocean, in the centre of the Atlantic and Indian Oceans as well between Africa and Europe and where India meets Asia.
3. Volcanoes are distributed around constructive and destructive plate boundaries. They are most common around the Pacific Rim, which is known as the 'ring of fire'.
4. At destructive plate boundaries, dense oceanic crust is subducted below the lighter but thicker continental plate. As it subducts, it melts, causing magma to rise to the surface and volcanoes form. At constructive plate boundaries, the crust pulls apart, forming new land. As the crust separates, magma can escape to form volcanoes.
5. See Figure 6.4 and 6.5 in the Student's Book.
6. Some volcanoes are found away from plate boundaries. They form above hot spots, where super-heated plumes of magma rise up through the mantle towards the crust. The magma forces its way through the crust to form volcanic features. The Hawaiian island chain is an example of this type of volcanic activity.
7. Over the next 50 million years, continental drift will continue to change the relative positions for the continents. Using current movements, it is possible to predict what the world will look like in 50 million years. The Atlantic Ocean will continue to grow, moving Europe and Africa further away from North and South America. Africa will move northward and close the Mediterranean Sea, colliding and folding up southern Europe into a new mountain range. Australia will drift north and collide with Papua New Guinea forming a new landmass. Antarctica will move further north and warm up.
8. An earthquake is a sudden violent shaking of the ground as a result of movements within the Earth's crust.
9. a) Focus – the point within the Earth's crust where an earthquake originates.
   b) Epicentre – the point on the Earth's surface directly above where an earthquake occurs.
   c) Magnitude – the strength of an earthquake.
10. Factors affecting earthquake impact:
    - the depth of the earthquake foci
    - the geology of the area – soft sedimentary rocks will vibrate more
    - the size or magnitude of the earthquake
    - the level of vulnerability of the population (wealth, building regulations, education, preparedness, emergency responses)
11. Earthquakes are measured either by their strength (magnitude) or by the intensity of the shaking felt.
12. The impact of an earthquake is directly influenced by the geological factors listed above. For example, a deep 7.0 magnitude earthquake under strong and stable rock will cause less damage than a very shallow 6.0 magnitude under soft sedimentary rocks – despite being 10 times less powerful. The level of vulnerability of the population and their capacity to cope will play a significant role in determining the scale of a disaster.
13. See supplementary case study on pages 106-107 of the Teacher's Guide.
14. Volcanoes are described as still active and erupting frequently, dormant (temporarily inactive but not fully extinct) or extinct (never likely to erupt again).
15. The size, shape and effects of an eruption depend on the viscosity of the lava that formed the volcano. Runny lava will form wider shield volcanoes such as Mauna Loa, Hawaii. Thicker, more viscous lava will build up a lava dome, or if combined with layers of ash, will form a stratovolcano.
16. See Figure 6.11 in the Student's Book.

17. A shield volcano is wider and flatter due to being formed by less viscous lava, whereas a stratovolcano is made of layers of lava and ash from more viscous lava, forming steeper and higher sides.
18. The strength of a volcanic eruption is measured on the Volcanic Explosivity Index (VEI) – an 8 point scale where each higher number is 10 times greater than the last. A VEI of 6 occurs every 50–100 years; an 8 occurs approximately every 50 000 years.
19. There is a range of different examples that students could use for this question – Mt St Helens, Mt Pinatubo, Mt Merapi or Eyjafjallajökull. The impact on people and the environment will depend upon the example used. Typical impacts are:
    - ash fall
    - disruption of air travel
    - lahars or mud flows
    - pyroclastic flows
    - trees knocked down
    - lava flows
    - short-term agricultural disruption due to ash fall
    - damage to property and risk to people
20. Earthquake risk can be reduced before the event by:
    - monitoring fault lines using lasers and satellite technology to see if there is an increase in strain
    - mapping faults accurately and looking at evidence of historical earthquakes
    - detecting radon gas (which is sometimes given off before earthquakes)
    - implementing rigorous building codes, so new buildings are fitted with earthquake-proof designs
    - retrofitting old buildings to reduce the damage in earthquakes
    - educating the population about how to prepare for and act in an earthquake
    - conducting large-scale earthquake drills with emergency services
    - ensuring that local governments have detailed emergency management plans.
21. Lower income countries will have lower levels of preparedness, less stringent building codes and lower levels of education. These factors increase the vulnerability of the local population to earthquakes. This often means damage is greater and requires a greater immediate response to help people. The lack of preparedness will then further exacerbate the disaster as people will be unable to be rescued or have food, shelter and health care in the immediate aftermath.
22. The risk from volcanoes can be reduced, but not eliminated completely by:
    - developing evacuation plans based on historical ash records
    - monitoring volcanoes from space as well as locally using tiltmeters that look at their shape
    - using seismometers to detect movements in magma below the surface
    - monitoring gas levels
    - predicting the likely ash fall – leading to hazard risk maps
    - evacuating people from areas likely to be hit by pyroclastic flows or lahars
    - educating local people about how to react if a volcano does erupt
    - building volcano shelters
23. Mt Merapi is the most active volcano in Indonesia – erupting every two to three years. Over 1 million people live within a 10-km radius. Hundreds have died in eruptions since 1990, with pyroclastic flows travelling down the volcano flanks at 240 km/h. A number of steps have been taken to reduce the risk to local people:
    i. setting up evacuation centres, which include room for livestock
    ii. resettling people to safer locations
    iii. setting up government funds to help farmers replace livestock
    iv. developing a volcano hazard map
    v. education of local people on warning signs
24. The Caribbean island of Montserrat suffered a series of large volcanic eruptions from the Soufrière Hills volcano from 1995–1997. The ash fall and pyroclastic flows devastating the then capital city, New Plymouth, caused a complete evacuation of the southern part of the island. Detailed hazard risk maps were issued, which controlled movement of people on the island. This was an effective technique as it allowed scientists to monitor the volcanic activity knowing that the local population were out of harm's way in the far north of the island. People were able to build new houses in the north or choose to leave the island. With a highly effective monitoring system in place, the local population that remain are less at risk than before.
25. a) Tropical cyclone – an intense spinning storm with high winds and torrential rain around a calm centre (the eye). At a certain point of intensity, it becomes a cyclone or hurricane.
    b) Storm surge – a significant increase in sea level due to sudden, very low air pressure and strong winds associated with storms.
    c) Coriolis effect – the effect that the rotation of the Earth has on moving objects such as tropical storms.
26. Tropical cyclones are formed in narrow belts between 5° and 20° north and south of the equator. They are more common in the North Atlantic Ocean and the west of the Pacific Ocean.
27. Tropical cyclones form over warm tropical water where the surface temperature is at least 27 °C and ocean depth of at least 60 m. Powerful convection of warm moist air occurs over the warm water. This rises, cools, condenses and forms storm clouds. Fuelled by the ocean temperatures, the storm grows and begins to rotate due to the Coriolis effect. The tropical disturbance turns first to a tropical depression, then storm, then a tropical cyclone.
28. Tropical cyclones are measured according to the strength of the sustained windspeed using the Saffir-Simpson scale.
29. A category 1 tropical cyclone on the Saffir-Simpson scale will have a sustained wind speed of between 119 and 153 km/h and come with a storm surge of 1.2–1.5 metres. They will cause damage to poorly constructed buildings and mobile homes as well as bring down power lines and cause coastal flooding. In contrast, a category 5 tropical cyclone on the Saffir-Simpson scale will have a sustained wind speed of 252 km/h or higher and an associated storm surge of over 5 metres. It will cause catastrophic damage to infrastructure and severe inland flooding. The area will be uninhabitable for some time and there is likely to be loss of life.
30. This response depends on the example chosen. The Student's Book uses Typhoon Haiyan, which hit the Philippines in 2013. There are other examples worth noting as case studies to investigate: Cyclone Nargis, Hurricane Katrina, Hurricane Sandy.

31. a) Precipitation – water deposited on the Earth's surface in a range of forms such as rain, hail, snow, sleet and dew.
    b) Infiltration – the downward movement of water through the soil and into the rock layer below.
    c) Interception – water that is caught and stored by vegetation.
    d) Surface run-off – the movement of water over the ground surface following precipitation – also known as overland flow.
32. See Figure 6.27 in the Student's Book.
33. Factors affecting flooding risk:
    - **Weather** – Rain that falls for a prolonged period can cause the soil to become saturated. Any further rainfall will not be absorbed into the soil and instead will run off the surface rapidly – increasing flood risk. Flooding can occur when very heavy rain falls – even in short bursts. Sometimes water will not even flow into rivers, but instead will accumulate and cause flooding away from rivers. Heavy rain can also cause rapid surface run-off, which causes rivers to burst their banks.
    - **Geology** – In some places, the underlying geology is permeable – which means water can pass through the rocks. However, in places where the underlying rock is impermeable, water cannot pass through, which leads to the soil above becoming saturated more quickly – increasing flood risk.
    - **Relief** – The height and shape of the land is an important factor in determining how water behaves when it falls as precipitation. Steep slopes lead to faster surface run-off, whereas gentle slopes allow water the time to infiltrate and enter rivers more slowly. When floods occur, flat land will allow floodwater to spread easily from the river across the floodplain.
    - **Urbanisation** – Urban areas are full of impermeable concrete and tarmac areas. Furthermore, roofs catch rainwater and efficiently channel it to drain systems below. Growth of urban areas can also lead to river channel modification. Combined, these factors can lead to a rapid increase in the speed at which water enters rivers. Unrestricted building on flood plains will further increase the risk from flooding.
34. See pages 160-161 of the Student's Book.
35. There are many strategies that can be used to reduce the risk of flooding before it occurs:
    - developing flood risk maps
    - examine historical floods to establish the recurrence interval
    - use storm hydrographs to predict how a river will respond to changes in input
    - flood proof housing – and ensure insurance is taken out
    - use land-use zoning
    - build flood defences such as:
        - hard engineering – building dams, levees, flood-relief channels, concrete embankments, control gates
        - soft engineering – planting trees, preserving marshland and wetlands, controlled flooding
36. When establishing whether a place should be protected by flood defences, local planners will conduct a cost benefit analysis to measure the cost of the defences against the cost of the property protected. They will examine the probability of floods of a certain size occurring and the frequency. Engineers will consider the impact the defences will have downstream as well as on the natural operation of the systems in the river.
37. Evaluation of flood defences:

Type of flood defence	Evaluation
Dams	• Expensive to build and disruptive to river systems. • Effective at controlling river flow downstream and reducing flooding. • Can be multipurpose schemes to generate power and provide freshwater and recreation activities.
Afforestation	• A natural solution – trees intercept rainfall and slow surface run-off. • The newly-forested areas provide habitat for animals and absorb CO_2. • Often needs to be done as part of a larger scheme.
Levees	• These walls protect surrounding areas from flooding. • The raised water level poses a significant risk if the levees break. • The levees interrupt a natural system, increasing the speed of the river and increasing the risk of flooding downstream.
Flood relief channels	• Expensive to construct, these channels give the river space to expand into if there is a flood. • They divert water away from urban areas and allow the channels to flood, taking pressure from the main channel. • They can provide new habitats and leisure opportunities.
Controlled flooding	• Rivers that have dams are sometimes flooded deliberately in a controlled way. This can be to reduce the pressure on the dam if it is filling up, or to mimic the natural benefits a small flood can have on natural flood plains. • Sometimes levees are deliberately breached to sacrifice certain areas to the flood water, in order to protect a more valuable urban area.

38. Causes of drought:

Physical causes of drought	Human causes of drought
• Weather patterns • Climate change • El Niño • Local climatic factors	• Poor farming practices • Over abstraction of water • Deforestation • War and conflict

39. As with other natural hazards, the impact of a drought will vary significantly depending upon the level of vulnerability of the population affected, as well as the capacity of the region to cope with the effects. For example, drought in the UK might inconvenience people as the water authorities restrict use of hosepipes, whereas drought in Sudan will cause crops to fail and famine, which can lead to mass migration and conflict.
40. Desertification is the degrading of land through soil erosion in dryland areas to such an extent that the environment comes to resemble a desert.
41. Areas that experience frequent drought can reduce the risk by:
    - forecasting drought in advance and issuing warnings
    - transferring water from other parts of a country
    - developing desalination
    - exploiting unused groundwater in aquifers
    - working to reduce water consumption on an ongoing basis through education
    - building up food supplies to cope with a possible famine
42. Natural hazards such as volcanoes provide opportunities for:
    - farming the fertile soils
    - mining the minerals
    - tourism
43. Batur in Indonesia provides a range of opportunities for local people, who despite the risk, live nearby the active volcano. The volcano is a source of income for thousands of people on Bali who benefit from:
    - fertile volcanic soil for growing rice and many other crops
    - volcanic stone for construction
    - tourism opportunities
    - a volcanic lake that provides water to thousands of people
    - a lake for leisure and tourism opportunities
44. See case study on pages 170-172 of the Student's Book.
45. See case study on pages 173-175 of the Student's Book.
46. Answers will vary depending on students' choice of topic and investigative focus. See Section 6 of the Student's Book and the supplementary case studies in the Teacher's Guide for more information. See also www.collins.co.uk/EnvMgmtIGCSE

7 The atmosphere and human activities: answers to Student's Book questions (pages 257-259)

1. Key features of the atmosphere:

Name	Height	Temperature	Features
Troposphere	Surface to 8–14.5 km high	Decreases with height at 6.5 °C/km	Most dense part containing almost all atmospheric water vapour.
Stratosphere	14.5–50 km high	Stable, then increases with altitude from -50 °C to 0 °C	A zone of dry, thin air that is cold and clear. It contains the ozone layer.
Mesosphere	50–85 km high	Decreases with altitude to about -100 °C	The coldest layer of the atmosphere. Meteors burn up in this layer.
Thermosphere	85–600 km high	Rises continually up to 1000 °C	This layer is so thin, that although the air molecules are hot, to us it would be freezing. The ISS orbits in this layer.
Exosphere	600–10 000 km	Highly variable	This is the uppermost part of our atmosphere ,which merges into space. This is where many satellites orbit the Earth.

2. Almost all atmospheric water vapour and all weather is found in the troposphere. As it is the densest layer, it is also vital for life on Earth as this is where the oxygen we breathe is found.
3. The temperature of the atmosphere declines at a steady rate with altitude in the troposphere. At the start of the stratosphere, the temperature is steady before warming again back to 0 °C. As altitude increases to 50 km, temperature begins to decline. This is the start of the mesosphere. Temperature declines steadily until 85 km where it begins to rise again in the thermosphere.
4. The majority of the atmosphere is made up of nitrogen (78 per cent), oxygen (21 per cent) and argon (0.9 per cent). The rest is made up of trace gases such as carbon dioxide, ozone and methane.

5. Greenhouse gases such as water vapour, carbon dioxide, methane and ozone interact with incoming and outgoing solar radiation and warm the atmosphere.
6. Ozone in the atmosphere filters out parts of the incoming ultraviolet radiation from sunlight and protects plants, animals and humans from the damaging effects of the sun.
7. Greenhouse gases like carbon dioxide absorb energy from the sun – creating a natural greenhouse effect that warms the Earth's surface. This makes planet Earth habitable for life. Without this, the average temperature of the Earth's surface would be −18 °C, instead of today's average of 15 °C.
8. Atmospheric pollution is generally comprised of smog, acid rain, ozone depletion and greenhouse gas emissions.
9. London suffered from episodes of severe smog in the 1950s. This was caused by a combination of stable air conditions, low winds and excessive burning of coal. The suffocating mixture of smoke and fog led to 12 000 deaths over four days. The worst event in 1952 led to changes in the law, which banned the burning of coal in houses, and a shift toward other heating systems in houses. The UK government developed forecasts that could warn of likely problems and led to advice and warnings being issued.
10. Factors causing the build-up of atmospheric pollution in cities:
    a) Calm conditions: When there are low winds, air pollution from vehicle engines and factories will not blow away. Instead they will accumulate over the city and reduce air quality.
    b) High air pressure: This leads to stable air, low wind speeds and calm conditions. The air is descending – trapping any atmospheric pollution next to the surface.
    c) City in a valley surrounded by steep hills: Los Angeles lies in a flat coastal plain, surrounded by hills and the sea. This often leads to the build-up of smog as the pollution becomes trapped by the steep hills and sits over the city until there is a change in wind direction.
11. Acid rain is caused when atmospheric water mixes with sulfur dioxide and nitrogen oxide – emitted from thermal power stations, vehicle pollution and industry. These gases are converted into sulfuric and nitric acid, which can fall as rain.
12. Sulfur dioxide emissions shown on the proportional map are highest in the USA, China and Eastern Europe. They are lower in South Asia, Africa and South America. This is likely to be because the more developed industrial economies of the world will burn more coal for power generation and for use in industry. There is also more likely to be more vehicles on the roads and more air travel – both of which contribute to sulfur dioxide emissions.
13. Acid rain can cause significant damage to the environment through the acidification of water. The sulfuric and nitric acid damage ecosystems by harming the most sensitive species and destroying food chains. Acid rain also impacts on fish populations. It will cause fish eggs not to hatch and with increasing acidity will kill adult fish or their sources of food – reducing biodiversity.
14. The ozone layer is vital for life on Earth. Ozone is highly reactive and is constantly being formed and broken down, which leads to global variation each year in the amount of ozone present in the atmosphere. Ozone reacts and is broken down by chemicals such as chlorine – which has been released into the atmosphere in large quantities over time. A cause of ozone depletion is the use of chemicals called chlorofluorocarbons (CFCs). These were commonly found in aerosol cans and refrigerators used in high income countries in the past century. The CFCs react with sunlight and form chlorine, which destroys ozone.
15. Ozone depletion, smog and acid rain are often described as transboundary environmental issues – as they affect more than one nation. Managing these is complex as the source of the pollution may not be the country most adversely affected. This is the case with the Southeast Asian haze where uncontrolled burning in Indonesia is affecting air quality in Malaysia and Singapore. The Malaysian and Singaporean governments are unable to tackle the issue at source. Instead they rely upon pressure placed upon the Indonesian government to take action. Direct lawsuits have been launched by private individuals against the companies most responsible for the burning in attempts to prevent future clearing of the forests of Indonesia using slash and burn techniques. The same issues occur in dealing with acid rain, where the most polluting countries are responsible for acid rain across the border of other nations. Intergovernmental agreement is at its most difficult where global agreement is required, for example, with ozone depletion where agreement on the global ban of CFCs was needed.
16. The natural greenhouse effect is vital in keeping the planet habitable. Greenhouse gases absorb incoming solar radiation, which warms the atmosphere. Sources of natural greenhouse gases include volcanic eruptions. The enhanced greenhouse effect refers to the addition of greenhouse gases from human activity into the atmosphere. The release of carbon that was 'locked' away in rocks over millions of years in the course of 200 years of human history has led to a significant elevation of carbon dioxide levels in the atmosphere – well above any natural level attained in the past 650 000 years. These elevated levels are enhancing the natural greenhouse effect, warming the atmosphere and causing climate patterns to change.
17. Since 1880, there has been a rise in CO_2 concentration from 290 ppm to around 385 ppm by 2009. The rate of increase has accelerated since 1980. This is likely to be because of an increase in demand for and consumption of fossil fuels associated with increasing levels of wealth and technological development. There are also now a greater number of people on the planet who are demanding more energy. The acceleration in the availability of cheap air travel and the globalisation of food supplies and industrial production has further contributed to the rate of acceleration.
18. Carbon dioxide and methane are greenhouse gases. They absorb the incoming solar radiation. As the levels of greenhouse gases in the atmosphere increase, the level of absorption will increase, leading to a warming of the atmosphere, which in turn will increase surface temperatures.

19. Projected impacts of climate change:

<table>
<tr><th></th><th colspan="3">Projected rise in temperature:</th></tr>
<tr><th>Potential impact on:</th><th>1 °C</th><th>3 °C</th><th>5 °C</th></tr>
<tr><td>Water</td><td>1 billion with increased water stress.</td><td colspan="2">1.1–3.2 billion with increased water stress.</td></tr>
<tr><td>Ecosystems</td><td>Amphibian extinction, coral bleaching.</td><td>20–30 per cent of species at risk of extinction.</td><td>Extinction of major species around the world.</td></tr>
<tr><td>Food</td><td colspan="2">Decreased crop productivity in low latitudes; some increases at higher latitudes.</td><td>All cereals decrease in lower latitudes.</td></tr>
<tr><td>Coasts</td><td>Increased damage from floods and storms; up to 3 million at risk of coastal flooding.</td><td colspan="2">30 per cent loss of coastal wetlands; 2–15 million people at risk of coastal flooding.</td></tr>
<tr><td>Health</td><td>Increase in risk from heatwave, drought, floods and malnutrition.</td><td colspan="2">Substantial burden on health services.</td></tr>
<tr><td>Events</td><td>Local retreat of ice in Greenland and Antarctica.</td><td>Long-term commitment to several metres of sea level rise, weakening of global ocean current conveyor.</td><td>Low lying coastal areas inundated.</td></tr>
</table>

20. The global nature of climate change means that some countries are more likely to feel the adverse effects first, or are more likely to suffer due to the existing level of vulnerability and low capacity to cope. For example, low lying coastal areas or small islands are most likely to suffer from the early stages of a rise in sea levels. This issue will take some time to affect other areas in the same way. Equally, the retreat of glaciers in the Himalayas or Andes is more likely to affect water supplies in the countries dependent on glacier melt for their water. Countries such as India and Peru will be more worried about this than other higher income countries who may be able to adapt to changing conditions.
21. Managing atmospheric pollution requires action from government and individuals to reduce carbon footprints, reduce use of fossil fuels and increase energy efficiency. These can be achieved by:
    - Using public transport
    - Flying less
    - Using less energy and switching sources – installing solar panels
    - Eating more locally produced food
    - Switching to more renewable energy sources to adjust the energy mix
    - Installing smart meters
    - Switching off electrical appliances
22. See case study on pages 191-192 of the Student's Book.
23. Palm oil is often an invisible ingredient in many of the products we consume. The West African oil palm tree is highly productive and is used in plantations in tropical areas around the world. The fruit is processed and turned into vegetable oil. Palm oil is the cheapest form of vegetable oil and growing plantations of trees is highly lucrative for some groups. The tropical and subtropical climates of South and Southeast Asia are perfect for growing these plantations. Tropical rainforests are cleared, then burnt to remove the remaining vegetation. These areas are then planted with palm oil. The growth in the use of palm oil is directly responsible for large-scale deforestation of tropical forests.
24. This question provides an opportunity to engage with a complex argument. It is without doubt that deforestation and burning of tropical forests in Indonesia causes the haze issue in Southeast Asia. The majority of the deforestation is driven by palm oil production so it stands to reason that the demand for palm oil is driving the deforestation. However, the degree to which consumers of palm oil products are responsible for the deforestation and haze is open to debate. The key part of the question is the command words – to what extent. It can be argued that the responsibility lies with the Indonesian government or the farmers. However, it could also be argued that multinational companies are equally to blame as they source unsustainable and cheap palm oil. Further to this, they might look at the role of consumers in taking a stand against the use of palm oil derived from tropical areas.
25. Answers will vary depending on students' choice of topic and investigative focus. See Section 7 of the Student's Book and the supplementary case studies in the Teacher's Guide for more information. See also www.collins.co.uk/EnvMgmtIGCSE

8 Human population: answers to Student's Book questions (pages 260-262)

1. Population distribution – the way in which a population is spread out over an area.
   Population density – the average number of people living in a 1 sq km area.
2. Overpopulation occurs when the resource demands of people living in an area, particularly for food, exceed the capacity of the environment to provide for them. This is sometimes referred to as the number of people exceeding the carrying capacity of the environment.

3.

Factor	Influence on distribution and density
Climate	People are attracted to temperate areas with mild temperatures and evenly distributed rainfall, which offers greater opportunities for farming than areas with more extreme weather patterns.
Relief	Flat, lower-lying and gently-undulating landscapes attract because they are easier to settle, farm and to construct transport links. Higher, steeper, colder more rugged land with thin acidic soils is generally avoided.
Soils	Places with deeper, more fertile soils often have higher population densities because farming is more productive than locations with shallow and infertile soils where fewer people can be supported.
Natural resources	Locations with rich naturally-occurring materials, for example, minerals, forests and water, which boost economic activity, attract, whilst places with little to exploit commercially tend to be avoided.
Accessibility	Areas that are easily reached such as river valleys or coastal locations tend to have higher concentrations of people than more remote and inaccessible inland areas.
Vegetation	Areas with dense or potentially hazardous vegetation generally have fewer people than more open grassland areas where the environment is more easily managed.

4. The factor is communications or accessibility. Manufacturing industry and services are attracted to places with very good transport links such as road and railway networks and air and sea routes. Such high accessibility levels reduce their transport costs. In turn, people are attracted to industrial areas because of the employment prospects and the opportunity to improve their own life chances. As a result, areas of dense population density can arise as towns and cities grow adjacent to industrial areas.
5. Population density tends to be highest along the southern and western coastlines of the four most southerly islands. Population density is lowest in the most northerly island. Generally, the northern coastline is less densely populated than the southern coastline. Much of the central area of the largest island has a lower population density compared with the southern coastline. This is because most of this area is mountains with a very cold climate, poor soils and very little flat land. Farming is hard and building roads and railways difficult. Industry is not attracted here. As a result, it is not an attractive place to live. In comparison the coastal plain to the south has a milder climate, less rain and some flat land. Farming is easier and industries have set up here because roads and railways and ports have been built along the coast. The availability of jobs has attracted millions of people who live at high density in huge cities such as Kawasaki.
6. In the first or lag phase the population grows slowly but in the second or log stage the population growth rate is exponential or constantly expanding. This is because the population is able to take advantage of unlimited resources such as food and water in the environment it inhabits. The S phase sees population growth slow as the availability of resources to support the population become more limited or scarce. A fourth or stable phase is reached when the size of the population matches the carrying capacity of the environment to support it. Carrying capacity means the maximum number that the resources of the environment can sustain. Lastly the decline stage is reached when population growth exceeds the carrying capacity of the environment, which can lead to a sudden catastrophic crash in numbers when events such as famines occur.
7. The maximum number of species of living things that the resources of an environment can support.
8. a) population – the persons inhabiting a specified area
   b) birth rate – the average number of live births in a year per 1000 people
   c) death rate – the average number of deaths in a year per 1000 people
   d) natural increase/decrease – the rise or fall in a population calculated by subtracting the death rate from the birth rate
9. 7.8 per 1000 people per year
10. -1.5 per 1000 people per year
11. Infant mortality rate – the proportion of children dying at birth or before their first birthday per 1000 live births.
    Life expectancy – the average number of years that a newborn is expected to live.
12. The two most important factors affecting the birth rate are infant mortality and life expectancy at birth. When infant mortality is high and life expectancy low, the birth rate will tend to be high. This is because many women will have more children in a situation where a high proportion may die at a young age because of disease, poor health care and inadequate sanitary conditions. Good health care (like that shown in the photograph) is one factor that will reduce infant mortality and increase life expectancy. As a result, the birth rate will tend to drop as fewer children die at a young age and most people in the country live longer lives than before.
13. a) Diets and levels of nutrition – Eating a well-balanced and nutritious diet on a regular basis from a young age will contribute to lowering death rates in a country, particularly amongst children and women of child-bearing age. Poor nutrition or malnutrition will make people, particularly children, much more vulnerable to contracting life threatening diseases.
    b) The availability of clean drinking water – Access to an improved supply of freshwater that is safe for drinking and cooking will be a factor reducing the death rate whilst unsafe supplies that carry water-borne diseases such as malaria and cholera will contribute to raising the death rate amongst people in a country.
    c) The quality of sanitation and hygiene – Improved sanitation is sewerage and household waste disposal that safely separates human faeces from human water supplies. Over 1 billion people in the world do not have access to improved sanitation. These people tend to live in the poorest countries such as those of Sub-Saharan Africa where death rates are high compared with MEDCs. The rate is high because a lack of sanitation means people are vulnerable to contracting water-borne diseases such as bilharzia.
    d) Age-sex structure and sex ratio – Death rates will tend to be lower in communities with a higher proportion of younger people than older dependents because on average, women tend to live longer than men. Death rates will often be higher in places with a sex ratio of more men than women than in communities consisting of greater numbers of women compared with men.

14. a) Migration – the movement of people from one place to live in another location.
    b) Immigration – the movement of people into a population, for example, into a country, having moved from somewhere else.
    c) Emigration – the movement of people away from a population to live somewhere else.
15. An anti-natalist policy is one that encourages couples to reduce the number of children they anticipate having compared with a pro-natalist policy, which governments sometime introduce in order to persuade young couples to have more children.
16. Because by then, the population of the country was growing by 18 million people every ten years and the government was worried that it would not be able to provide sufficient food, housing and public services for everyone in the future.
17. On the one hand, it offered incentives (things to persuade) for young couples to have only one child, such as free child care and priority for receiving a house or pension in the future. On the other hand, it put pressure on couples, like setting up family planning teams that checked all women were using contraceptives. It also influenced women to be sterilised after they had had one child.
18. Many couples who followed the one child policy felt it much more important to have a boy child rather than a girl. This is because in China, family lineage is traced through sons, and boy children continue the family name and are responsible for providing for their parents in old age. Because of this, some women had abortions when they discovered they were having a girl baby. Other parents deliberately abandoned girl children immediately after birth so that they could try again for a boy. This has meant that there are now many more adult males in China than adult women – about 118 men for every 100 women. This is gender imbalance. In the future, millions of men may never find a woman to marry and with whom to have children.
19. The population pyramid reveals that there are currently approximately twenty-four million people in France aged between 40 and 65 years. Most of these will be presently economically active, which means they are in employment and contributing to the tax base of the country. However, over the next forty years or so, all of these people will retire from work. Many will cease to pay income tax entirely, which the government relies upon to pay for social services such as pensions, hospitals and education. In contrast, there are only about sixteen million young dependents in France who will over the next twenty years or so become economically active when they join the workforce. This means that the dependency ratio (the number of old dependents aged over sixty-five per economically active member of the population aged 15-64) will be at least 1:1.5. With a greater proportion of old dependents compared to the economically active, the government is unlikely to raise enough tax to cover the increasing costs of public pensions, health care and social housing for the elderly. This may mean that income tax may have to rise, or social benefits, such as free public transport, for the elderly may be cut. The quality of life for many elderly people will fall.

9 Natural ecosystems and human activities: answers to Student's Book questions (pages 263-266)

1. The biotic element of an ecosystem is the community of living plant, animal and microorganism species, whereas the abiotic element refers to the non-living components such as rocks, soil and water.
2.

Biotic	Abiotic
plant	rainfall
bird	rock
snake	temperature
insect	light
fungus	wind

3. Because there is competition for resources such as food within an ecosystem, every living creature tends to adapt in particular ways to ensure that it can obtain what it requires to survive. As a result, each living organism comes to inhabit its own ecological niche within an ecosystem. This is the unique way in which it is adapted to living in a habitat, such as the food it eats or the times when it is active. For example, some organisms may only hunt at night whilst others may have skin colouring that conceals their presence within the habitat.
4. Every living creature requires food, which it obtains by eating other organisms within the habitat in which it lives. Because of this, every organism forms part of a food chain, which shows what occurs when individual living things eat each other to obtain the food they require to survive. There are five positions known as trophic levels within a food chain. At the first trophic level are producers. These are living things such as plants and algae that produce through photosynthesis the food compounds (such as glucose) on which all other living things depend. Animals that can't make their own food have to eat other animals to obtain the energy they require. These organisms are known as consumers and are found at the next trophic level of the food chain. Primary consumers are herbivores that feed on plant producers. They use aerobic respiration to release the energy from the plants they have consumed. Secondary consumers are carnivores or omnivores that eat primary consumers and also release the energy from the food they have consumed through respiration. At the very top of a food chain is normally a tertiary or apex consumer that eats both primary and secondary consumers and has no predators itself. All living things eventually die and within a food chain, decomposers, such as bacteria, fulfil the vital role of breaking down dead matter and recycling the nutrients that they contain.
5. A food chain suggests that all living things are consumed by just one predator and always occupy just one trophic level within an ecosystem. Nature is much more complex than this. A single living organism may be part of many food chains. For example, a rabbit will be part of the food chain of foxes, badgers, stoats, eagles and snakes. A food web shows these links between food chains and indicates much more accurately how everything living within a habitat is both interconnected and interdependent.
6. The graph is called an ecological pyramid of numbers. Each bar in the pyramid represents a different feeding level, starting with the producers at the base and ending with the apex consumer at the top. The width of each bar is drawn in proportion to the number of living things at each level.
7. Carbon dioxide in the atmosphere is converted through photosynthesis into carbon compounds like glucose by producers such as plants. Plants will consume some of these compounds through respiration to create the energy they need to stay alive. During respiration some of the fixed carbon returns to the atmosphere as carbon dioxide. The plants store the remaining carbon compounds they have 'fixed' from the atmosphere. In turn, primary and secondary consumers will obtain the energy they require from stored carbon compounds such as carbohydrates through respiration. At each trophic level, more carbon dioxide returns to the atmosphere as consumers process the stores of energy contained in the living things they eat. Finally, decomposers consume the remaining chemical compounds in dead organisms through respiration and release further amounts of carbon dioxide. In this

way, carbon is constantly being extracted from the atmosphere by producers and returned by way of respiration of consumers and decomposers.

8. The Atacama Desert is very hot during the day and sometimes very cold at night. As well as this, it receives very little rainfall during the year. As a result, living things have to cope with extreme conditions including rugged mountains, and the photograph shows virtually nothing growing in a landscape of mostly bare rock and sand. On the other hand, North Island in New Zealand clearly has a more moderate climate, more rain, low rounded hills and soils in which plants are able to grow. Because abiotic conditions in the Atacama Desert are so extreme you would expect to find less variety of living things here than in North Island and also they will have to be adapted to cope with the heat and drought.
9. Adaptation describes the different ways in which living things have evolved or changed to help them survive better in the habitat in which they live. As a result, every organism comes to occupy a special ecological niche within the habitat. The Atlantic walrus is likely to have thick skin or blubber to protect it from freezing temperatures in the water and in the wind when out on the ice. The tree in Ecuador has wide roots at its base to help it remain upright and balanced. Perhaps the soils are thin here and the tree quite tall. The cactus is living in a desert environment with little or no rain and therefore will store water to survive during long periods of drought. The Fennec fox has very large ears in proportion to the size of the rest of its body. This could be to help it hear the sounds and movements of smaller creatures that it eats, or perhaps to keep cool in hot environments such as deserts.
10. This kind of interaction is called predation as one living organism is eating another. Pollination is another example of interaction when pollen moves from one flower to another, which leads to fertilisation and the production of seeds. Mutualism, in which two organisms both benefit from living together or in close proximity like oxpeckers and buffalos in parts of Africa, is also a type of interaction. When living things try to gain resources in short supply (such as males fighting over available females in the breeding season), this interaction is known as competition.
11. Biodiversity is the word used to describe the total number and variety of living things occupying a habitat, ecosystem or biosphere (the entire global ecosystem). Genes occur in the nucleus of cells and determine all of the characteristics of living things. A gene pool is another word for the set of genes required to replicate a species, which is passed on from one generation to the next.
12. Deforestation involves entirely felling and permanently destroying forests and woodlands. The main cause of deforestation in the world is the clearance of trees to make way for more farmland in order to feed more people. The world's population is expected to rise by three billion by 2100. Other important reasons include using timber as a resource for furniture and paper manufacture. Clearing forests to make way for huge surface mines, or the spread of towns and cities and building new roads and railways are also important reasons for deforestation.
13. All plants extract or 'fix' carbon dioxide from the atmosphere and through the process of photosynthesis, to create carbon compounds such as glucose and carbohydrates that they store. When trees are burnt, all of this stored carbon is released back into the atmosphere as carbon dioxide. Each year this totals at least one billion tonnes. Carbon dioxide, along with methane and nitrous oxide, is an important greenhouse gas. Once in the atmosphere, it helps to trap infrared radiation from the planet's surface, which is making the surface of the Earth warmer – perhaps by as much as 3 °C by 2100. This global warming is altering climate patterns in the world as well as causing the melting of glaciers and polar ice sheets.
14. Soil erosion is the washing or blowing away of topsoils by heavy rain or strong winds. Serious soil erosion can lead to the loss of all nutrients and eventually to desertification. This is where once fertile land with plants and trees comes to resemble a desert. Tree felling is a major cause of soil erosion because it removes the roots that hold the soil in place. Once the trees are gone, the soil is quickly blown or washed away. Farming practices such as overgrazing animals close to water holes, ploughing up and down hill slopes, which create channels for the rain to wash the soil away, and removing natural wind breaks like hedges, all contribute to soil erosion. Ploughing the soil in places that are too dry or have sandy soils can lead to serious disasters caused by soil erosion such as the Dust Bowl, which occurred in the southern United States in the 1930s.
15. Extreme soil erosion can lead to the process of desertification, where once fertile lands resemble deserts in that they become stripped of vegetation and almost all topsoil. As a result, almost nothing grows. Tree and plant roots help to bind the soil and keep it in place. When these are cut down by people, or farmers allow their herds of cattle or goats to overgraze places so that all the plants disappear, then no roots remain. As a result, the soil is blown or washed away by strong winds or heavy rainfall. The same thing can happen when people remove natural wind breaks that protect the soil, such as hedges or plough up and down hillsides rather than around them following contours.
16. Tree roots grow into soils and as they develop, they create a network that helps to hold the soil in place. Tree roots also help to stop the soil become too compact or dense. This is important because it means that rainwater will soak into the air pockets that the roots create within the soil, rather than just running off its surface, carrying particles with it. The foliage of trees also helps to protect the soil below from the impact of heavy raindrops that can break up and wash particles away.
17. Genes are found in every cell of plants and animals, and they determine the characteristics of living things such as the amount of meat on an animal or how much seed a plant will produce. These characteristics are passed on through reproduction from one generation to another. Human beings depend on plants and animals (and therefore their genes) in order to survive. In fact, people use over 40 000 species of plants and animals for food, medicines, building materials, clothes and energy. If a plant or animal becomes extinct, its genes are lost forever. It is essential therefore to make sure that genes are conserved for the future by not letting living organisms we already know about become extinct and also making sure we identify new genes in organisms that have yet to be discovered.
18. Ecotourists tend to travel only in small groups and ensure that their impact on the environment is as minimal as possible. For example, they may camp rather than stay in hotels and walk from one location to another rather than using vehicles. They tend to be interested in activities such as wildlife watching and visiting cultural sites in more remote and unspoilt places. They pay local travel companies and guides rather than foreign-owned companies for their holiday experiences, which means local communities benefit directly. Wherever possible, they use local shops and services to buy their food or to provide guides for excursions. Jobs are then created for local people that give them a strong reason for ensuring the environment and its wildlife is conserved for future generations. For this reason, ecotourism is sometimes described as a good example of sustainable development.
19. A quadrat consists of a square frame often subdivided into smaller internal squares. A common size is a square metre. It is laid over an area of living things in a habitat. An ecologist will then estimate the number, variety and spread of living things within it. Living things within quadrats tend only to be plants and slower moving animals such as snails. Once recorded, the ecologist will

then usually move the quadrat along a transect (a line between two points) and record the results for the next location. A line transect involves laying a measuring tape or rope with marked points along it across a habitat. All of the species of living things touching the tape or rope at given locations (such as intervals of five metres) are then recorded. Pooters are small jars used to collect insects in a habitat. It involves the ecologist sucking up the insects into the jar where they can then be studied, named and recorded. A pitfall trap is a small container that is mostly buried in the ground with its rim level with the surface. Insects and ground crawling animals that are passing fall in and cannot climb back out. Once trapped, they can be identified and recorded.

20. Sustainable development involves exploiting the resources of an ecosystem in a way that does no lasting damage to the habitat and ensures the long-term health and richness of all the living things within it. It is more about resource stewardship and the harvesting of raw materials that will then regenerate themselves. Forests can be exploited sustainably through forestry that ensures that as trees are felled, they are replaced with seedlings and areas with particularly rare or rich biodiversity are avoided altogether. Ecotourism is another example of how a forest resource can be exploited sustainably. Tourists may pay to wildlife watch, camp or hike but leave no negative impact on the forest ecosystem.

21. The water cycle describes the constant movement or 'cycling' of water vapour from the oceans and vegetation of the world to the atmosphere and then back again by way of condensation, rainfall and run-off and collection by rivers. About 10 per cent of water vapour rising up into the atmosphere originates from plants and trees. During photosynthesis, plants and trees release water vapour through small pores called stomata on their stems and the underside of their leaves. This is known as transpiration. This water vapour then rises into the atmosphere where it condenses to form clouds and raindrops, which fall back to Earth to be taken up once again by plants and trees.

22. About 20 000 sq km of tropical forest are being destroyed on the island of Borneo each year. It has lost over half of its forest cover since the 1970s. Clearing the land to make way for agro-industrial crops, particularly palm oil plantations, is the main cause of forest loss. Deforestation is also being caused as new farmland is created to grow maize and rice for a fast-growing population in Indonesia. Over half of the world's tropical timber comes from Borneo, so logging by commercial companies and illegal traders is another important cause of tree loss. The most serious effect of deforestation has been the rapid drop in biodiversity on the island, and today, dozens of species such as the clouded leopard and orang-utan are critically endangered. In addition to this, deforestation is releasing millions of tonnes of stored carbon into the atmosphere as carbon dioxide as the trees are burned. This is contributing to global warming and changes in weather patterns around the world associated with climate change. The removal of trees is causing soil erosion that is silting up rivers and causing serious flooding, which is threatening the traditional water supplies and ways of life such as fishing of the indigenous Penang people.

23. a)

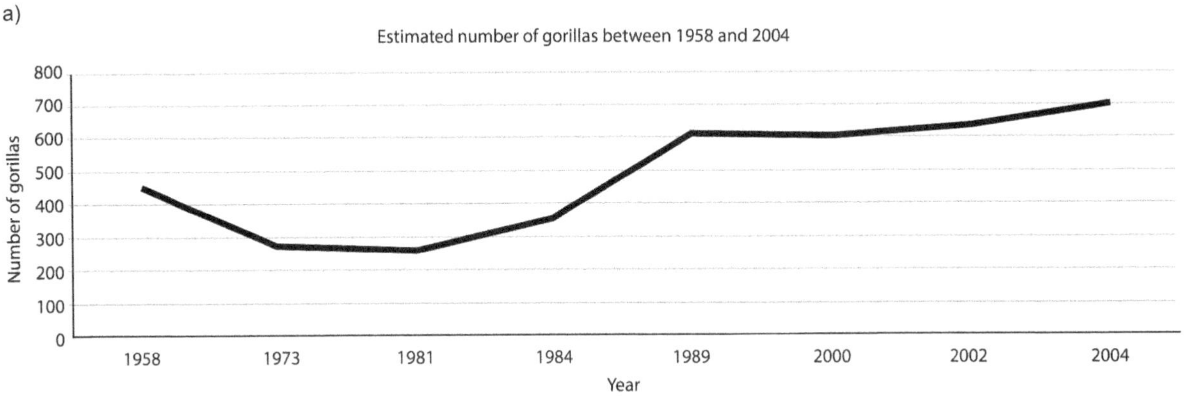

b) 42.4%

c) Numbers of mountain gorillas in countries such as Rwanda have been massively reduced in the last hundred years for a number of reasons. The loss of their forest habitat as more land is cleared for farming has caused the gorillas to be split up into fragmented groups that can no longer contact each other. This has led to inbreeding and offspring that find it very hard to adapt to environmental changes around them. Many gorillas are killed each year as they move across the farmland that separates the pockets of forest in which they live. Gorillas are also hunted for trophies like their heads, and many young animals are captured for the pet trade. Other gorillas die because they contract common human diseases such as the flu – spread by people visiting the forest – against which they have no immunity. Over twenty years of war in central Africa has also contributed to the death of gorillas as they are killed by mines, or captured and sold to raise money for weapons.

d) 70.3%

e) This increase is a result of many international organisations and governments working together on successful conservation measures. These have included increasing the number of anti-poaching patrols in the forest, removing snares that have been laid to catch other animals such as deer that also injure and kill gorillas, replanting trees and increasing the area of protected forest. A lot of work has also been done with local communities, such as education programmes in schools and supporting people to set up their own ecotourism businesses. This has been an important way of giving local people a strong reason to protect the gorilla and its forest habitat as they earn money from organising visits of tourists to view them.

Syllabus delivery chart

Core topic	Learning objectives	Student's Book	Teacher's Guide
1 Rocks and minerals and their exploitation	**a) Formation of rocks**		
	• describe and interpret the rock cycle	pp. 11–12 (238)	p. 41
	• state and explain the formation and characteristics of named igneous, sedimentary and metamorphic rocks	pp. 10–11 (238)	
	b) Extraction of rocks and minerals from the Earth		
	• describe surface and subsurface mining methods of extracting rocks and minerals from the Earth	pp. 12–13 (238)	p. 7
	• discuss the factors that affect the decision to extract rocks and minerals	pp. 13–15 (239)	p. 7
	c) Impact of rock and mineral extraction		
	• describe and explain the environmental, economic and social impacts of rock and mineral extraction	pp. 15–18 (239)	pp. 8–9, 25, 159
	d) Managing the impact of rock and mineral extraction		
	• describe and evaluate strategies for restoring landscapes damaged by rock and mineral extraction	pp. 18–19 (239)	pp. 13–14
	e) Sustainable use of rocks and minerals		
	• define *sustainable resource* and *sustainable development*	p. 20	p. 10
	• describe and evaluate strategies for the sustainable use of rocks and minerals	pp. 20–21	p. 10
	f) Case study		
	• study the development, impact and management of a mine including land restoration after the mine has closed	pp. 21–23	pp. 13–14
2 Energy and the environment	**a) Fossil fuel formation**		
	• describe the formation of the fossil fuels: coal, oil and gas	pp. 28–30 (241)	
	b) Energy resources and the generation of electricity		
	• classify the following energy resources as non-renewable or renewable: fossil fuels, nuclear power, biofuels, geothermal power, hydro-electric power, tidal power, wave power, solar power, wind power	p. 31 (241)	pp. 6, 26–27, 47–48, 81
	• describe how each of these energy resources is used to generate electricity	pp. 32–36 (241)	
	• describe the environmental, economic and social advantages and disadvantages of each of these energy resources	pp. 32–36 (241)	pp. 26–27
	c) Energy demand		
	• describe and explain the factors affecting the demand for energy	pp. 36–38 (242)	pp. 6, 24, 26–27, 120, 139, 146
	d) Conservation and management of energy resources		
	• describe and explain strategies for the efficient management of energy resources	pp. 38–42 (242)	
	• research and development of new energy resources	pp. 41–42 (242)	pp. 28–30, 47–48, 81

	e) Impact of oil pollution		
	• describe the causes and impacts of oil pollution on marine and coastal ecosystems	pp. 42–44 (243)	p. 61
	f) Management of oil pollution		
	• discuss strategies for reducing oil spills in marine and coastal ecosystems	pp. 44–45 (243)	
	• discuss strategies for minimising the impacts of oil spills on the marine and coastal ecosystems	pp. 45–46 (243)	
	g) Case study		
	• study the impact and management of an oil pollution event	pp. 46–49 (243)	
3 Agriculture and the environment	**a) Soil composition**		
	• describe and explain the composition of soils	p. 54 (244)	pp. 5, 41, 49–50
	b) Soils for plant growth		
	• describe soils as a medium for plant growth	pp. 54–58 (244)	pp. 41, 49–50
	• describe the differences between a sandy and clay soil	pp. 57–58 (244)	p. 41
	c) Agriculture types		
	• describe the different types of agriculture	pp. 58–59 (245)	p. 61
	d) Increasing agricultural yields		
	• describe techniques used to increase agricultural yields	pp. 59–68 (245)	pp. 43–44, 100, 159
	e) Impact of agriculture		
	• describe and explain the impact of agricultural practices on the environment and people	pp. 68–70 (245)	pp. 45–46, 100, 159
	f) Causes and impacts of soil erosion		
	• describe the causes of soil erosion	p. 70 (245)	
	• describe and explain the impacts of soil erosion	pp. 70–72 (245)	pp. 5, 100, 120
	g) Managing soil erosion		
	• describe and explain strategies to reduce soil erosion	pp. 73–74 (246)	pp. 49–50
	h) Sustainable agriculture		
	• describe and explain strategies for sustainable agriculture	pp. 75–76 (246)	
	i) Case study		
	• Study an example where agriculture has had severe environmental consequences including soil erosion and strategies for the conservation of the soil	pp. 77–79 (246)	
4 Water and its management	**a) Global water distribution**		
	• describe the distribution of the Earth's water	p. 84 (247)	pp. 41, 61

	b) The water cycle		
	• describe and interpret the water cycle	pp. 84–85 (247)	p. 61
	c) Water supply		
	• describe the sources of fresh water used by people	pp. 86–89 (247)	pp. 5, 61
	d) Water usage		
	• describe the different ways in which fresh water can be used	pp. 90–92	
	e) Water quality and availability		
	• compare the availability of safe drinking water (potable water) in different parts of the world	pp. 92–96 (248)	pp. 41, 61, 63–65, 121
	f) Multipurpose dam projects		
	• describe and evaluate multipurpose dam projects	pp. 96–100 (248–249)	pp. 71–73
	g) Water pollution and its sources		
	• describe the sources of water pollution	pp. 100–103 (249)	pp. 66–68
	h) Impact of water pollution		
	• describe and explain the impact of pollution of fresh water on people and on the environment	pp. 100–103 (249)	pp. 61, 69–70
	i) Managing pollution of fresh water		
	• describe and explain strategies for improving water quality	pp. 104–107 (249)	
	j) Managing water-related disease		
	• describe the life cycle of the malaria parasite	pp. 107–108 (249)	
	• describe and evaluate strategies to control malaria	pp. 108–111 (249)	
	• describe strategies to control cholera	pp. 111–112 (249)	
	k) Case studies		
	• the impact of a named multipurpose dam scheme	pp. 112–114 (249)	pp. 71–73
	• the causes, impact and management of pollution in a named body of water	pp. 114–117 (250)	
5 Oceans and fisheries	**a) Oceans as a resource**		
	• outline the resource potential of the oceans	pp. 122–125 (251)	pp. 61, 81
	b) World fisheries		
	• distribution of major ocean currents	pp. 125–126 (251)	pp. 83–86
	• explain the distribution of major marine fish populations	pp. 127–128 (251–252)	
	• describe the El Niño Southern Oscillation (ENSO) phenomenon and its effects on fisheries along the Pacific coast of South America	pp. 128–129 (252)	p. 100

	c) Impact of exploitation of the oceans		
	• describe and explain the impact of exploitation of fisheries	pp. 130–132 (253)	
	• describe how farming of marine species reduces the exploitation of fisheries	p. 132 (253)	p. 81
	d) Management of the harvesting of marine species		
	• describe, explain and evaluate strategies for management of the harvesting of marine species	pp. 133–136 (253)	pp. 61, 81
	e) Case studies		
	• the resource potential, exploitation, impact and management of a marine fishery	pp. 136–138 (253)	
	• an example of farming of marine species, the source of food, pollution from fish waste and impact on the natural habitat	pp. 138–139 (253)	
6 Managing natural hazards	**a) Earthquakes and volcanoes**		
	• the structure of the Earth	pp. 144–145 (254)	p. 41
	• describe and explain the distribution and causes of earthquakes and volcanoes	pp. 145–147 (254)	
	b) Tropical cyclones		
	• describe and explain the distribution and causes of tropical cyclones (storms, hurricanes and typhoons)	pp. 152–153 (255)	pp. 25, 100, 120
	c) Flooding		
	• describe and explain the causes of flooding	pp. 157–160 (255)	pp. 25, 100, 120
	d) Drought		
	• describe and explain the causes of drought	p. 164 (256)	pp. 100, 120
	e) The impacts of natural hazards		
	• describe and explain the impacts of natural hazards on people and the environment	pp. 147–149, 154–156, 160–161, 165–166	pp. 25, 67–68, 100, 102–105, 106–107
	f) Managing the impacts of natural hazards		
	• describe and evaluate the strategies for managing the impacts of natural hazards before, during and after an event	pp. 149–152, 156–157, 161–163, 166–168 (256)	p. 100
	g) Opportunities presented by natural hazards		
	• describe and explain the opportunities presented by natural hazards to people	pp. 168–169 (256)	
	h) Case studies		
	• compare and contrast the strategies for managing the impacts of tectonic events between a named more economically developed country (MEDC) and a named less economically developed country (LEDC)	pp. 170–172 (256)	pp. 104–105
	• study the strategies for managing the impacts of a tropical storm, flood or drought	pp. 173–175 (256)	

7 The atmosphere and human activities	**a)**	**The atmosphere**		
	•	describe the structure and composition of the atmosphere	pp. 180–181 (257)	
	•	describe the natural greenhouse effect	p. 181 (257)	
	b)	**Atmospheric pollution and its causes**		
	•	describe and explain the causes of atmospheric pollution, with reference to: – smog – acid rain – ozone layer depletion – enhanced greenhouse effect	pp. 181–182 (257) pp. 182–183 (257) pp. 183–184 (257–258) p. 185 (258) pp. 186–187 (258)	pp. 61, 122–123 p. 120 p. 120 pp. 101, 120, 123
	c)	**Impact of atmospheric pollution**		
	•	describe and explain the impact of atmospheric pollution	pp. 186–187 (258)	pp. 122–123
	d)	**Managing atmospheric pollution**		
	•	describe and explain the strategies used by individuals, governments and the international community to reduce the effects of atmospheric pollution	pp. 188–190 (259)	pp. 128–129
	e)	**Case study**		
	•	study the causes, impact and management of a specific example of atmospheric pollution	pp. 191–192 (259)	pp. 128–129
8 Human population	**a)**	**Human population distribution and density**		
	•	identify where people live in the world	pp. 196–199 (260)	pp. 5, 141–142
	b)	**Changes in population size**		
	•	describe and explain the growth curve of populations	pp. 199–200 (261)	p. 24
	•	describe and explain the changes in human populations	pp. 200–202 (261–262)	pp. 100, 120, 143–144
	c)	**Population structure**		
	•	describe population structure in MEDCs and LEDCS	pp. 203–204	pp. 100, 144
	d)	**Managing human population size**		
	•	evaluate strategies for managing human population size	pp. 204–205 (262)	p. 145
	e)	**Case study**		
	•	study the strategies a named country or region has used to manage population size	pp. 206–207 (262)	
9 Natural ecosystems and human activities	**a)**	**Ecosystems**		
	•	define the terms *ecosystem*, *population*, *community*, *habitat* and *niche*	p. 212 (263)	
	•	describe the biotic (living) and abiotic (non-living) components of an ecosystem	p. 212 (263)	pp. 6, 61
	•	describe biotic interactions	p. 212 (263)	pp. 6, 61
	•	describe the process of photosynthesis	p. 212 (263)	

	• describe energy flow using food chains, food webs and trophic levels	pp. 212–214 (263)	
	• describe and explain ecological pyramids based on numbers and energy	p. 215 (263)	
	• describe the process of respiration	p. 213 (263)	
	• describe the carbon cycle	p. 214 (263)	
	b) Ecosystems under threat		
	• describe and explain causes and impacts of habitat loss	p. 216 (266)	pp. 25, 82, 121, 161–163
	c) Deforestation		
	• describe and explain the causes and impacts of deforestation	pp. 217–219 (264–265)	pp. 100, 120
	d) Managing forests		
	• describe and explain the need for the sustainable management of forests	pp. 219–222 (266)	
	e) Measuring and managing biodiversity		
	• describe and evaluate methods for estimating biodiversity	pp. 222–225 (266)	
	• apply sampling techniques to unfamiliar situations	pp. 223–225 (266)	
	• evaluate national and international strategies for conserving the biodiversity and genetic resources of natural ecosystems	pp. 225–227 (265–266)	pp. 41, 164–166
	f) Case studies		
	• study the causes and impacts of deforestation in a named area	pp. 228–230 (264)	
	• study the conservation of a named species	pp. 231–232 (266)	pp. 168–169
	• study a named biosphere reserve	pp. 233–235	

Acknowledgements

Cover and title page image: Silvia Iordache / Shutterstock

1.1 Roy Westlake / LGPL / Alamy; 1.2 Robert Buchanan Taylor / Alamy; 1.3 vvoe / Shutterstock; 1.4 Collins; 1.5 Ivan_Sabo / Shutterstock; 1.6 Collins; 1.7 David Weatherly / Collins; 1.8 gabriel12 / Shutterstock; 1.9 Collins; 1.10 Collins; 1.11 Gingerss / Shutterstock; 1.12 Edward Haylan / Shutterstock; 1.13 Collins; 1.14 Bahnfrend / Wikipedia / CC BY-SA 4.0; 1.15 Jürgen Matern / Wikipedia / CC BY-SA 2.5; 1.16 Daniel Gale / Shutterstock; 1.17 Sergey Uryadnikov / Shutterstock; 1.18 Ainars Aunins / Shutterstock; 1.19 bernard bradley / Wikipedia / CC BY-SA 2.0; 1.20 David Havel / Shutterstock; 1.21 Collins; 1.22 Collins; 1.23 Friedrich Stark / Alamy

2.1a Collins; 2.1b Collins; 2.2 Collins; 2.3a © Google/Google Earth; 2.3b © Google/Google Earth; 2.4 Collins; 2.5 Collins; 2.6 Collins; 2.7 Jim West / Alamy; 2.8 ZUMA Press Inc / Alamy; 2.9 Jim West / Alamy; 2.10 Stephen Saks Photography / Alamy; 2.11 © NASA / NOAA; 2.12 Collins; 2.13 Collins; 2.14a Collins; 2.14b Collins; 2.15 imageBROKER / Alamy; 2.16 Ricardo Ribas / Alamy

3.1 Collins; 3.2 Eye Ubiquitous / Alamy; 3.3 Collins; 3.4 chombosan / Shutterstock; 3.5 Paul Mayall Australia / Alamy; 3.6 Collins; 3.7 Collins; 3.8 MMCez / Shutterstock; 3.9 Collins; 3.10 Andrew Baskott / Alamy; 3.11 Collins; 3.12 Collins

4.1 Collins; 4.2 Collins; 4.3 Collins; 4.4 ZUMA Press, Inc. / Alamy; 4.5 Christian Vinces / Shutterstock; 4.6 Global Warming Art / Wikipedia / CC BY-SA 3.0; 4.7 © NASA/GISS; 4.8 Yory Frenklakh / Shutterstock; 4.9 Pontificia Universidad Católica de Chile / Wikipedia / CC BY-SA 2.0; 4.10 Collins; 4.11 Collins; 4.12 Fotos593 / Shutterstock; 4.13 Collins; 4.14 Tupungato / Shutterstock; 4.15 Collins; 4.16 Collins; 4.17 Wikpedia / public domain; 4.18 San Francisco, Ca. : H.M. Alexander Ptg. Co., 1910 / Wikipedia / public domain; 4.19 March of Dimes / Wikipedia / public domain; 4.20 Asianet-Pakistan / Shutterstock; 4.21 Collins; 4.22 Orlova-tpe / Wikipedia / CC BY-SA 3.0; 4.23 Eye Ubiquitous / Alamy; 4.24 meunierd / Shutterstock; 4.25 Anton_Ivanov / Shutterstock; 4.26 Collins; 4.27 Collins; 4.28 Collins; 4.29 Collins; 4.30 John Brown / Alamy; 4.31 [and text extract on page 77] © Water for Cambodia; 4.32 Sean Sprague / Alamy; 4.33 Olivier Asselin / Alamy; 4.34 James Heilman, MD / Wikipedia / CC BY-SA 4.0; 4.35 Oliver Lynton / Alamy; 4.36 corlaffra / Shutterstock

5.1 New Zealand Defence Force / Wikipedia / CC BY 2.0; 5.2 LegoLostAtSea / Wikipedia / public domain; 5.3 Collins; 5.4 Rick Rickman / NOAA / public domain; 5.5 Collins; 5.6 Konrad Mostert / Shutterstock; 5.7 Ethan Daniels / Shutterstock; 5.8 Citizen of the Planet / Alamy; 5.9 Citizen of the Planet / Alamy; 5.10 Rosanne Tackaberry / Alamy; 5.11 © The Ocean Cleanup – www.theoceancleanup.com; 5.12 © The Ocean Cleanup – www.theoceancleanup.com; 5.13 © AquaMaps / www.aquamaps.org; 5.14–5.15 Food and Agriculture Organization of the United Nations, 2016, The State of World Fisheries and Aquaculture – Contributing to food security and nutrition for all (www.fao.org/3/a-i5555e.pdf); reproduced with permission; 5.16 © Global Fishing Watch

6.1–6.4 © EM-DAT: The OFDA/CRED International Disaster Database / www.emdat.be, Université Catholique de Louvain, Brussels (Belgium); 6.5 © Nicholas Sheehan; 6.6 Concept use / Shutterstock; 6.7 Neil Cooper / Alamy; 6.8 dave stamboulis / Alamy; 6.9 Alex Proimos / Wikipedia / CC BY 2.0; 6.10 Aurora Photos / Alamy; 6.11 Barry Lewis / Alamy; 6.12 Aflo Co., Ltd. / Alamy; 6.13 Collins; 6.14 Archive Image / Alamy; 6.15 Collins; 6.16 Mikenorton / Wikipedia / CC BY-SA 3.0; 6.17 © GNS Science; 6.18 © GNS Science; 6.19 © GNS Science; 6.20 Collins; 6.21 © GNS Science; 6.22 © Chris Mance/GeoNet; 6.23 Collins

7.1 Dr. Morley Read / Shutterstock; 7.2 Collins; 7.3 © Google Earth; 7.4 Collins; 7.5 Collins; 7.6 Ruslan Kerimov / Shutterstock; 7.7 mailer_diablo / Wikipedia / CC BY-SA 3.0; 7.8 Calvin Teo / Wikipedia / CC BY-SA 2.5; 7.9 toonman / Shutterstock; 7.10 Environmental Protection Agency. Headquarters: Washington, D.C., U.S.A. / Wikipedia / public domain; 7.11 NOAA/NCDC / Wikipedia / public domain; 7.12 Collins; 7.13 Collins; 7.14 © Jesse Allen / NASA Earth Observatory; 7.15 © Jesse Allen / NASA Earth Observatory; 7.16 Collins; 7.17 Chumash Maxim / Shutterstock

8.1 Collins; 8.2 Collins; 8.3 Collins; 8.4 Collins; 8.5 Collins; 8.6 Collins; 8.7 John Linnell / Wikipedia / CC BY 4.0; 8.8 Everett Historical / Shutterstock; 8.9 Collins; 8.10 Collins; 8.11 Demmo / Wikipedia / public domain; 8.12 Demmo / Wikipedia / public domain; 8.13 Collins; 8.14 YGLvoices / Wikipedia / CC BY 2.0; 8.15 paul prescott / Shutterstock; 8.16 Richard Thornton / Shutterstock; 8.17 Collins; 8.18 AT2663 / Wikipedia / CC BY-SA 3.0; 8.19 Collins; 8.20 Collins; 8.21 Collins; 8.22 Collins; 8.23 Nigel Cattlin / Alamy; 8.24 ton koene / Alamy; 8.25 Universal Images Group North America LLC / DeAgostini / Alamy; 8.26 sombo sombo / Alamy; 8.27 Collins; 8.28 Zoonar GmbH / Alamy; 8.29 reportage / Alamy; 8.30 Friedrich Stark / Alamy; 8.31 adrian arbib / Alamy

9.1 Julian W / Shutterstock; 9.2 Adwo / Shutterstock; 9.3 Ninaras / Wikipedia / CC BY 4.0; 9.4 Ninaras / Wikipedia / CC BY 4.0; 9.5 dbimages / Alamy; 9.6 N Mrtgh / Shutterstock; 9.7 © Dartmoor National Park; 9.8 Sergei Aleshin / Shutterstock; 9.9 DrimaFilm / Shutterstock; 9.10 Martyn Williams Photography / Alamy; 9.11 Max Earey / Shutterstock; 9.12 kojihirano / Shutterstock; 9.13 stockphoto-graf / Shutterstock; 9.14 Tatiana Dyuvbanova / Shutterstock; 9.15 Troutnut / Shutterstock; 9.16 Piotr Krzeslak / Shutterstock; 9.17 Udo Schröter / Wikipedia / public domain; 9.18 Shanti Hesse / Shutterstock; 9.19 Rich Carey / Shutterstock; 9.20 KYTan / Shutterstock; 9.21 KYTan / Shutterstock;9.22 Collins; 9.23 Collins; 9.24 Chris Collins / Shutterstock; 9.25 West Coast Scapes / Shutterstock; 9.26 Dave Watts / Alamy; 9.27 © Roger Graveson / www.saintlucianplants.com; 9.28 LiveIImages / Shutterstock; 9.29 M. Timothy O'Keefe / Alamy; 9.30 Ocean Image Photography / Shutterstock; 9.31 Collins; 9.32 © SMMA

Answers: Section 3, Q19: Jouve; Section 4, Q13: Jouve; all other images in answer section: Collins